Introduction to English Text-linguistics

Textbooks in English Language and Linguistics (TELL)

Edited by Magnus Huber and Joybrato Mukherjee

Volume 2

PETER LANG

Frankfurt am Main · Berlin · Bern · Bruxelles · New York · Oxford · Wien

Jürgen Esser

Introduction to English Text-linguistics

PETER LANG
Internationaler Verlag der Wissenschaften

Bibliographic Information published by the Deutsche Nationalbibliothek
The Deutsche Nationalbibliothek lists this publication in the Deutsche Nationalbibliografie; detailed bibliographic data is available in the internet at <http://www.d-nb.de>.

ISSN 1862-510X
ISBN 978-3-631-56003-7
© Peter Lang GmbH
Internationaler Verlag der Wissenschaften
Frankfurt am Main 2009
All rights reserved.

All parts of this publication are protected by copyright. Any utilisation outside the strict limits of the copyright law, without the permission of the publisher, is forbidden and liable to prosecution. This applies in particular to reproductions, translations, microfilming, and storage and processing in electronic retrieval systems.

www.peterlang.de

For Anne (aged 4), Laura (3) and Matthias (2),
whom I wanted to see more often
when they developed so marvellously
while I was writing this book.

Preface

This book aims at covering those areas of text-linguistics that have enjoyed widespread attention in English linguistics, as laid down for example in the two classic monographs by Halliday/Hasan (1976), *Cohesion in English*, and by Beaugrande/Dressler (1981), *Introduction to Text Linguistics*. Besides these two approaches more recent ones have entered the stage. Notably, there are corpus linguistic studies in lexical patterns and classifications of texts, and psycholinguistic and cognitive studies in text constitution and decoder-orientation. One special feature of this book is that it not only covers medium-independent elements and structures but also medium-dependent written and spoken presentation.

I am grateful for many discussions with my dear younger colleagues Rolf Kreyer, Sebastian Patt and Sharmila Vaz while I wrote the manuscript. Finally, I also want to thank Joybrato Mukherjee for his invitation to write this volume in the TELL Series.

Bonn   Jürgen Esser
July 2008

Table of Contents

Typographical Conventions — xiii

1 The Scope of Text-linguistics — 1
1.1 Defining 'text': the terms 'text' and 'discourse' — 1
1.2 Studying 'text': the heterogeneity of approaches — 10
1.3 Textuality — 12
1.4 Essentials of text-linguistics — 20
1.5 Questions and exercises — 21
1.6 Further reading — 21

2 Formal Texture I: Medium-independent Elements and Structures — 23
2.1 Order and realization of elements — 24
    2.1.1 General framework — 24
    2.1.2 Order of clause elements: signalling information flow — 29
        2.1.2.1 Objective and subjective order — 29
        2.1.2.2 Linear thematic progression — 32
    2.1.3 Realization of clause elements: referencing and establishing cohesion by referring back and forward — 34
        2.1.3.1 Pronouns — 37
        2.1.3.2 Determiners — 37
        2.1.3.3 Comparison — 39
        2.1.3.4 Substitution — 41
        2.1.3.5 Ellipsis — 41
        2.1.3.6 Lexical cohesion — 42
        2.1.3.7 Place relators — 45
        2.1.3.8 Time relators and tense marking — 47
        2.1.3.9 Referring forward — 49
    2.1.4 Connecting clauses in clause complexes and beyond — 50
        2.1.4.1 Syntactic coordination — 51
        2.1.4.2 Syntactic subordination — 53
        2.1.4.3 Textual linkage of clause complexes — 57
2.2 Corpus-linguistic approaches to the study of words in texts — 59
    2.2.1 Lexical patterns — 61
    2.2.2 Collocation and naturalness — 68

2.3 Corpus-linguistic approaches to the classification of texts — 73
    2.3.1 Genres, registers and text-types — 75
        2.3.1.1 Genres — 75
        2.3.1.2 Registers — 77
        2.3.1.3 Text-types — 79
    2.3.2 Styles — 91
2.4 Questions and exercises — 92
2.5 Further reading — 93

3 Formal Texture II: Medium-dependent Presentation — 95
3.1 Written presentation — 97
    3.1.1 Orthography and Punctuation — 97
    3.1.2 Script unit — 103
    3.1.3 Layout — 104
    3.1.4 Classification of texts — 111
3.2 Spoken presentation — 117
    3.2.1 Phonological word-forms in tone units — 117
    3.2.2 Tone units and tone unit sequences — 120
    3.2.3 Talk unit — 125
3.3 Questions and exercises — 128
3.4 Further reading — 129

4 Semantic Texture: Psycholinguistic and Cognitive Aspects of Text Constitution — 131
4.1 Lexical priming — 131
4.2 Scenes and frames semantics — 135
4.3 Coherence — 140
4.4 Rhetorical structures — 146
4.5 Macrostructures and superstructures — 154
4.6 Thematic progression and hyperthemes — 158
4.7 Questions and exercises — 162
4.8 Further reading — 163

5 Decoder-orientation — 165
5.1 Textual rhetoric — 165
5.2 Processibility — 173
5.3 Optimizing texts — 176

5.4	Questions and exercises	180
5.5	Further reading	180

6 Textual Intentions — 181
6.1	Deep structure genres	183
6.2	Discourse types	188
6.3	Questions and exercises	194
6.4	Further reading	195

List of References — 197

Index — 207

Typographical Conventions

<abc>	Written word-form(s)
>abc<	Medium-independent word-form(s)
ABC	Lexeme
a̱ḇc̱	Nucleus of a tone unit
abc/	Spoken word-form(s) with rising tone at tone unit boundary
abc\	Spoken word-form(s) with falling tone at tone unit boundary
/abc/	Spoken word-form(s) presented in phonological transcription
[abc]	Spoken word-form(s) presented in phonetic transcription
'abc'	Terms, notions, concepts, meanings
"abc"	Quotation
abc	Object language unspecified as to medium (usually understood as medium-independent), emphasis in written presentation, titles of written documents
a̲b̲c̲	Highlighted linguistic elements in examples
Abc Def	[Initial capital letters] Theoretical models and methods derived thereof, names of corpora

In quotations, spelling variants and graphic styles for emphasis are kept in their original form, even if they differ from the conventions used in this book. With reference to sexually unspecified encoders and decoders the generic *he* is used.

1 The Scope of Text-linguistics

1.1 Defining 'text': the terms 'text' and 'discourse'

In our everyday language, a text is something that we can see or touch: a book or any other piece of writing. A text is a written document or part of it. This is reflected in the following definitions of *text* from the *Cobuild English Dictionary* (Sinclair 1995), "any written material" (definition 2), and the *Oxford English Dictionary* (Burchfield 1989), "the wording of anything written or printed" (definition 1a). We should first note that these definitions of the word *text* not only refer to words but also, and specifically, to their material embodiment, i.e. the written words as we perceive them in their physical substance, for example on paper. We can say that this notion of text is bound to the written medium, it is medium-dependent. But this is not the whole story.

We can also use the word *text* to refer to the words used in a speech, broadcast, or sound recording if they are converted from their original material embodiment of sound waves into a different physical medium, namely paper. This usage of *text* is reflected in definition 3 of the *Cobuild English Dictionary* and its illustrative example from the Cobuild database, The Bank of English:

> 3 The **text** of a speech, broadcast, or recording is the written version of it. *A spokesman said a text of Dr Runcie's speech had been circulated to all of the bishops.*

In the quoted example *text* is again something that can be seen, touched and even circulated, i.e. something material. But this time *text* is also meant as something independent of the medium. In our example the text has been transferred from its embodiment in the original medium, sound waves, to a different medium, paper. The change of medium does not mean, of course, that the sound waves have been transferred to paper by a physical process. What has been transferred are rather the immaterial words that were used, i.e. the words that were understood as abstract entities regardless of their physical properties. This means, then, that *text* according to definition 3 of the *Cobuild English Dictionary* and the given example refers not only to something material but also to a medium-independent structure of words which can be embodied in either of the two mediums, spoken or written. This meaning of the word *text* is also covered by the term "wording" in definition 1a from the *Oxford English Dictionary*, quoted in the first paragraph above.

That is, in everyday language two senses of *text* can be distinguished, which often go together unreflectingly but each of which can receive more or less prominence:

(i) medium-dependent: a written document or part of it,

(ii) medium-independent: the wording of language material regardless of its medial embodiment.

We should note that sense (ii) is more abstract than sense (i) and that while (i) implies (ii), (ii) does not imply (i). While a written document has an underlying structure in terms of its wording, the wording as an abstract entity exists independent of its medial embodiment, i.e. it is medium-independent.

It is only natural that in everyday language we are not always aware of these two senses of *text* and are happy with the vagueness between the two notions. They are also implied in the other meanings that we have not mentioned so far. Besides definition 2 and 3 quoted above, the *Cobuild English Dictionary* offers us also:

1 The **text** of a book is the main part of it, rather than the introduction, pictures, notes, or index.

4 A **text** is a book or other piece of writing, especially one concerned with science or learning.

5 A **text** is a written or spoken passage, especially one that is used in a school or university for discussion or in an examination.

By mentioning science, learning, school and university, definitions 4 and 5 hint at one further general sense of the everyday use of *text*, namely that it is a meaningful unit. This is an important aspect that must be clearly spelled out: If we understand a text to be the medium-dependent or medium-independent wording of language material, we also take it for granted that it is meaningful and devoted to one topic or a limited number of topics.

There is a further sense in definitions 1, 3, 4, and 5 which has not been mentioned yet but which is usually implicitly understood, namely that the written material or the wording comprises more than just a word or a sentence. With the exception of definition 2 from the *Cobuild English Dictionary*, "any written material", all the definitions and illustrative examples refer to language material that comprises multiple sentences. Thus, prototypically we imagine a text to be longer than just a sentence or a word. A less typical case, still covered by "any written material", would be a text message on the mobile phone.

If we summarize our short exploration into the everyday meanings of *text* as explained in the *Cobuild English Dictionary*, we get the following prototypical senses of *text*:

In everyday language, *text* is a piece of language that is:

(i)   written (medium-dependent aspect),

(ii) the wording of language material regardless of its medial embodiment (medium-independent aspect),

(iii) meaningful and devoted to one topic,

(iv) typically more than just a word or a sentence.

In the following we will compare our everyday understanding of *text* with a word which has meanings similar to those of *text*, namely *discourse*. The *Cobuild English Dictionary* gives this definition and truncated corpus example:

1 Discourse is spoken or written communication between people, especially serious discussion of a particular subject. ...*a tradition of political discourse*.

First we have to note that this definition of *discourse* refers to something more general than *text*. *Discourse* is a topic-bound exchange of views in which more than one party is engaged. We should also note that the first definition of *discourse* stresses the medium-independent aspect: you cannot see, touch or circulate (a) discourse. This medium-independent sense is partly reflected by the fact that in this case *discourse* is grammatically treated as a non-count noun.

In its second meaning the noun *discourse* is grammatically treated as a count noun in the *Cobuild English Dictionary*. It comes fairly close to our everyday understanding of *text*. The entry with its illustrating example reads as follows:

2 A discourse is a serious talk or piece of writing which is intended to teach or explain something; a formal use. *Gates responds with a lengthy discourse on deployment strategy*.

Although this second definition refers to the contribution of only one party, it is embedded in a larger interactional setting such as argumentation or teaching. Since there is no restriction to the realization in one particular medium, this notion of *discourse* is completely medium-independent. Although it is not mentioned explicitly, a discourse is always more than just a word or a sentence.

A summary of the everyday meanings of the noun *discourse* based on the *Cobuild English Dictionary* yields the following prototypical senses of *discourse*:

In everyday language, a *discourse* is:

(i)   a multi-party exchange of views OR

(ii) the contribution of one party in a larger interactional setting regardless of its medial embodiment (medium-independent aspect),

(iii) bound to one topic,

(iv) always more than just a word or a sentence.

If we compare the everyday meanings of *text* and *discourse* we can see that there is a remarkable affinity between the respective senses (ii), (iii) and (iv). The basic difference is that while *text* is only viewed as a product, e.g. written words, *discourse* is also viewed as a process in a larger communicative setting, for example the strife for the best arguments in politics.

After dealing with the everyday meanings of *text* and *discourse*, we can now turn to the meanings that these words have acquired as technical terms in linguistics. The earliest appearance of the terms 'text' and 'discourse' (certainly not of the words *text* and *discourse*) in linguistics that I am aware of can be found in the seminal article "Discourse analysis" by Harris (1952). In this paper Harris purports to present "a method for the analysis of connected speech (or writing)" (p. 1). This method should enable the linguist to describe the occurrence of morphemes beyond the limits of a single sentence.

To understand this, one should bear in mind that at that time linguists were studying the distribution of phonemes and morphemes and the hierarchical structure of sequences of morphemes in words and sentences with a procedure called Immediate Constituent Analysis; that is, the largest domain whose internal structure was analysed was the sentence. As Harris (ibid.) puts it, "descriptive linguistics generally stops at sentence boundaries." These limitations should be overcome by discourse analysis.

The new object of linguistic description is referred to by Harris as 'connected discourse', or in short, 'discourse' or 'text'. One has to admit that, at the beginning of a new linguistic discipline, these are pre-theoretical notions, which are used tentatively and which are not yet properly defined. Harris speaks of "the discourse under investigation" and "the particular text we are studying" in one and the same paragraph (ibid.). The object of study, 'connected discourse', refers to the whole range of spoken and written language activities in both physical embodiments:

> We consider just the sentences of a particular connected discourse - that is, the sentences spoken or written in succession by one or more persons in a single situation. [...] Language does not occur in stray words or sentences, but in connected discourse - from a one-word utterance to a ten-volume work, from a monolog to a Union Square argument. (Harris 1952: 3)

Connected discourse as the object of linguistic investigation is manifest in spoken or written, i.e. medium-bound, forms. On the other hand, the aim of linguistic analysis is to establish abstract, medium-independent entities and properties. The important aspect to note is, however, that in Harris' article both 'discourse' and 'text' refer to the language material under investigation which now goes beyond the limitations of a sentence.

A similar view is held by Chafe (1992: 356), who remarks about the terms 'discourse' and 'text': "Both terms may refer to a unit of language larger than the sentence: one may speak of 'a discourse' or 'a text'." This formulation by Chafe, however, does not indicate whether "unit of language" refers to the medium-dependent aspect of language (something that can be read or heard), as do the instantiations of 'connected dicourse' ("from a one-word utterance ...") in the quotation from Harris above, or to the medium-independent aspect, i.e. the wording as abstract entities regardless of their physical embodiment.

In our attempt to describe the meanings that 'text' and 'discourse' have as technical terms in linguistics, we can summarize the views held by Harris and Chafe as follows:

In linguistics, 'text' and 'discourse' may refer to:

(i) actually spoken or written words (medium-dependent aspect) AND/OR

(ii) an abstract unit of language larger than the sentence (medium-independent aspect).

While the definitions given by Harris and Chafe appear to be straightforward, additional meanings have developed which complicate the picture. Some linguists like Halliday/Hasan (1976: 1) and Kallmeyer/Meyer-Hermann (1980: 242-243) reserve sense (i) exclusively for 'text' (not for 'discourse') and they understand 'text' as 'parole' or 'performance', i.e. the actual language use. As Halliday/Hasan put it:

The word TEXT is used in linguistics to refer to any passage, spoken or written, of whatever length, that does form a unified whole. (Halliday/ Hasan 1976: 1)

The first part of this definition, "any passage, spoken or written, of whatever length", captures the idea of naturally occuring language material. This is a feature that we have seen above in the quotation by Harris, "from a one-word utterance to a ten-volume work, from a monolog to a Union Square argument". 'Text' in this usage is something that we can hear, see or touch. However, unlike Harris, Halliday/Hasan define a text as a "unified whole", which is a semantic definition, and not a structural one.

Halliday/Hasan expressly reject the idea that 'text' is an abstract, structural unit of language, larger than the sentence, cf. (ii). This becomes apparent in their second definition of 'text':

> A text is a unit of language in use. It is not a grammatical unit, like a clause or sentence; and it is not defined by its size. [...] A text is not something that is like a sentence, only bigger; it is something that differs from a sentence in kind. A text is best regarded as a semantic unit: a unit not of form but of meaning. (ibid.: 1-2)

In structuralism there is the widespread idea of ranks, i.e. of levels of constituency, whereby smaller units combine to form larger units and larger units consist of smaller units. These relations are mutually defining. For example, words pattern into phrases, phrases pattern into clauses, clauses pattern into sentences. Reversely, sentences consist of clauses, clauses consist of phrases, phrases consist of words. The types and numbers of relations are determined by the grammar of the language. For example, a sentence consists of at least one independent clause and potentially further, though structurally defined, dependent clauses. Such a restriction does not exist for 'text'. There is no grammatical rule which says that texts consist of a certain number of sentences or certain types of sentences. Graphically this may be represented as follows:

words ⇆ phrases ⇆ clauses ⇆ sentences ←?→ text

On the other hand, some linguists, in contrast to Halliday/Hasan, do understand 'text' as a unit of linguistic description which is in fact larger than the units 'word', 'phrase', 'clause' and 'sentence', cf. sense (ii) of 'text' and 'discourse' above. Since this usage of 'text' refers to a theoretical construct in the minds of linguists it can neither be seen nor touched. In his earlier writings van Dijk (1977: 3), for example, distinguishes 'text' and 'discourse'. For him 'text' refers to an abstraction – a theoretical construct, cf. (ii) – and 'discourse' to its realization, cf. (i):

> These are reasons which have lead us to assume that utterances should be reconstructed in terms of a larger unit, viz that of TEXT. This term will here be used to denote the abstract theoretical construct underlying what is usually called a DISCOURSE. Those utterances which can be assigned textual structure are thus acceptable discourses of the language [...].

In this model a 'narrative', for example, is seen as a structural configuration of semantic entities called 'superstructure' to which belong 'setting', 'complication', 'resolution' and 'moral'. They may be exemplified as follows:

(1) It was late in Portobello and the sky was dark [setting] when I was attacked by a stranger. He demanded my purse [complication]. I defended myself successfully with my umbrella [resolution]. Therefore I never go without an umbrella on my night walks [moral].

The superstructure of a narrative can be represented in the form of a tree diagram or formation rules (like generative syntactic rules) as for example in Figure 1.1. We have to note that the categories of a superstructure need not to be directly relatable to surface clauses and not all categories have to be present in a text, cf. example (1) where there is no evaluation.

As yet another kind of semantic differentiation some linguists reserve the term 'text' for the (monologic) product of writing and contrast it with 'talk', as van Dijk (1997: 3) does in his later writings:

> Thus, in the same way as 'text' is mostly used to refer to the product of writing, 'talk' is often studied as the product of speaking or as ongoing interaction [...].

This distinction focuses on the medium difference of the language production and characterizes 'text' as a medium-dependent notion.

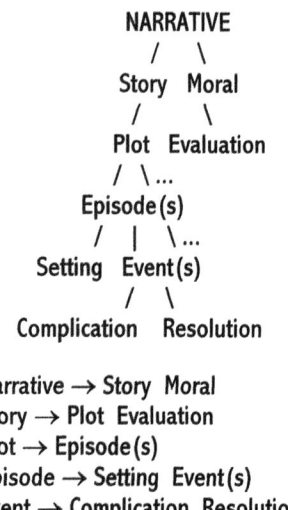

Figure 1.1: Superstructure of a narrative

For other linguists the notion of 'text' as 'parole' or 'performance' can be extended to comprise something larger, something that cannot be surveyed straightforwardly like a letter or a book, namely a corpus. This is one of the definitions of *text* given by Bussmann (1996): "the total of all linguistic expressions in the sense of a **corpus.**" This use is nicely exemplified in the following quotation from a classic book on corpus linguistics, Sinclair (1991: 1): "Large quantities of 'raw' text are processed directly in order to present the researcher with objective evidence." 'Text' understood as 'corpus' refers to a collection of texts, which have as their first embodiment the written or the spoken medium. Therefore a distinction is made between written and spoken corpora.

The different meanings of the linguistic notion of 'text' that we have discussed may be summarized (in a changed order of appearance) as follows:

In linguistics, 'text' is defined as one of the following:

(i) the (monologic) product of writing (medium-dependent aspect),

(ii) a spoken or written unit of language in use (medium-dependent aspect),

(iii)   a corpus (medium-dependent aspect),

(iv)   a unit of linguistic description larger than the sentence (medium-independent aspect),

(v)   a semantic unit (medium-independent aspect).

While (i), "the (monologic) product of writing", is restricted to the written medium, (ii), "a spoken or written unit of language in use", refers to either medium. Therefore (ii) can imply (i), but not vice versa. Furthermore, one can say that (iii), "a corpus", consists of a large number of spoken or written units of language in use, cf. (ii). Therefore (iii) implies (ii).

Our litte survey indicates that it is impossible to give a comprehensive definition of the linguistic notion of 'text' in terms of logically neccessary and sufficient features which would allow the linguist to distinguish 'texts' from 'non-texts'. As a student of linguistics one should rather conceive of 'text' as a prototype category, i.e. a category which has typical and less typical characteristics. In this view (i) and (iv) are the most typical features of 'text'. That is, prototypically, we conceive of a 'text' as a monologic product of writing constituting a unit larger than a sentence. This does not preclude Plato's *Dialogues* from being texts, nor the oral epic *Beowulf*, nor a bumper sticker, which consists only of a few words, for example *In God We Doubt*, which alludes to the motto *In God We Trust*.

Our very limited discussion of different understandings of the linguistic notion of 'text' has made it clear that 'text' is a highly polysemous term, i.e. it can adopt different, though related, meanings. As with many other linguistic concepts, for example 'word', 'sentence' and 'style', the meanings of the term 'text' are bound to specific theories and must be explained with more basic concepts. Enkvist (1973: 14-15) describes such terms as "notational terms". As we shall see, it is particularly the medium-independent senses (iv) and (v) which divide text-linguists and ask for more theoretical explanation.

However, before we move on to sketch the various approaches to text-linguistics, a few final remarks about the linguistic term 'discourse' are necessary. While we have seen that in everyday language the words *text* and *discourse* share some features, and in linguistics the terms 'text' and 'discourse' may be even used synonymously, it must be stated that 'discourse' is also a highly polysemous, notational term. In order to highlight this, we may look at the meanings of the term 'discourse' listed in Bussmann (1996):

> Connected speech, the product of an interactive process in a socio-cultural context, performance, talk, conversational interaction, language in context across all forms and modes, process (vs. product).

'Discourse' is extensively dealt with in the volume *Introduction to English Pragmatics* (Schneider forthcoming) in the TELL Series. Discourse analysis, which can be seen as complementary to text-linguistics, is studied from numerous perspectives. Perhaps most prominently, it gains insight into social interaction. It is chiefly concerned with language material that originated in speech. With this kind of analysis, 'discourse' or 'text' is partly constructed by the decoder, that is the hearer or reader. Therefore this approach is less interested in the distribution of word-forms and their functional interpretation in terms of the language system.

1.2 Studying 'text': the heterogeneity of approaches

The diversity of approaches to text-linguistics is a result of different interests in knowledge. All text-linguists aim at describing how sentences combine to form a text. That is, they want to detect and describe some sort of texture. However, their interests often differ in terms of medium, level of abstraction and contextualization. For example, describing the semantic structure or the intention of a letter needs a higher degree of abstraction and contextualization than the mere description of its pronouns, conjunctions or focusing constructions.

It is possible to distinguish between three basic approaches in text-linguistics. Without undue commitment to terminology they can be briefly named as follows:

(i) Formal texture

(ii) Semantic texture

(iii) Textual intentions

(i) Formal texture The approaches whose basic interest is in formal texture can be divided into two groups. First, there are those approaches that are based on the medium-dependent presentation of texts. Here, texts are more than just the wordings. For the written medium, the wording may be accompanied by pictures as in comic strips or by other visualizations, e.g. tables or figures, or layout features as in the stanzas of poems or in hypertexts, where we may find non-verbal elements like navigators and links. For the spoken medium, the interest of some researchers is in the intonational macrostructure that accompanies the medium-independent wording. For example, in reading out news items, a new topic may be indicated intonationally by a higher pitch of voice and the end of a topic by a lower pitch of voice.

Second, there are those approaches that are based on linguistic units abstracted from their medial embodiment. Here the interest is in the formal arrangement and functional interpretation of medium-independent lexical or grammatical units. Of the various research lines within this direction it will suffice here to mention just three.

One research line is interested in what is commonly called 'cohesion'. Linguists pursuing this interest, study, for example, the introduction of new topics (cf. *a king* and *a daughter* in the example below) and the continuity of referring items such as pronouns (cf. *He* and *She*):

(2) Once upon a time there was a king. He had a daughter. She was very pretty.

A second research line is interested in statistical patterns of word-forms in text. This study of lexical patterns is carried out with corpus-linguistic methods. It has been found out, for instance, that the verb *cause* "carries bad news around with it" (Hoey 2006: 22). Therefore, words like *accident, cancer, death* or *pain* are likely to co-occur with *cause*.

A third research line, also based on corpus-linguistic methods, is interested in the statistic study of lexical and grammatical patterns of co-occurrence in different text-types. There is, for example, a statistical tendency for past tense forms and personal pronouns to co-occur in reporting texts (cf. Biber 1986).

(ii) Semantic texture The approaches whose basic interest lies in semantic texture deal with the meanings that the medium-independent elements convey and with their cognitive models. One important research line is the study of 'coherence'. It describes the connectedness of sentences which are not formally linked, for example, by conjunctions or pronouns. Take the following example from Quirk et al. (1985: 1428):

(3) The policeman held up his hand. The car stopped.

It is only by our world knowledge that we understand the policeman's action to be the reason for the stopping of the car. Although the relation between these two sentences is not cohesive, it is nevertheless coherent.

(iii) Textual intentions Approaches whose basic interest lies in the study of textual intentions deal with global functions of texts. Some linguists have extended the notion of the speech act and apply it not only to sentences but also to whole texts, as for example in the case of 'description' or 'instruction'. Van Dijk (1980: 212), for instance, speaks of 'macro acts' ("sprachliche Makrohandlungen"). This is sometimes mirrored in everyday designations for standardized texts such as, for example, a letter of complaint or an invitation. 'Complaint', 'invitation' as well as 'description' and 'instruction' can be regarded as intentional text-types in contradistinction to text-types based on formal texture.

The main approaches in text-linguistics and a selection of the most important subdivisions can be summarized as in Figure 1.2 below. It is obvious that almost any text can be described with most or all of the approaches mentioned in this list. However, some approaches have found more attention than others. For example, the study of medium-dependent formal texture has been less extensive than the study of medium-independent formal texture, semantic texture and textual intentions. The dominant interest in cohesion, coherence and textual intentions, which can be studied in almost any text, has led some linguists to give cohesion, coherence and intention a special status not only in the description of texts, but also in the definition of what texts are. This has been captured under the term 'textuality', to which we will turn next.

Formal texture
    Medium-dependent
        Written medium
            e.g. study of layout
        Spoken medium
            e.g. study of intonational macrostructure
    Medium-independent
        Lexical and grammatical units
            e.g. study of cohesion
        Statistical patterns of word-forms
            e.g. study of lexical patterns
        Statistical co-occurrence
            e.g. study of text-types
Semantic texture
        e.g. study of coherence
Textual intentions
        e.g. study of macro acts
        (intentional text-types)

Figure 1.2: Approaches in text-linguistics

1.3 Textuality

In chapter 1.1 above we accepted the idea that the linguistic notion of 'text' is a prototype concept which cannot be defined with sufficient and necessary features. This idea, which is gaining ground (cf. Sandig 2000, Adamzik 2004: 47), is opposed to an older, although influential, idea proposed by Beaugrande/

Dressler (1981: 3), according to which 'texts' can be distinguished from 'non-texts' by criteria of 'textuality':

> A TEXT will be defined as a COMMUNICATIVE OCCURRENCE which meets seven standards of TEXTUALITY. If any of these standards is not considered to have been satisfied, the text will not be communicative. Hence, non-communicative texts are treated as non-texts.

The seven standards of textuality are: cohesion, coherence, intentionality, acceptability, informativity, situationality and intertextuality. The first two standards, cohesion and coherence, are "**text**-centered notions, designating operations directed at the text materials" (p. 7). The remaining standards are "**user**-centered notions which are brought to bear on the activity of textual communication at large, both by producers and by receivers" (ibid.). A more detailed classification of the user-centered notions is given in an earlier publication by Beaugrande (1980: 21), which describes all seven standards:

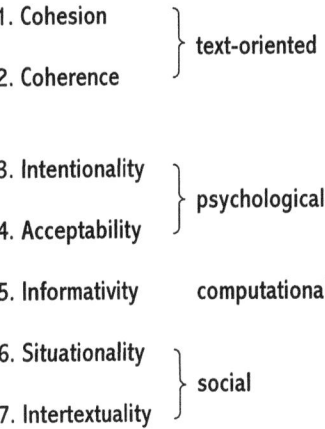

Figure 1.3: Seven standards of textuality

In the following we will briefly look at the seven standards and discuss their main features.

1. Cohesion This is the first of the two text-oriented notions which focus on the text as a product. We have already mentioned the linguistic concept of 'cohesion' above in connection with example (2). Here is how Beaugrande/ Dressler (1981: 3) define it:

The first standard will be called COHESION and concerns the ways in which the components of the SURFACE TEXT, i.e. the actual words we hear or see, are mutually connected within a sequence. The surface components **depend** upon each other according to grammatical forms and conventions, such that cohesion rests upon GRAMMATICAL DEPENDENCIES.

With regard to this quotation there are two aspects that must be pointed out. First, cohesion deals with actual word-forms. Second, grammatical dependencies exist both within a sentence and between sentences. Beaugrande/Dressler (1981: 50) note: "Cohesion *within* a phrase, a clause, or sentence is more direct and obvious than cohesion among two or more such units." You will note that this echoes Harris' attempts to extend the range of structural analysis beyond the sentence, referred to above in section 1.1.

The following lines from a nursery rhyme illustrate both cohesion within a sentence and between sentences:

(4) Old Mother Hubbard went to the cupboard to fetch her poor dog a bone. But when she got there the cupboard was bare and so the poor dog had none.

Without going into syntactic details we can say that at sentence level there is, for example, a cohesive relation between the subject *Old Mother Hubbard*, the verb *went* and the adverbials *to the cupboard* and *to fetch her poor dog a bone* in the main clause of the first sentence. These types of grammatical dependencies are part and parcel of every conventional syntactic description. More interesting from a text-linguistic perspective are the cohesive relations that exist between word-forms across sentence boundaries. They can be summarized in tabular form as in Figure 1.4 below. As we can see, the continuity of referents, i.e. of elements that are talked about, is achieved by proforms in the widest sense (*she, there, none*) and by repetitions (*cupboard, dog*). We will see in section 2.1.3 that proforms and repetitions are important, though not the only, cohesive devices.

First sentence	Second sentence
Old Mother Hubbard	*she*
to the cupboard	*there, the cupboard*
her poor dog	*the poor dog*
a bone	*none*

Figure 1.4: Cohesive relations across sentence boundaries in example (4)

2. Coherence This is the second of the two text-oriented notions. The standard of coherence is defined as follows:

> The second standard will be called COHERENCE and concerns the ways in which the components of the TEXTUAL WORLD, i.e. the configuration of CONCEPTS and RELATIONS which underlie the surface text, are mututally accessible and relevant. (Beaugrande/Dressler 1981: 4)

In the textual world that is created in the story of Old Mother Hubbard and her dog many of the concepts and their mutual relations are taken over from the real world. So the reader will assume that Old Mother Hubbard is in her house, that houses have cupboards and that *went to the cupboard* involves only a few steps and not an hour's walk. It is also understood that we store edible things not on the floor but in a cupboard. These concepts and relations are part of our understanding of the text. It is obvious that the word-forms of the surface text help to create the textual world in our minds. Therefore cohesion helps to create coherence. But not everything that is understood can be made explicit nor has it to be made explicit. Nevertheless, the distinction between what is explicit and what is not is important. Therefore Beaugrande/Dressler (1981: 13) point out that "the distinction between connectivity of the surface and connectivity of underlying content is indispensable".

Coherence is concerned with cognitive models that help us to understand texts. Important components of such models are causality and temporal relations, as we have seen in connection with example (3) above, which is repeated here as (5):

(5) The policeman held up his hand. The car stopped.

Our world knowledge tells us that the policeman's action is the cause for the driver to stop his car and that the policeman's action is temporally prior to the stopping of the car. This knowledge is used in the interpretation of (5). It establishes a connectivity between the two sentences, which show no overt links of cohesion.

3. Intentionality This is the first of the user-centered notions and describes the psychological rationale of the text producer. Beaugrande/Dressler (1981: 7, 116) define this standard of textuality as follows:

> The third standard of textuality could then be called INTENTIONALITY, the text **producer**'s attitude that the set of occurrences should constitute a cohesive and coherent text instrumental in fulfilling the producer's intentions, e.g. to distribute knowledge or to attain a GOAL specified in a PLAN.

In a wider sense of the term, intentionality designates all the ways in which text producers utilize texts to pursue and fulfil their intentions.

In other words, a speaker/writer aims at producing cohesive and coherent language in order to pursue a certain goal. Conversely, a listener/reader assumes that the language material presented is purposeful and is meant to follow a certain aim. These assumptions are described in the framework of the 'cooperative principle' by Grice (1975), cf. Schneider (forthcoming). Very often we are not consciously aware of the intentions that underlie verbal behaviour, but they may become focal when cohesion is distorted. This can be due to imperfect speech planning or imperfect mastery of the language if, for example, the language used is not the mother tongue. Beaugrande/Dressler (1981: 7) quote an instance of a fragmented syntactic structure:

(6) Well where do – which part of town do you live?

The goal of this utterance is, of course, to find out the address of the person spoken to. The fragmented structure impedes understanding, but, as Beaugrande/Dressler (1981: 7) point out:

> Text users normally exercise TOLERANCE towards products whose conditions of occurrence make it hard to uphold cohesion and coherence altogether, notably in casual conversation.

One could even go as far as to say that tolerance towards lacking and/or faulty cohesion is a typical characteristic of successful face-to-face communication.

4. Acceptability While intentionality relates to the psychological rationale of a message producer, acceptability relates to the rationale of a message receiver. This standard of textuality is defined as follows:

> The fourth standard of textuality would be ACCEPTABILITY, concerning the text **receiver**'s attitude that the set of occurrences should constitute a cohesive and coherent text having some use or relevance for the receiver, e.g. to acquire knowledge or to provide co-operation in a plan. (Beaugrande/Dressler 1981: 7)

The notion of acceptability addresses the good will of a listener/reader (i) to assume that the wording in question is meaningful and purposeful and (ii) to work out the intended meaning and goal. That is, the recipient of a text expects that the text is cohesive, coherent and purposeful. If these expectations are not met, the recipient has to make his own contribution and work out, i.e. infer, the coherence and intention of the given text.

On the other hand, a text producer has to anticipate the acceptability of his text to a potential reader. In doing so, the writer has to strike a balance between offering too little or too much information. Beaugrande/Dressler (1981: 8) quote the by now famous warning of the Bell Telephone Company:

(7) Call us before you dig. You may not be able to afterwards.

In this short text, the text producer has deliberately not mentioned the cause for the statement made in the second sentence. The wording for a more explicit text, guided by the same intention, would be:

(8) Call us before you dig. There might be an underground cable. If you break the cable, you won't have phone service, and you may get a severe electric shock. Then you won't be able to call us.

If we compare the original text (7) and its elaboration (8), we must say that the additions made in (8) are necessary for a proper understanding of (7). These additions correspond to the contribution that the recipient has to make if he wants to work out the coherence and intention of text (7). However, Beaugrande/Dressler point out that it is intriguing that (7) is more effective, i.e. makes a stronger impression, than (8), which is more explicit.

5. Informativity Related to acceptability is informativity. It deals with how the mind computes information. This standard of textuality is defined by Beaugrande/Dressler (1981: 8-9) as follows:

> The fifth standard of textuality is called INFORMATIVITY and concerns the extent to which the occurrences of the presented text are expected vs. unexpected or known vs. unknown/uncertain.

Referring to examples (7) and (8) one can say that the last sentence is more unexpected in (7) than it is in (8). From the point of view of information theory, which is based on calculations of likelihood, the last sentence in (7) is more informative than the last sentence in (8). However, there is a trade-off between informativity and processing ease. That is, the higher information value of the last sentence in (7) corresponds to more processing effort on the part of the recipient.

6. Situationality This standard of textuality "concerns the factors which make a text RELEVANT to a SITUATION of occurrence" (Beaugrande/Dressler 1981: 9). As we have seen in Figure 1.3 above, situationality is classified as a social standard. The example that Beaugrande/Dressler provide is the now also famous text of a road sign:

(9) SLOW

    CHILDREN

    AT PLAY

Note that with this example the medium-dependent layout is crucial for a proper understanding of the text. The short text under (9) is appropriate for a motorist who has only limited time and attention at his disposal as he is driving along. This has been taken into consideration by the text producer who has produced a maximally economic text. The aspect of economy is also relevant for a reader of newspapers, who has to decide which article to read. Here the headers must arouse interest in due brevity. Similarly, situations in which the minimal texts *Help!* or *Fire!* are produced do not lend themselves to long-winded verbosity.

   7. Intertextuality This last standard of textuality deals again with social aspects of text interpretation. It is defined as follows:

> The seventh standard of textuality is to be called INTERTEXTUALITY and concerns the factors which make the utilization of one text dependent upon knowledge of one or more previously encountered texts. (Beaugrande/Dressler 1981: 10)

A very obvious and simple example of intertextuality would be a road sign placed at some distance after (9):

(10) RESUME SPEED

It is evident that the relevance of (10) depends on the knowledge of (9).
   The notion of intertextuality can be understood in two ways. Firstly, it can refer to the relation of the present text to other texts. This is what we have encountered with the examples (9) and (10). This sense of intertextuality is systematically exploited in numerous text-types or parts of texts, where a more or less explicit relation between two texts is established. The most explicit connection between two texts can be seen in quotations, mottos, letters to the editor and translations. In these cases the reference to the first text is explicitly documented. But there are also implicit references. In these cases the text producer must hope that the text receiver knows the earlier text or quotation that is referred to. We have seen such a case of intertextuality above in connection with the bumper sticker *In God We Doubt*, which is a parody of the motto of the state of Florida *In God We Trust* and of a line in the American national anthem, *The Star-Spangled Banner*: "And this be our motto: 'In God is our trust'".
   If we consider that most of our knowledge today is mediated and does not come from personal experience or observation, it is clear that almost any text or

thought is related to some prior texts or thoughts as we do not live in a vacuum. This touches, of course, on the issue of cultural knowledge and general education. Part of this is, for example, to know and recognize quotations from important authors and the Bible. Thus, intertextuality is ultimately a very elusive concept.

Secondly, the notion of intertextuality can refer to text-types and the common features that texts of the same type share. Beaugrande/Dressler (1981: 10) explain:

> Intertextuality is, in a general fashion, responsible for the evolution of TEXT TYPES as classes of texts with typical patterns of characteristics.

This means that we often can classify a text on the ground of medium-dependent or medium-independent features as, for example, a death notice, a page from a dictionary or a narrative and an official document. Such classifications are possible because we have seen many instances of similar texts. Therefore, in this case intertextuality is not related to specific wordings or thoughts but to text-types.

After our cursory discussion of the seven standards of textuality, we must come back to the question of what a 'standard' actually is. When Beaugrande/ Dressler introduce the term, as we have seen at the beginning of this section 1.3, they give the impression that 'standards' are defining features, i.e. necessary conditions, for texts. Later on, however, they seem to distance themselves from such a position. Standards are then seen in relation to 'appropriateness', which is a pragmatic term and not a grammatical one. Beaugrande/Dressler write (1981: 11): "The APPROPRIATENESS of a text is the agreement between its setting and the ways in which the standards of textuality are upheld."

In a later publication, Beaugrande (1997: 15) is at pains to clarify the confusion about what the standards of textuality are. He writes:

> We need to emphasize that they designate the **major modes of connectedness** and not [...] the **linguistic features** of text-artefacts nor the borderline between 'texts' versus 'non-texts' [...]. The principles apply wherever an artefact is textualized, even if someone judges the results 'incoherent', unintentional', 'unacceptable', and so on. Such judgements indicate that the text is not appropriate (suitable to the occasion), or efficient (easy to handle) or effective (helpful for a goal); but it is still a text.

In the course of their book Beaugrande/Dressler (1981: 113) stress the importance of the text-centred notions of 'cohesion' and 'coherence'. They write:

The **cohesion** of surface texts and the underlying **coherence** of textual worlds are the most obvious standards of textuality. They indicate how the component elements of the text fit together and make sense. However, they cannot provide absolute borderlines between texts and non-texts in real communication. People can and do use texts which, for various motives, do not seem fully cohesive and coherent.

That is, the creation of cohesion and coherence rests on the freedom of choice to employ certain linguistic means or not. This option was discussed in connection with examples (7) and (8) above. But we have also seen in connection with example (5) that coherence may exist without cohesion. Therefore it is reasonable to agree with Vater (2001: 54), for whom 'coherence' appears to be the most important standard of textuality.

The last quotation from Beaugrande/Dressler can be fully supported as it corroborates the idea expressed earlier that 'text' is a prototype concept. Ideally it is cohesive and coherent, but much depends on the user-centred notions of intentionality, acceptability, informativity, situtionality and intertextuality, which all describe general prerequisites for successful communication and are as such not restricted to text-linguistics.

1.4 Essentials of text-linguistics

Our discussion of the scope of text-linguistics has shown that it must be distinguished from neighbouring disciplines such as discourse analysis or pragmatics and that there is a heterogeneity of approaches due to differing research interests. We have seen that text-linguistic research interests are concerned with the formal and functional analysis of sequences of word-forms (medium-independent aspect) and their material embodiment (medium-dependent aspect). We have also seen that this fundamental distinction plays an important role in the different meaning components of 'text' and 'discourse'. It is therefore reasonable that this distinction is also reflected in the organisation of the present book. It deals with medium-independent elements and structures in chapter 2 (Formal texture I) and with their medium-dependent presentation in chapter 3 (Formal texture II).

Medium-dependent presentation has not been a major concern of text-linguistic efforts but it is indispensable for at least two reasons. On the one hand, it is gaining more attention in the wake of the generally increasing interest in the media, especially the Internet. On the other hand, it is only reasonable to study medium-dependent presentation in a systematic way and not only intermittently. It must be added, however, that in this book the medium-dependent presentation is limited to alpha-numeric strings and therefore excludes pictures, figures, tables, etc. and their contribution to the verbal structure.

As we have also seen in our survey, the study of formal texture must be complemented by functional aspects, namely the study of semantic texture, decoder orientation and textual intentions. These essentials will be dealt with in chapters 4, 5 and 6.

1.5 Questions and exercises

1. What do 'text' and 'discourse' as linguistic terms have in common and how are they distinguished?

2. What are the most typical features of 'text' as a prototype category?

3. What is meant by 'formal texture' and 'semantic texture'?

4. What is the difference between 'cohesion' and 'coherence'?

5. What are the meanings of 'intertextuality'?

6. Give an example of coherent sentences which show no cohesion.

7. Take a text passage from a children's book and find out the cohesive links between sentences.

8. Why should coherence be more important than cohesion?

1.6 Further reading

Adamzik (2004) provides an overview of different conceptions of text, with a bias towards German and German studies. Vater (2001) offers, inter alia, text definitions and discusses textuality in chapter 2. Beaugrande/Dressler (1981) started the discussion of textuality and propagated a procedural approach to text-linguistics. Esser (2006) gives information on medium-transferability as well as medium-independent and medium-dependent structures.

2 Formal Texture I: Medium-independent Elements and Structures

In this chapter we shall deal with formal text constituents that are overtly expressed in either medium: actual words that we hear or see. More precisely, we should say that we are dealing with strings of 'word-forms' that were actually spoken or written. However, we are not interested in the physical medium-bound manifestations of word-forms but rather in their abstract realizations (cf. Halliday 1961: 250). Put in the words of Halliday/Hasan (1976: 5), we are interested in "lexicogrammatical forms", the "wording", but not in "phonological and orthographic expressions". They write (ibid.): "Meaning is put into wording, and wording into sound or writing." Following this distinction, we are interested in the lexicogrammatical forms of texts, i.e. the wording, but not in how the wordings are pronounced or written. This is a matter of abstraction.

Spoken word-forms and written word-forms are closer to the substance in which language is transmitted: sounds for your ears and graphic symbols for your eyes. As competent language users and as linguists we abstract from the medium-bound properties and the different morphological shapes (especially morphological endings) that a word may have and speak of a 'lexeme'. The lexeme is an abstract unit of the mental or linguistic lexicon. For example, the verb lexeme HELP can be instantiated by the written word-forms <help helps helped helping> and the corresponding spoken word-forms /help helps helpt helpɪŋ/. Note that due to the pervasive features of homophony and homography in present-day English, there is not allways a one-to-one relation between the written and the spoken forms of a lexeme.

For our purpose it is irrelevant, for example, whether the lexeme YOUR is written with or without a capital letter at the beginning, namely <Your> or <your>, and whether the spoken word-forms [jɔː] or [jʊər] are used. Features such as capitalization in writing or a British or an American accent in speech are irrelevant from the point of view of the abstract medium-independent language system. All of the four medium-bound word-forms are instantiations of a medium-independent word-form that may be symbolized >your<.

The phonetician Abercrombie (1967: 1) has described the relation between the different mediums and the language system as follows:

> We have recognized, in effect, that the piece of spoken English and the piece of written English are the same *language* embodied in different *mediums*, one medium consisting of shapes, the other of noises.

It is a commonplace that we can transfer messages from one medium to the other. We can write down what we hear and we can pronounce what we read; the message will be the same. This relation between speech, writing and the language system has been described with the notion of 'medium-transferability' by Lyons (1972: 65), who explains this important design feature as follows:

> People can learn, fairly easily and successfully for the most part, to transfer from one medium to the other, holding invariant much of the verbal part of language.

The restriction "much of the verbal part of language" refers exactly to the message that can be transferred from one medium to the other in terms of words and structures, i.e. the "wording" in the sense of Halliday/Hasan (1976: 5) quoted above. This is what linguists are normally interested in when they discuss lexicology, syntax and text-linguistics. Medium-bound information such as an American accent or a capital letter (for example, at the beginning of a sentence) is irrelevant outside phonology and graphology because it cannot be transferred from one medium to the other. When [jɔː] and [jʊ°r] are transferred from speech to writing, the information of a British or an American accent gets lost. Likewise, the spelling differences between <Your> and <your> have no equivalent in pronunciation: we cannot hear the capital letter. Thus, what can be transferred from one medium to the other are medium-independent word-forms and the structures to which they belong, in other words, the wording.

In the medium-independent approach to text-linguistics that is developed in this chapter, we will concentrate on those linguistic elements and structures that are subject to medium-transferability, which means that such elements and structures can be transferred from speech to writing and from writing to speech without loss of information. Therefore medium-bound expression systems such as intonation and layout will not be considered here but will be dealt with in chapter 3.

2.1 Order and realization of elements

2.1.1 General framework

Our descriptive model draws on fundamental ideas first formulated by Halliday (1961) in an attempt to develop a metatheory for structural linguistics. In what follows I do not want to explain his theory in detail but focus on two aspects that still enjoy general acceptance. The two metatheoretical aspects are 'rank' and 'instantiation'. (Halliday does not use the now fashionable term 'instantiation' but rather speaks of "exponent", which is to be understood as "example", p. 271.)

The notion of 'rank' refers to the generally acknowledged idea that we can and must distinguish descriptive entities of different size (cf. section 1.1 above). Linguists distinguish levels of constituency, whereby smaller units combine to form larger units and larger units consist of smaller units. The highest rank in grammatical description is occupied by the unit 'clause complex' and the lowest rank by the unit 'morpheme'. In between there are 'clause', 'phrase' and 'word'. Note that the concept 'clause complex' reflects our restriction to medium-independent units. In this I follow Halliday (1985: 193), who says: "A sentence is a constituent of writing, while the clause complex is a constituent of grammar." The ranks and units of grammar are listed in Figure 2.1.

Rank	Units
highest	clause complex
	clause
	phrase
	word
lowest	morpheme

Figure 2.1: Ranks and units of grammar

Clause complexes consist of clauses, clauses consist of phrases, phrases consist of words, words consist of morphemes. Reversely, morphemes pattern into words, words pattern into phrases, phrases pattern into clauses, clauses pattern into clause complexes. (Note that in the extreme case a clause complex may consist of just one clause, one phrase and one word, as e.g. in the directive *Go!*)

The second metatheoretical aspect that describes our general framework is 'instantiation'. It relates the units of grammar to the linguistic data ('exponence' in Halliday's framework) at various levels of abstraction ('delicacy' in Halliday's framework). This can be exemplified with the second orthographic sentence of example (4). This 'written sentence' corresponds at the medium-independent level to the 'clause complex' under (1), where the symbols > < indicate the medium-independent status:

(1) >but when she got there the cupboard was bare and so the poor dog had none<

With reference to (1) we can say that the clause complex is instantiated by three clauses: (i) a dependent clause (*but when she got there*), which is part of (ii); an independent clause (*the cupboard was bare*); and (iii) a further, coordinated independent clause (*and so the poor dog had none*). The combination of the three clauses is an instance of a clause complex. The different ranks and their instantiations can be summarized as in Figure 2.2. (For our purpose the connectors and the morphological level can be ignored, e.g. the information that the word-form *had* has a 'past' meaning.)

Unit	Instantiated by									
Clause complex	dependent clause			independent clause			independent clause			
Clause	[SVA]A			SVC			SVO			
Phrase	NP	VP	AdvP	NP	VP	AdjP	NP		VP	NP
Word class	Pron	V	Adv	Det	N	V	Adj	Det	Adj	N	V	Pron
Word	she	got	there	the	cupboard	was	bare	the	poor	dog	had	none

Figure 2.2: Units and their instantiations

At the rank of the clause, we can describe the clause elements of the three clauses. Following Quirk et al. (1985: 49), we distinguish five elements of clause structure: subject (S), verb (V), object (O), complement (C) and adverbial (A). Clause (i) is an instance of the clause pattern SVA, which functions as an adverbial in (ii); clause (ii) instantiates the pattern (A)SVC and clause (iii) has the pattern SVO. Disregarding the connectors *but, when, and* and *so*, the clause elements are instantiated at the phrase level as follows: [SVA:] NP+VP+AdvP, [SVC:] NP+VP+AdjP, [SVO:] NP+VP+NP. The phrases have the following instantiations by word classes: [NP:] Pron, [VP:] V, [AdvP:] Adv; [NP:] Det+N, [VP:] V, [AdjP:] Adj; [NP:] Det+Adj+N, [VP:] V, [NP:] Pron. Finally, at the rank of the word we have the following instantiations in terms of word-forms: [Pron:] *she*, [V:] *got*, [Adv:] *there*; [Det:] *the*, [N:] *cupboard*, [V:] *was*, [Adj:] *bare*; [Det:] *the*, [Adj:] *poor*, [N:] *dog*, [V:] *had*, [Pron:] *none*.

Example (1) instantiates grammatically units at different ranks, namely clause complex, clause, phrase, word class and word. This means that we can give for (1) structural descriptions of varying abstraction or generalization.

The instantiations of the clauses in Figure 2.2 are stated in terms of clause elements and their functions as subject (S), verbal element (V), adjunct (A), complement (C) and object (O), cf. Quirk et al. (1985). The instantiation of the clause patterns in terms of the realized phrases is, however, not the only type of instantiation of clause patterns. A different type is given if we consider structures that are in a systematic correspondence with the clause patterns that are regarded as basic and are therefore used in the abstract description of clause types. Examples of such correspondences are modifications of word order and of focusing constructions.

If we take the clause pattern SVO, this pattern can be instantiated, for example, at the level of word-forms as *I like that*. For purposes of emphasis the same clause pattern SVO can also be instantiated by the word-forms *that I like* (fronted object) or *that's what I like* (cleft construction). This means that there is variation of the pattern SVO not only in terms of the constitutive phrases, but also in terms of corresponding structures which instantiate the same pattern SVO. Such corresponding structures are called 'allo-sentences' by Daneš (1964: 233).

Daneš introduced the notion of the 'allo-sentence' to refer to the fact that the syntactic structure of a string of word-forms can be described at different levels of abstraction. Just as the concept of the phoneme /l/ is more abstract and removed from the physical data than the allophones [l] (clear 'l') and [ɫ] (dark 'l'), so the clause pattern /SVO/ is more abstract than its instantiations [SVO] and [OSV], cf. Figure 2.3.

Clause pattern	SVO	
	↗	↖
Allo-sentence	SVO	OSV
	↑	↑
Word-form	*I like that*	*that I like*

Figure 2.3: Instantiations of clause pattern and allo-sentence

The relation of instantiation (X → Y, to be read 'X instantiates Y') plays an important role in recent cognitive linguistics, which also describes concrete word-forms at various layers of abstraction (cf., for example, Langacker 1988).

It should also be noted that the contents of a clause pattern, i.e. the meaning in terms of a statement or a proposition, does not change as a rule in its allo-sentences. (One exception are quantifiers whose scope of meaning depends on their relative positions in the clause, cf. *few people know many languages* vs. *many languages are known by few people.*)

The concept of the allo-sentence, though not the term, is already discussed in Halliday (1961). With regard to exponents, i.e. instantiations, he writes:

> Since sequence is a variable, and may or not be an exponent of structure, we find difference in sequence without difference in structure, or difference in structure without difference in sequence. (ibid.: 255)

"Difference in sequence without difference in structure" describes exactly the situation that the allo-sentences *I like that* and *that I like* have the same meaning and both instantiate the clause pattern SVO. In the heyday of generative transformational grammar this situation was called 'structural synonymy'. The converse relation, 'structural homonymy' or ambiguity, is described with the words "difference in structure without difference in sequence" in Halliday's quotation above. An example that Halliday gives is the following:

(2) the man came from the gas board

Here, the prepositional phrase *from the gas board* can be given two analyses with two different meanings: it can postmodify the noun phrase *the man* in an SV clause pattern or it can be an adjunct in an SVA pattern.

It was mentioned above that related allo-sentences express the same proposition in a different word order or in a focusing construction. In Figure 2.4 there is a representative, although not exhaustive list of constructions by which pairs of allo-sentences are systematically related. The modified examples are taken from Quirk et al. (1985: 58-59, 1377-1402).

Example pair	Construction type
a number of people saw the accident ~ *the accident was seen by a number of people*	Active-passive relation
she sent Jim a card ~ *she sent a card to Jim*	Dative shift
you call it relaxation ~ *relaxation you call it*	Fronting
her oval face was especially remarkable ~ *especially remarkable was her oval face*	Inversion
I shall ignore his callousness ~ *it is his callousness that I shall ignore*	Cleft construction
you need most a good rest ~ *what you need most is a good rest*	Pseudo-cleft construction
to hear him say that surprised me ~ *it surprised me to hear him say that*	Extraposition
it is a pleasure to teach Elizabeth ~ *Elizabeth is a pleasure to teach*	Raising
they pronounced every one of the accused guilty ~ *they pronounced guilty every one of the accused*	Postponement
plenty of people are getting promotion ~ *there are plenty of people getting promotion*	Existential *there*

Figure 2.4: Systematic correspondences between allo-sentences

2.1.2 Order of clause elements: signalling information flow

2.1.2.1 Objective and subjective order

The choice of allo-sentence depends on the verbal context of the clause, i.e. its co-text, usually the preceding clauses. The relation of an allo-sentence to its co-text has been described in various theoretical frameworks and terminologies. Widdowson (1978: 25), for example, speaks of 'propositional development':

> Sentences are contextually appropriate when they express propositions in such a way as to fit into the propositional development of the discourse as a whole. [...] Generally speaking we can say that propositions are organized in such a way that what is known, or given, comes first in the sentence, and what is unknown or new, comes second.

For Widdowson (ibid.) the exchange (3) is odd, because B's answer does not start with what is mutually known or given, i.e. common ground.

(3) *A*: What did the rain do?

  B: The crops were destroyed by the rain.

On the other hand, B's alternative answers to A's question in (4) are felicitous:

(4) *A*: What happened to the crops?

  B: The crops were destroyed by the rain.

  They were destroyed by the rain.

  Destroyed by the rain.

Here we have cohesive, i.e. coreferential, links between the topic of crops (common ground) in A's question and B's answers. As B's answers show, the given topic can be taken up, for example, by repeating the noun phrase right at the beginning (a case of lexical cohesion), by referring to it with a pronoun (a case of reference) or by simply leaving it out (a case of ellipsis). B's answers in (4) can be viewed as allo-sentences which instantiate the clause pattern SVO, which, quite generally, could also be instantiated by the active allo-sentence *The rain destroyed the crops*. And we should note that the variants *They were destroyed by the rain* and *Destroyed by the rain* are possible instantiations of *The crops were destroyed by the rain* that could be regarded as 'allo-sentences of an allo-sentence'.

Widdowson (1978: 26) expressly relates the notion of cohesion, which will be dealt with in detail in section 2.1.3, to propositional development:

The notion of cohesion, then, refers to the way sentences and parts of sentences combine so as to ensure that there is propositional development.

Here is an authentic example of a felicitous propositional development, in which the author Peter Carey in his novel *Jack Maggs* (1997: 72) uses a fronted object (*him*) in an allo-sentence that enables an information flow from known to noteworthy:

(5) Mr Constable, the footman. Him you had sworn to murder in his bed.

The propositional development had already been a topic in the Prague School and its theory of Functional Sentence Perspective (FSP). Here the semantic notions of 'given' and 'new' are couched in the terms of 'theme' and 'rheme'. Mathesius, the leading figure of the Prague School, recognizes two kinds of arrangement: the objective order, corresponding to the concerns of Widdowson, and the subjective order, which gains a special status. Here is what Mathesius (1975 [1961]: 156) has to say:

> The usual position of the theme of an utterance is the beginning of the sentence, whereas the rheme occupies a later position, i.e. we proceed from what is already known to what is being made known. We have called this order o b j e c t i v e, since it pays regard to the hearer. The reversed order, in which the rheme of the utterance comes first and the theme follows, is s u b j e c t i v e. In normal speech this order occurs only in emotionally coloured utterances in which the speaker pays no regard to the hearer, starting with what is most important for himself.

The subjective order can be nicely demonstrated in a corny joke taken from Lewis (1977: 36)

(6) *Diner*: waiter there's a fly in my soup

Waiter: then perhaps you'd prefer a red wine sir

In the complaint of the diner the rheme of the utterance, *a fly*, comes first and is followed by the theme *in my soup*. The emotive order gives the utterance an appropriate emotional colour. As an alternative the diner could also have chosen the objective order as in (7), which has a less dramatic effect.

(7) *Diner*: waiter in my soup there is a fly

Note that we are not considering the medium-bound effects of intonation, which could render (7) dramatic after all.

2.1.2.2 Linear thematic progression

Propositional development in terms of 'theme' and 'rheme' was described by Daneš (1970, 1974) as 'thematic progression'. Daneš was not only concerned with the relation between two adjacent clauses, as was Widdowson, but rather with the text structuring potential of the thematic elements:

> The TP [thematic progression] might be described in terms of FSP [Functional Sentence Perspective], *i.e.* each utterance will be represented as a nexus of T-R [theme-rheme]; and as we must assume that each T [theme] (as an already known, old piece of information) has to be chosen (derived) from the subject matter already presented in the given discourse (text) or from the common stock of knowledge of the participants of the discourse (potential readers of the text), our task is to find out this contextual or situational connection for each T [theme]. This connection will be indicated here by means of a vertical arrow ↓ (while the horizontal arrow → indicates the T-R [theme-rheme] nexus in an utterance). Thus the TP [thematic progression] might be defined as the concatenation of particular T's [themes] and their connection with a text, its subparts and situation. (Daneš 1970: 137)

There are basically three types of thematic progression: two operate at the level of overt word-forms (i.e. lexically and grammatically) and one at the level of semantics. In other words, the first two types deal with the themes of clause complexes (sometimes called 'sentence themes') and the third with 'text themes'; the latter will be dealt with in section 4.6 of chapter 4 on semantic texture.

The first type of overt thematic progression is the 'simple linear progression'. It can be graphically symbolized as in Figure 2.5 (T stands for 'theme' and R stands for 'rheme') and exemplified as in (8), which is taken from Daneš (1974: 118).

$$T_1 \rightarrow R_1$$
$$\downarrow$$
$$T_2 (= R_1) \rightarrow R_2$$
$$\downarrow$$
$$T_3 (= R_2) \rightarrow R_3$$

Figure 2.5: Simple linear progression

(8) The first of the antibiotics was discovered by Sir Alexander Flemming in 1928. He was busy at the time investigating a certain species of germ which is responsible for boils and other troubles.

T_1, *the first of the antibiotics*, is related to R_1, *Sir Alexander Flemming*. The referent of R_1 is taken up with the pronoun *he* in the next clause complex as T_2. T_2 is related to R_2, *a certain species of germ*, which in turn is taken up as T_3 by the relative pronoun *which*, which is in turn related to R_3, *responsible for boils and other troubles*.

The stylistic device of simple linear progression does not describe whole texts but rather portions of them. It can be found in simple narratives and fairy tales, cf. example (2), which is repeated here as (9).

(9) Once upon a time there was a king. He had a daughter. She was very pretty.

The second type of overt thematic progression is 'progression with a continuous theme'. It can be symbolized graphically as in Figure 2.6 and exemplified as in example (10), again taken from Daneš (1974: 118-119).

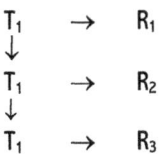

Figure 2.6: Progression with a continuous theme

(10) The Rousseauist especially feels an inner kinship with Prometheus and other Titans. He is fascinated by any form of insurgency... He must show an elementary energy in his explosion against the established order and at the same time a boundless sympathy for the victims of it... Further the Rousseauist is ever ready to discover beauty of soul in anyone who is under the reprobation of society.

The continuous theme is here "the Rousseauist", which is taken up several times, by the pronoun *he* and the repetition *the Rousseauist*. Example (10) shows that there is a connection between the clause themes and the theme of a paragraph (or even a larger portion of a text). Therefore, *the Rousseauist* can also be regarded as a local text theme which is overtly expressed.

We have seen in this section that information flow can be studied from various perspectives which all relate to the same cohesive devices (pronouns and lexical linkage): propositional development of theme and rheme from one clause to the next, clause-internal arrangement of theme and rheme, and thematic progression over several clauses. In the following section 2.1.3 a further aspect will be discussed, namely the referring function of grammatical and lexical elements.

2.1.3 Realization of clause elements: referencing and establishing cohesion by referring back and forward

We have noted in section 1.1 that Halliday/Hasan (1976: 2) regard 'text' as a semantic unit: "a unit not of form but of meaning". Surely, for the linguist, a text consists of a sequence of word-forms. But the word-forms are structurally related only in clause complexes and not beyond. The point is that 'text' is not a grammatical unit in the system of ranks (cf. Figure 2.1 in section 2.1.1 above). In the words of Halliday/Hasan (1976: 27): "There are no structural units defined by the cohesive relation." It is therefore the cohesive relation between word-forms in separate clause complexes that is regarded as meaningful. This type of meaning has to be worked out in the decoding process:

> Cohesion occurs where the INTERPRETATION of some element in the discourse is dependent on that of another. The one PRESUPPOSES the other, in the sense that it cannot be effectively decoded except by recourse to it. (ibid.: 4)

Halliday/Hasan (1976: 2) demonstrate the meaning of a cohesive relation with the help of the following example from a cookery book:

(11) Wash and core six cooking apples. Put them into a fireproof dish.

Referring to this sequence they write:

> What is the MEANING of the cohesive relation between *them* and *six cooking apples*? The meaning is that they refer to the same thing. The two items are identical in reference, or COREFERENTIAL. (ibid.: 3)

Coreference means that the items *six cooking apples* and *them* refer to the same entities in the extralinguistic world or in the world created by the text. This may be visualized as in Figure 2.7.

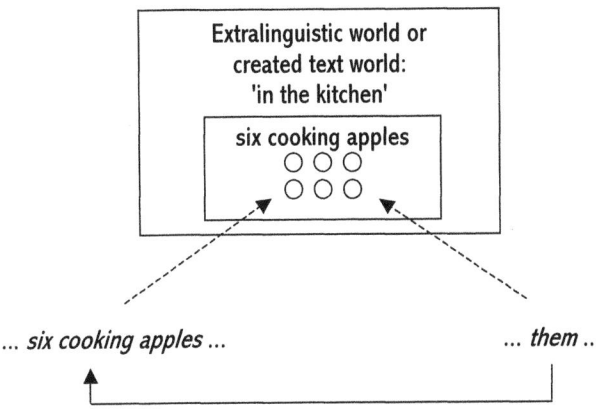

Figure 2.7: *Endophoric and exophoric reference*

There are two kinds of link symbolized by the two kinds of arrows. The solid arrow links the two textual items *them* and *six cooking apples*; this link in the text itself is classed as 'endophoric reference' (reference within the text) by Halliday/Hasan (1976: 33), more specifically, 'anaphoric reference' (reference to preceding text) because the item *them* refers back to the earlier mentioned item *six cooking apples*. On the other hand, the broken arrows link the textual items to the situation of the extralinguistic or textual world; this is called 'exophoric reference' (reference to the context of situation) by Halliday/Hasan (ibid.). It is clear that endophoric and exophoric reference interact in the creation of a text world by a decoder. Coreference can be understood as the feature that textual items refer to the same classes or entities in the extralinguistic world or in the created text world.

When Halliday/Hasan speak of the cohesive device of 'reference' they mean text-internal relations. There is, however, a slight terminological problem in that 'reference' is generally understood in its exophoric meaning, while Halliday/Hasan use it to designate a type of endophoric cohesive relation.

The standard use of the term 'reference' in semantics and speech act theory describes the relation between a linguistic expression and an object of the extralinguistic reality, more specifically, the attempt by a speaker/writer to identify for a listener/reader objects of reality about which he wants to say/write something (cf. Lyons 1977: 177). This attempt of 'referencing' can be more or less successful and depends on the kinds of referring expressions that are used in a communication situation.

In face-to-face communication it is normal to treat the surrounding objects as mutually accessible and therefore as common ground between the speaker and the listener; the encoding will typically make use of deictic expressions like *this, that, here, there* and personal pronouns like *he, she* and *they*. On the other hand, when the communication partners do not share the situation as in writing or telephoning, the linguistic items that refer to the objects that we want to speak or write about must be properly introduced with descriptive noun phrases to create successfully an image in the textual world. The use of deictic expressions and endophorically referring items is inappropriate for a first mention in such communication situations.

The two styles of referencing were discussed more than thirty years ago under the sociolinguistic terms 'restricted code' and 'elaborated code' (cf. Bernstein 1971). Halliday/Hasan (1976: 35) exemplify these two styles by quoting two prototypical descriptions of a picture story verbalized by five-year-old children. The wordings are given here as examples (12) and (13).

(12) they're playing football and he kicks it and it goes through there and it breaks the window and they're looking at it and he comes out and shouts at them because they've broken it so they run away and then she looks out and she tells them off

(13) three boys are playing football and one kicks the ball and it goes through the window the ball breaks the window and the boys are looking at it and a man comes out and shouts at them because they've broken the window so they run away and then that lady looks out of her window and she tells the boys off

Example (12) is meant to illustrate features of a restricted code while example (13) is meant to illustrate features of an elaborated code. From a textlinguistic point of view it is interesting to note that referencing in (12) relies heavily on exophoric reference, i.e. the items *they, he, it, there*, etc. point to the picture which, however, the listener or reader cannot see. Therefore it is unclear for the decoder what the items refer to, and this makes the establishment of cohesive relations and the creation of a textual world difficult. On the other hand, (13) makes more use of lexically filled noun phrases (*three boys, the ball, the window* etc.) which can then be a target of endophoric reference for the anaphoric items *one* [boy], *it* [ball], etc.

These general differences in referencing were described later by Kay (1977) with the terms 'non-autonomous style' and 'autonomous style'. Example (12) is non-autonomous because it depends on the shared situation by the speaker and the listener, i.e. it depends on common ground. That is, the speaker assumes that the listener can also see the pictures that are described. On the other hand, example (13) is fairly autonomous because it is independent of a shared situation between the communication partners. New entities are properly introduced into the world created by the text and can then be referred to with endophoric reference.

It is evident that the non-autonomous style is appropriate for spoken face-to-face communication while the autonomous style is appropriate for writing. None of the two is better than the other; the choice is a matter of appropriateness. But it is also clear that children first acquire the non-autonomous style while the autonomous style has to be properly learnt at school.

Halliday/Hasan (1976) describe the various types of grammatical and lexical devices that can be employed to refer back to items mentioned earlier in a text, both within clause complexes and, more interesting from the point of view of text-linguistics, across the borders of clause complexes. In the following sections we will discuss various grammatical and lexical means that can be used for textual reference that establishes cohesion.

2.1.3.1 Pronouns

Pronouns have a signposting function, especially the third person pronouns *he, she, it* and *they*. They refer to noun phrases that are mentioned earlier in a text. Their interpretation is highly variable. *He*, for example, means 'I am still talking/writing about a male person/animal that was identified earlier and I assume that this entity is still in your short-term memory'. We already saw an example of the referring function of personal pronouns in example (9) above. Here is an adapted corpus example from Sinclair (1990: 385) with a personal pronoun (*her*) and a possessive pronoun (*hers*) referring back to *Mary*:

(14) Mary was in my arms. I held her very close. My cheek was against hers.

While *Mary* and *her* are in a relation of coreference (both referring in the extralinguistic world to the same female person) the relation of *hers* to *Mary* is different. *Hers* is a noun phrase head that is in a relation to the noun phrase *my cheek* with the difference that the referent of *my*, i.e. *I*, is replaced by the referent *Mary*. We could say that *hers* substitutes the noun phrase *my cheek* with a new possessor. The possessive pronouns *mine, yours, his, ours* and *theirs* function in the same way.

2.1.3.2 Determiners

Determiners such as the definite article *the*, the demonstrative pronouns *this* and *that*, and the possessive pronouns *his* and *her* are linguistic means to indicate that the things or persons you want to talk about are identifiable. They are therefore suitable to establish a cohesive relation between a noun phrase constructed with one of these determiners and a noun phrase mentioned earlier in the text.

Halliday/Hasan (1976: 71-72) distinguish five uses of the definite article *the*, of which only one is cohesive. In the following I want to discuss some of their examples. There are three exophoric uses. Firstly, it refers to a specific situation as in example (15).

(15) Don't go; the train's coming. ('the train we are both expecting')

Secondly, the definite article refers to something that exists only once, like *the sun, the government* ('of our country') or *the baby* ('our baby'). Thirdly, the definite article can refer to a whole class, as is the case with *the snail* in (16), a use which is called 'generic'.

(16) The snail is considered a great delicacy in this region.

Of the two endophoric uses of *the*, one points backward (anaphoric reference), as in (17). This use only is cohesive.

(17) She found herself in a long, low hall which was lit up by a row of lamps hanging from the roof. There were doors all round the hall, but they were all locked.

Note that *the* not only signals referential identity between *in a long, low hall* and *the hall*. The definite article *the* can also be used to indicate something that is closely connected with something mentioned earlier. This kind of cohesive link exists between *hall* and *roof*, the roof being part of the hall. The semantic relations that exist between two nouns related in this way is a topic of coherence and will be discussed in section 4.3.

Lastly, there is the cataphoric use of *the*. But its forward-pointing function is only within a noun phrase, i.e. to point to the specifying postmodification as in *the ascent of Mount Everest*. From a textlinguistic perspective this clause-internal use of the definite article is not cohesively relevant.

The next group of determiners that can be used cohesively are the demonstratives *this, these, that* and *those*. Here are some corpus examples from Sinclair (1990: 387):

(18) The concert began with his Second Piano Sonata. This is a work that has usually been considered as fundamentally negative.

(19) Only small pines are left. Many of these have twisted and stunted shapes.

(20) There's a lot of material there. You can use some of that.

(21) The rooms are inhabited by boys from twelve to sixteen years of age. The majority of those boys have reached the stage of caring for comfort and decorations.

The examples show that determiners can occur with an overtly expressed noun phrase, as in example (21), or on their own, as the preceding examples show. Thus, *this* in (18) can be understood and paraphrased as *this work*, *these* in (19) as *these pines*, and *that* in (20) as *that material*.

As a last class of determiners we must mention possessive pronouns. Their cohesive function is within a clause and across clause complex boundaries, as the following corpus examples from Sinclair (1990: 50) demonstrate.

(22) I took off my shoes.

(23) Her husband remained standing. He had his hands in his pockets.

Note that the possessive determiner *his* can fulfil two functions: It can function as a determiner with an overt noun phrase as in (23), but it can also, like demonstratives, stand on its own for the whole noun phrase as in example (24) taken from Sinclair (1990: 33).

(24) David Lodge? I've just read a novel of his.

The other possessive determiners, i.e. *my, your, her, its, our, their*, have distinct formal counterparts as possessive pronouns, i.e. *mine, yours, hers* (*its* is not attested in Sinclair's corpus-based grammar), *ours* and *theirs*. As we have seen, possessive pronouns themselves stand for noun phrases and are not just determining parts of these (cf. section 2.1.3.1).

2.1.3.3 Comparison

The cohesive link between two clause complexes can also be established by making a comparison. Hereby we indicate that something mentioned explicitly or implicitly before is the same, similar or different. An important item that can fulfil this function is *such*. It is used with a noun phrase head that refers to an entity mentioned explicitly or implicitly before. *Such* can occur as a determiner, as a predeterminer and as an adjective, as the following corpus examples from Sinclair (1990: 392-393) show respectively.

(25) New business on a small scale has been found to provide the great majority of new jobs. By their nature such businesses take risks.

(26) They lasted for hundreds of years. On a human time scale, such a period seems an eternity.

(27) Mr Bell's clubs were privately owned. Like most such clubs everywhere, they were organizations of congenial people who shared a certain interest.

Besides *such*, there are several adjectives that can be used to make comparisons. The item *same* can premodify a noun phrase as in (28, 29) and also stand on its own as the head of a noun phrase as in (30) (Sinclair 1990: 393).

(28) The door opened and a man popped his head into the room and said 'Next please'. About ten minutes later, the same man returned.

(29) We accept that thought is a common property of the human race. But we cannot make the same assumption about machines.

(30) The conversion process is inefficient and about two-thirds of the energy is wasted. The same is true of nuclear power stations.

Examples (28) and (29) show that the link established with the comparison can be understood coreferentially as in (28), *a man – the man*, and to refer to something implicit as in (29). Example (29) and also (30) show that the noun phrase with *same* (as premodifier or head) has no direct nominal antecedent but rather the contents of the preceding clauses, i.e. propositions. Note that *the same assumption* in (29) refers to *thought is a common property of the human race*, and *The same* in (30) refers as a whole or in part to *The conversion process is inefficient (and about two-thirds of the energy is wasted)*.

Among the adjectives that can be used for comparison are *contrasting, different, equal, analogous, comparable* and *similar*, cf. Sinclair (1990: 393-394) and his following corpus example:

(31) West Germany, Denmark and Italy face declines in young people. Ireland is confronted with a contrasting problem.

As a last group Sinclair (1990: 394) mentions the adjuncts *in the same/similar way, similarly, likewise, otherwise* and *differently*, cf. (32):

(32) She spoke of Jim and Karl tolerantly but with frowns and sighs. And presumably she spoke to them of me in the same way.

The examples (31) and (32) show again that the comparison is made not with an anteceding nominal referent but rather with the contents, i.e. the propositions, of the preceding clauses.

2.1.3.4 Substitution

'Substitution' is the name of a further type of link between two textual items. Halliday/Hasan explain it as follows:

> Substitution is a relation between linguistic items, such as words or phrases; whereas reference is a relation between meanings. (Halliday/ Hasan 1976: 89)

Therefore, substitution does not indicate referential identity but only identity of lexicogrammatical forms or categories. We have seen this difference already in connection with example (14) in section 2.1.3.1 above. Similarly, in example (33) below, *one* substitutes *building*, i.e. a noun slot that is realized by a word-form of the lexeme BUILDING. Halliday/Hasan distinguish between 'nominal', 'verbal' and 'clausal substitution' which may be signalled by the substitutes *one*, *do* and *so* respectively as the following examples from the British National Corpus (BNC) show. (Information about the BNC and other corpora mentioned in this book can be found in Kennedy (1998).)

(33) They didn't stop at the nearest building, but drove on to a bigger o̱ne̱ with many more vehicles outside. ['building'] (BNC CEU 3012)

(34) You think Joan already knows? – I think everybody do̱e̱s̱. ['knows/already knows'] (BNC FRL 1763)

(35) She stopped being really French, everyone says s̱o̱. ['she stopped being really French '] (BNC GUK 483)

As example (34) shows, verbal substitution can refer not only to the verbal element but also to accompanying adjuncts or complementations.

2.1.3.5 Ellipsis

Halliday/Hasan regard ellipsis as 'substitution by zero'. It is not simply something unsaid but something that is understood in terms of a structural presupposition:

> When we talk of ellipsis, we are not referring to any and every instance in which there is some information that the speaker has to supply from his own evidence. That would apply to practically every sentence that is ever spoken or written, and would be of no help in explaining the nature of a text. We are referring specifically to sentences, clauses, etc whose structure is such as to presuppose some preceding item, which then serves as the source of the missing information. An elliptical item is one which, as it were, leaves the specific structural slots to be filled from elsewhere. This is exactly the same as presupposition by substitution, except that in substitution an explicit 'counter' is used, eg: *one* or *do*, as a place-marker for what is presupposed, whereas in ellipsis nothing is inserted into the slot. This is why we say that ellipsis can be regarded as substitution by zero. (Halliday/Hasan 1976: 143)

As with substitution, a distinction is made between 'nominal', 'verbal' and 'clausal ellipsis'. Nominal and verbal ellipsis can be seen in examples (36) and (37), which are taken from the BNC; example (38), taken from Halliday/Hasan (1976: 221), demonstrates clausal ellipsis.

(36) It was quite a surprise, therefore, to find that most galaxies appeared red-shifted: nearly all [Ø] were moving away from us! ['galaxies'] (BNC H78 59)

(37) The scramble might be a training exercise, or it might not [Ø]. ['be a training exercise'] (BNC CDA 3066)

(38) The cheque is still valid. The Bank can tell them [Ø]. ['that it is still valid']

2.1.3.6 Lexical cohesion

The cohesive devices described so far were grammatical in nature. Pronouns (cf. 2.1.3.1) and determiners (cf. 2.1.3.2) are classes of grammatical units. Comparison (cf. 2.1.3.3), substitution (cf. 2.1.3.4) and ellipsis (cf. 2.1.3.5) are based on structures, namely noun phrases, verb phrases (with or without an adjunct and complementation) and clauses. Lexical cohesion, however, is not based on grammatical units or structures but rather on the relation between lexical items. For Halliday/Hasan (1976: 274) 'lexical cohesion' is "the cohesive effect achieved by the selection of vocabulary". This means that lexical cohesion is described not with the help of grammatical structure but with lexical structure.

Lexical structure is a topic of structural semantics. It regards the vocabulary of a language not as completely unrelated items but rather as related by features and relations. To these belong 'synonymy' (sharing all or essential features, e.g. *girl – lass*), 'hyperonymy' (having fewer features, e.g. *child – girl*), 'antonymy' (complementarity of features, e.g. *single – married*) and 'metonymy' (change and transfer of features, e.g. *the crown – monarch*). These relations are classed as 'paradigmatic relations' because they affect the choice of words in a position of a text, cf. Lipka (2002).

Halliday/Hasan (1976: 274) mention a special type and use of 'hyperonym' which they call 'general noun'. It is chiefly used anaphorically to refer back in a text, e.g. *man, person, thing, move, place*, etc. as in example (39) from Halliday/Hasan (1976: 274-275):

(39) Didn't everyone make it clear they expected the Minister to resign? - They did. But it seems to have made no impression on the man.

In their explanation of the concept 'general noun' and as an interpretation of example (39) Halliday/Hasan (1976: 275) write:

> From a lexical point of view, they [general nouns] are the superordinate members of major lexical sets, and therefore their cohesive use is an instance of the general principle whereby the superordinate item operates anaphorically as a kind of synonym. From a grammatical point of view, the combination of general noun plus specific determiner, such as *the man, the thing*, is very similar to a reference item. There is little difference between *it seems to have made very little impression on the man* and *it seems to have made very little impression on him*: in both instances interpretation is possible only by reference to something that has gone before.

This description shows that Halliday/Hasan regard general nouns as sharing features of grammatical and lexical cohesion.

Recent research has shown that not only simple lexemes enter into cohesive relations in a text, but also derivations (especially nominalizations) and compounds (cf. Novak 1996). These must also be considered in the discussion of lexical cohesion, cf. examples (45) and (46) below.

And lastly, from a paradigmatic point of view, the repetition of a word (called 'reiteration' by Halliday/Hasan) belongs to the resources that establish a coreferential link between lexical items in a text. This leads us to the list of devices for paradigmatic lexical cohesion shown in Figure 2.8; examples (40) to (42) are taken from Halliday/Hasan (1976: 278), the others from the British National Corpus (BNC) and the Lancaster-Oslo/Bergen Corpus (LOB).

Device	Example
general noun	(39)
repetition	(40)
synonymy	(41)
hyperonymy	(42)
antonymy	(43)
metonymy	(44)
nominalization	(45)
compounding	(46)

Figure 2.8: Devices for paradigmatic lexical cohesion

(40) There was a large mushroom growing near her, about the same height as herself; and, when she had looked under it, it occurred to her that she might as well look and see what was on the top of it. She is stretched herself up on tiptoe, and peeped over the edge of the mushroom, ...

(41) Accordingly ... I took leave, and turned to the ascent of the peak. The climb is perfectly easy ...

(42) Henry's bought himself a new Jaguar. He practically lives in the car.

(43) The walk was scheduled to depart from Green Park Tube, and when I arrived I found a group of thirty or so walkers already tapping their feet. (BNC ABS 104)

(44) In regard to the latter, Ford deplored 'the inability of the White House to maintain control over the large federal bureaucracy'. [Gerald Ford was the 38th President of the USA from 1974 to 1977.] (BNC EAY 206)

(45) Profits jump. There is surprisingly good news this morning from Sir Ivan Stedeford, master of mighty Tube Investments. He reports a jump in profits of 3 million to a record 27 million. (LOB A16 75-77)

(46) The acid soils which have developed support a semi-natural cover of heath, or of deciduous wood-land consisting of oak and birch with some rowan and holly, and a bracken or heathy type of ground flora. ... Replanting

consisted mainly of pine, though some open, degenerate, dry oak-birch woodland remains. (LOB J03 63-72)

We have noted before that the cohesive relation between lexical items in a text is not limited to referential identity, i.e. to coreference. Coreference could be observed in the examples for general noun (39), repetition (40), synonymy (41) and hyperonymy (42). As further types of cohesive relation Halliday/Hasan in a later publication recognize besides coreference also 'co-classification' and 'co-extension'. Co-classification is defined as follows:

> In this type of meaning relation, the things, processes, or circumstances to which A and B refer belong to an identical class, but each end of the cohesive tie refers to a distinct member of this class. (Halliday/Hasan 1985: 74)

An example of co-classification from the LOB corpus is provided by Novak (1996: 132):

(47) ... and there they would be, cheerful and kind, ready for talk and paper-games ... Good heavens no, what nonsense we would say, and settled down to another paper game. (LOB K22 73, 77)

Here the items *paper-games* and *paper game* refer to the same class of referents, but to distinct members. (Note that the spelling variants are instances of the same medium-independent word-form >papergame<.)

Co-extension is defined by Halliday/Hasan (1985: 74) as follows: "Here the relationship [...] is [...] that both [members] refer to something within the same general field of meaning." The examples of antonymy (43) and metonymy (44) can be regarded as instances of co-extension. Departing and arriving in (43) are stages of a journey, and in (44) Ford as President of the United States resides in the White House.

2.1.3.7 Place relators

The creation of a textual world depends crucially on spatial and temporal orientation. Therefore the expressions that refer to places mentioned in a text deserve special attention. Place relators are a mixed category. First, there are the two demonstrative adverbs *here* and *there* that can refer to a place mentioned before in the text. Here are two corpus examples, (48) from the BNC, (49) from Sinclair (1990: 388):

(48) The legislative route adopted by the government with respect to the curriculum and assessment procedures for schools in England and Wales, contrasts with the situation found in Scotland. Here the restructuring of the curriculum and assessment practice has been gradually introduced ... (BNC CN5 13-14)

(49) I decided to try Newmarket. I soon found a job there.

Besides the grammatical items *here* and *there*, there are also lexical ways to establish spatial coreference. This is highly dependent on the situation of the external world described and the created text world. Therefore the place relators often have features of the restricted code in that the noun phrases are not made fully explicit but rely on our common and situational knowledge.

Some of the information that is not explicated can be recovered in terms of structural ellipsis. But there is also a situational ellipsis, which is on the border to semantic implication. This can be demonstrated with a short text from Quirk et al. (1985: 1448):

(50) On Tuesday evening, I was at the front door talking to a caller. Suddenly we heard a crash and two cars collided just opposite. We hurried across to see if we could help. One driver was scrambling out, bleeding profusely, and my visitor helped him over to the pavement. Then along came some people, running up the street. I dashed back in and phoned for help. When I went out again, the other driver was trying to move his car down the road a little and in to the side.

The full understanding of the place relators can be made explicit as follows:

(51) at the front door [of the speaker's house]
just opposite [to where the speaker and the visitor were standing]
across [the intervening space (of footpath and street)]
out [of the driver's car]
over [the space between the car and the kerb]
along [the street]
up the street [towards the speaker / up the hill]
back in [the speaker's house]
out [of the house]
down the road [away from the speaker / down the hill]
in to the side [of the street]

Here are two more examples from Quirk et al. (1985: 1449) that show how place relators rely on ellipsis:

(52) He examined the car. The front [of the car] was slightly damaged.

(53) The building was heavily guarded by police. The windows at the top [of the building] were covered with boards.

Examples (52) and (53) also show that nominal place relators can be viewed as cases of metonymy, since spatial orientation relates to parts of larger entities, namely *car* and *building*.

2.1.3.8 Time relators and tense marking

The cohesive relations in a text also depend on the time references that are made, as Quirk et al. (1985: 1451-1452) explain:

> Since time passes irrespective of location (which need not change), temporal cues to periods, and to references *before*, *after*, *within*, and *during* these periods, are more inherently essential than locational cues. [...] Once a time reference has been established, certain temporal adjectives and adverbs may order subsequent information in relation to the time reference.

The cohesive temporal relation that is established with adjectives and adverbs can be demonstrated in the following examples from Quirk et al. (ibid.):

(54) He handed in a good essay. His previous essays were all poor.

(55) I shall explain to you what happened. But first I must give you a cup of tea.

(56) The death of the President was reported this afternoon on Cairo radio. A simultaneous announcement was broadcast from Baghdad.

(57) Several of the conspirators have been arrested but their leader is as yet unknown. Meanwhile the police are continuing their investigation into the political sympathies of the group.

(58) I left him at 10 p.m. And he was almost asleep. But some later hour he must have lit a cigarette.

(59) The manager went to a board meeting this morning. He was then due to catch a train to London.

Examples (54) and (55) give time reference previous to a given time, (56) and (57) simultaneous with a given time and (58) and (59) subsequent to a given time.

Another important factor for the cohesion of a text and an understanding of the time references in a text world is tense marking. Quirk et al. (1985: 1454) explain:

> But, as a further indication of the importance of time in language, all finite clauses (and many nonfinite ones) carry a discrete indication of tense and aspect. Although the contrasts involved are severely limited in comparison with adverbial distinctions, they contribute to the texual cohesion and progression, and of course they cannot be absent.

The importance of tense marking can be demonstrated with the following alternatives given by Quirk et al. (ibid.):

(60) She told me all about the operation on her hip.

   (a) It seemed to have been a success. (It seemed *to her* ...)

   (b) It seems to have been a success. (It seems *to me* ...)

Example (60) nicely shows the difference between reported time in (a) and reporting time (b). The change between these can also be observed in the following text from Quirk et al. (ibid.):

(61) As a child, I LIVED in Singapore. It's very hot there, you know, and I never OWNED an overcoat. I remember being puzzled at picture books showing European children wrapped up in heavy coats and scarves. I believe I THOUGHT it all as exotic as children here think about spacemen's clothing.

Figure 2.9 shows how the different tense markings relate to the reporting time (now), i.e. the time of the text production, and to the reported time in the text producer's past (THEN).

Formal Texture I

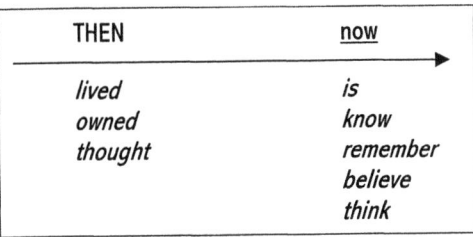

Figure 2.9: Reported and reporting time in example (61)

2.1.3.9 Referring forward

Although grammatical and lexical cohesive devices are mainly used anaphorically to refer back, there is also cataphoric, i.e. forward-pointing reference in texts. First, we must distinguish between cataphoric reference within the clause complex on the one hand, and beyond clause complex boundaries on the other. The first situation is given in complex noun phrases with a defining relative clause, when the definite article of a noun or a pronoun points forward to the defining relative clause as in examples (62) and (63) from Halliday/Hasan (1976: 72, 56).

(62) the people who predicted a dry summer

(63) He who hesitates is lost.

Then there is the case of 'left dislocation'. This occurs if the first, pronominal realization of a noun phrase is repeated in its more explicit form as in example (64) from Halliday/Hasan (ibid.: 56), which combines exophoric reference (reference to the situation) with cataphoric reference.

(64) They're good these peaches.

From the point of view of text-linguistics cataphoric reference across clause complex boundaries is more important. This is achieved by the demonstrative pronouns *this* and *these*, which point to noun phrases or propositions in the following clause complexes in examples (65) from Halliday/Hasan (1976: 17) and (66) from Sinclair (1990: 395).

(65) This is how to get the best results. You let the berries dry in the sun, till all the moisture has gone out of them. Then you gather them up and chop them very fine.

(66) These were the facts: on a warm February afternoon, Gregory Clark and a friend were cruising down Washington Boulevard in a Mustang.

Halliday/Hasan (1976: 56) also give an example of the cataphoric use of *it* that is cohesive:

(67) You would never have believed it. They've accepted the whole scheme.

Sinclair (1990: 395) mentions lexical items referring cataphorically to ideas, texts or pieces of writing that follow next in a text, for example:

(68) I draw the following conclusions: that natural childbirth and rooming in should be available for all who want them.

It must be pointed out that cataphoric reference is often not used to establish an overt referential relation in a text world (i.e. coreference) but rather to inform the reader of what comes next.

2.1.4 Connecting clauses in clause complexes and beyond

The ideas that are put into wording are expressed in clauses. There are several ways how the clauses of a text can be syntactically or textually related. Relating clauses syntactically means that the clauses form a syntactic unit called 'clause complex'. One way of relating clauses in a clause complex is by 'syntactic coordination'. This makes use of 'coordinators' like *and* and *but*, which signal that a clause beginning with these elements is part of a bigger structure, namely the clause complex. This will be discussed in section 2.1.4.1.

Another way of relating clauses in a clause complex is by 'syntactic subordination'. This means that dependent, i.e. subordinate, clauses are structurally part of a superordinate, independent clause, which is sometimes called 'matrix clause'. The structural dependency is mainly signalled by 'subordinators' like *if* and *because* and/or a nonfinite verb phrase. This will be discussed in section 2.1.4.2.

Since the clause complex is the largest syntactic unit, textual relations beyond clause complex boundaries can only be established semantically, either overtly by linking words like the 'conjunct' *therefore* or implicitly by coherence. Linking words will be discussed in section 2.1.4.3 and coherence in section 4.3.

2.1.4.1 Syntactic coordination

Syntactic coordination is formally signalled by what are called 'coordinators' or 'coordinating conjunctions'. Clear cases of coordinators are *and* and *or*. Quirk et al. (1985: 927) regard *and* and *or* as 'central coordinators', cf. Figure 2.10 below. They are at one end of a coordination-subordination gradient with 'conjuncts' in between.

The central coordinators *and* and *or* can link more than two clauses and when they do, all but the final instance of the linking items can be omitted, cf. example (69) from Quirk et al. (1985: 925).

(69) The battery may be disconnected, [or] the connection may be loose, or the bulb may be faulty.

This property does not hold for the (less central) coordinator *but* nor for the conjuncts *yet* and *therefore* (cf. below).

The coordinators *and*, *or* and *but* (like some of the conjuncts and all of the subordinators) are restricted to the initial positions in a clause. Thus when they coordinate subordinate clauses they stand in front of the subordinator, cf. example (70) from Quirk et al. (1985: 924).

(70) I wonder whether you should go and see her or whether it is better to write to her.

Conjuncts do not possess the property of linking subordinate clauses (cf. *and if ... / *yet if ...*) and are different in this respect from coordinators. Another difference is that coordinators can also link constituents in a clause, e.g. noun phrases, which only a subclass of conjuncts, e.g. *yet*, can do (e.g. *a firm yet gentle hand*). The conjunct *therefore* belongs to a different subclass: it has the property that it is not restricted to the initial position of the clause, cf. example (71) from Quirk et al. (1985: 643).

(71) Because Jennifer foresaw this well in advance, she therefore had the necessary time to take preventive action.

At the other end of the gradient there are subordinators like *if*, *because* and *although*. Subordinators are distinguished from coordinators and the conjunct *yet* by the property that they can link only clauses but not clause constituents, (cf. below).

Figure 2.10 summarizes important distinctions of Quirk et al.'s coordination-subordination gradient.

Gradient	Examples
central coordinators	*and, or*
(less central) coordinator	*but*
conjuncts	*yet, ...* *therefore, ...*
subordinators	*if, because, although, ...*

Figure 2.10:The coordination-subordination gradient

The following examples from Quirk et al. (1985: 921) show that equivalent semantic relations between clauses in a clause complex can be achieved by using a coordinator (72), a conjunct (73) or a subordinator (74); the idea of disappointment is expressed in all three examples.

(72) He tried hard, but he failed.

(73) He tried hard, yet he failed.

(74) He tried hard, although he failed.

Based on corpus observations, Sinclair (1990: 374) notes that if clauses having the same subject are coordinated, the subject is not usually repeated if the connector is *and, or* or *then*, cf. examples (75) to (77), but that it is usual to repeat the subject if the connector is *but, so* or *yet*, cf. (78) to (80).

(75) He took her hands from her eyes and [he] led her towards the house.

(76) It's a long time since you've bought them a drink or [you've] talked to them.

(77) When she recognized Morris she went pale, then [she] blushed.

(78) I try and see it their way, but I can't.

(79) I had no car, so I hired one for the journey.

(80) He lost the fight, yet somehow he emerged with his dignity enhanced.

If two actions are performed by the same thing, person or group, the two verbs can be coordinated. In some cases it is difficult to distinguish between the coordination of two clauses (with subject ellipsis) and two verbs (cf. Sinclair 1990: 377):

(81) We both shrugged and [we] laughed.

(82) I shouted and [I] hooted at them.

Other constituents that can be coordinated are noun phrases, adjective phrases, adverb phrases and prepositions, as the following corpus examples from Sinclair (1990: 378-381) show.

(83) The jacket and shirt were skilfully designed.

(84) Ms Scott's house was large and imposing.

(85) Quickly but silently they darted out of the cell.

(86) We see them on their way to and from school.

Such cases of coordination are, however, cohesive only within a clause and therefore not of immediate text-linguistic interest.

Detailed semantic descriptions of coordinators and conjuncts can be found in standard reference grammars, e.g. Quirk et al. (1985: 634-647, 930-941) or Sinclair (1990: 373-383).

2.1.4.2 Syntactic subordination

Syntactic subordination at the level of the clause complex occurs if clauses are marked by features of structural dependency which relate them to other clauses in a clause complex. Structural dependency is signalled by subordinators (e.g. *if*, *because*), subject-operator inversion as in (87) or the absence of a finite verb as in (88), cf. Quirk et al. (1985: 1006).

(87) Had I been more forthright, I would have acquired more support.

(88) Denying any interest in politics, she claimed that she wished to continue in forensic medicine.

Subordinators in a wider sense comprise 'subordinating conjunctions' like *if* and *because*, *wh*-elements like *how*, *what* and *why*, and *that* used as a relative pronoun or introducing a nominal clause.

A subordinate clause may function either as a clause element or within a clause element. As a clause element it may function as subject (89), object (90), complement (91), or adverbial (92) in a superordinate clause. The examples (89) to (95) are from Quirk et al. (1985: 1047).

(89) That we need a larger computer has become obvious.

(90) He doesn't know whether to send a gift.

(91) One likely result of the postponement is that the cost of constructing the college will be very much higher.

(92) When you see them, give them my best wishes.

Within a clause element, a subordinate clause functions as a postmodifier in a noun phrase, i.e. relative clause, (93), prepositional complement (94) or adjectival complementation (95).

(93) [Few of the immigrants retained] the customs that they had brought with them.

(94) [It depends] on what we decide.

(95) [We are] happy to see you.

There are three major functional classes of subordinate clauses that depend on the function they fulfil as clause elements or within a clause element: 'nominal clauses', 'adverbial clauses' and 'relative clauses'.

Nominal clauses refer to events, facts, dates, and ideas rather than to perceptible objects as do noun phrases (cf. Quirk et al. ibid.). They function as subject, object or complement in a superordinate clause. Here are some further corpus examples of nominal clauses from Sinclair (1990: 314, 339, 369)

(96) He promised to give me the money. [object clause]

(97) Our hope is that this time all parties will cooperate. [complement clause]

(98) What he said was perfectly true. [subject clause]

(99) They did not like what he wrote. [object clause]

Adverbial clauses function as adverbial in a superordinate clause. They are classified according to the semantics that the subordinators express. Quirk et al. (1985: 1077-1118) give a very detailed classification, while the one by Sinclair (1990: 343) is more cursory. His classification is given in Figure 2.11 below. The following illustrative examples are also from Sinclair (1990: 344-362).

Formal Texture I 55

(100) Her father died when she was young.

(101) Government cannot operate effectively unless it is free from such interference.

(102) They had to take some of his land in order to extend the churchyard.

Type of adverbial clause	Usual subordinating conjunctions	Example
time clause	when, before, after, since, while, until	(100)
conditional clause	if, unless	(101)
purpose clause	in order to, so that	(102)
reason clause	because, since, as	(103)
result clause	so that	(104)
concessive clause	although, though, while	(105)
place clause	where, wherever	(106)
clause of manner	as, like, the way	(107)

Figure 2.11:Types of adverbial clauses and their usual subordinating conjunctions

(103) I didn't know that she had been married, since she seldom talked about herself.

(104) My suitcase had become damaged on the journey home, so that the lid would not stay closed.

(105) I used to read a lot although I don't get much time for books now.

(106) He said he was happy where he was.

(107) I was never allowed to do things the way I wanted to do them.

As a summary of the main possibilities to connect clauses and clause complexes the list in Figure 2.12 below may be helpful.

It will be noted that both coordination and subordination operate at the rank levels of clause and clause constituent. Furthermore, syntactic coordination by conjunct, especially *yet*, is similar to subordination since both a subordinator and *yet* show the features of being immobile – restricted to the initial position of a clause – and that they cannot link subordinate clauses, i.e. structures that are also introduced by subordinators (cf. section 2.1.4.1 above). The medial position of conjuncts on the coordination-subordination gradient is mirrored by the fact that conjuncts can be viewed as linking both, units at the level of the clause and units at the level of the clause complex.

> Syntactic subordination
>   clause as clause element
>   nominal clause
>   subject clause
>   object clause
>   complement clause
>   adverbial clause
>   clause within a clause constituent
>   relative clause
>   prepositional complement
>   adjectival complementation
> Syntactic coordination
>   of clauses
>   by coordinator
>   by conjunct
>   of clause constituents
>   by coordinator
>   by conjunct
> Textual linkage
>   of clause complexes
>   by conjunct

Figure 2.12:How to connect clauses and clause complexes

From the point of view of text-linguistics, as opposed to syntax, the cohesive relations at the level of the clause complex, which constitute the textual linkage of clause complexes, are of special interest. It is here that conjuncts play an important role as a cohesive device. To these we will turn next.

2.1.4.3 Textual linkage of clause complexes

The cohesive devices that we have discussed so far in this subchapter 2.1 (Order and realization of elements) were mainly concerned with cohesive devices that create coreference and serve to establish a textual world. Now that we are dealing with conjuncts, the perspective changes from the textual world that is described in the text to the text-producer. Quirk et al. (1985: 632) describe the function of conjuncts as follows:

> We relate conjuncts to the speaker's comment in one quite specific respect: his assessment of how he views the connection between two linguistic units. The units concerned may be very large or very small [...].

Conjuncts are adverbials that are grammatically distinct from adjuncts by the following features:

> The adverbial [i.e. conjunct] cannot be the focus of a cleft sentence; cannot be the basis of contrast in alternative interrogation or negation; cannot be focused by subjuncts. (ibid.: 631)

With reference to example (108) these features are demonstrated by Quirk et al. (1985: 631) in examples (109) to (111):

(108) She may be unable to attend the meeting. You should nonetheless send her the agenda.

(109) ... *It is nonetheless that you should send her the agenda.

(110) ... *Should you send her the agenda nonetheless or therefore?

(111) ... *You should only nonetheless send her the agenda.

Quirk et al. show that the semantic role of expressing a relation between two units can be fulfilled by an adjunct or a conjunct. This is demonstrated with the following examples:

(112) It was snowing, and in spite of this Mona went cycling.

(113) ... and it was in spite of this that Mona went cycling. [adjunct]

(114) It was snowing, and nonetheless Mona went cycling.

(115) *... and it was nonetheless that Mona went cycling. [conjunct]

Quirk et al. (1985: 633) summarize the situation displayed in these examples as follows:

Conjuncts thus *both* indicate the relation *and* are demonstrably outside the syntactically integrated clause structure which admits adjuncts.

Quirk et al. (ibid.: 634) see conjuncts "in the wider context of inter-sentence relations and discourse structure". As was stated above, conjuncts express how the text-producer views the text-semantic connection between linguistic units. Quirk et al. (1985: 634-640) distinguish different 'conjunctive roles', which are summarized in Figure 2.13.

	Conjunctive role		Examples
listing	enumerative		*first, second, next*
	additive	equative	*correspondingly, likewise*
		reinforcing	*moreover, in addition*
summative			*altogether, therefore*
appositive			*namely, that is*
resultive			*accordingly, as a result*
inferential			*otherwise, in that case*
contrastive	reformulatory		*rather, alternatively*
	replacive		*on the other hand*
	antithetic		*by contrast, conversely*
	concessive		*nevertheless, after all*
transitional	discoursal		*incidentally, by the way*
	temporal		*meantime, eventually*

Figure 2.13: Roles of conjuncts

It may be noted that the special category of 'conjunct' is not recognized in Sinclair's (1990) grammar, nor in Halliday/Hasan's (1976) work. The latter only allude to 'continuatives' which are vaguely comparable to conjuncts (cf. ibid.: 276).

2.2 Corpus-linguistic approaches to the study of words in texts

In section 2.1 we concentrated on bilateral, usually point-to-point relations of linguistic units. The two related units were (i) word-forms of specified grammatical or lexical classes that occur in one clause or clause complex and that refer to (ii) other, usually preceding clauses in a text. The relations that are thus established fulfil the function of creating cohesive coreference and temporal or spatial orientation in a text, and of indicating how the text-producer views the connection between linguistic units.

In this section 2.2 we are not so much concerned with the cohesive potential of individual classes of word-forms, i.e. with the paradigmatic (substitutional) aspects of cohesion, but rather with the syntagmatic (combinatorial) relations of elements in a text. As we have seen above, the paradigmatic aspect of cohesion concerns the choice, i.e. the realization, of individual clause constituents in a concrete textual environment. For example, given the first sentence in (116), possible choices to refer to *a king* would be a pronoun, a repetition, a synonym or a hyperonym.

(116) Once upon a time there was a king. *He/the king/the monarch/the ruler* had a daughter.

Hence we are concerned with the paradigmatic choices of a text-producer that he has in his head as associative possibilities and that will fill a given paradigmatic slot. The paradigmatic choices are defined as linguistic categories like pronoun, synonym, hyperonym, adverbial and conjunct. These paradigmatic choices may be represented as in Figure 2.14.

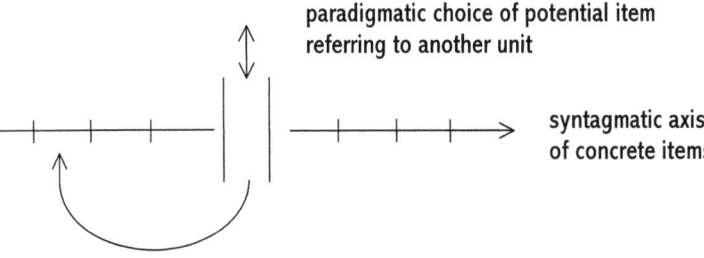

Figure 2.14: Paradigmatic choice in a syntagmatic chain

The syntagmatic aspect, on the other hand, does not focus on the associative potential, but rather on the actual string of word-forms in a text. This is where the corpus-linguistic approach becomes relevant. From a syntagmatic point of view we are no longer dealing with possibilities in the head of a text-producer or the model of a linguist, but rather with naturally occurring sequences of clause complexes in a text and the coreferential relations of concrete word-forms in a text (cf. Figure 2.15).

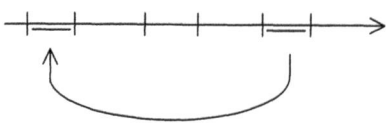

Figure 2.15:Syntagmatic relation of concrete items

The text itself is taken from a source called 'corpus'. This is usually a collection of texts that have been produced in real life communication and not in order to demonstrate a linguistic point, as we have seen in the potential sequence in (116). The source of (116) is, of course, not a corpus but intuition. The wording of (116) is what is disrespectfully termed an 'armchair example'.

Corpora can be explored in two ways: (i) on a small scale by 'textual analysis' and (ii) on a large scale by 'frequency-based observations' in a computerized corpus. Textual analysis seeks to show lexical patterns in a given text by relating items in the syntagmatic, actual chain of word-forms. Textual analysis is not limited to bilateral point-to-point relations but rather interested in uncovering the network of multilateral point-to-point relations in a real text (cf. Figure 2.16). This approach will be discussed in section 2.2.1.

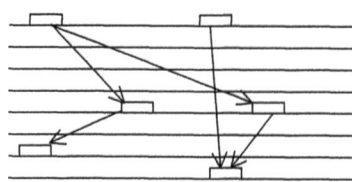

Figure 2.16:Network of word-forms in a text

Formal Texture I

On the other hand, the frequency-based corpus-linguistic study of words in texts is not interested in the syntagmatic relations of concrete items in one specific text, but rather in the likelihood that a given word-form co-occurs with another word-form in a larger collection of texts, i.e. in a computerized corpus. This approach is the subject of section 2.2.2.

2.2.1 Lexical patterns

Lexical patterns as networks are described, for example, by Halliday/Hasan (1985: ch. 5) and by Hoey (1991). Halliday/Hasan (1985: 70) offer for demonstration a short text, which seems to be the transcript of an orally produced children's story:

(117) once upon a time there was a little girl and she went out for a walk and she saw a lovely little teddy bear and so she took it home and when she got home she washed it

The network of lexical patterns in the five clause complexes can be represented as in Figure 2.17.

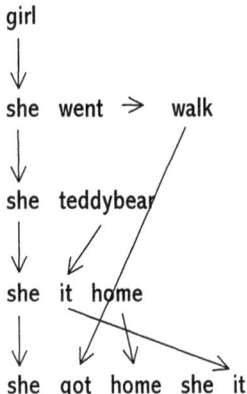

Figure 2.17:Lexical pattern of example (117)

It will be noted that the relations in this little text are of diverse types: (i) coreference between nouns (*girl, teddybear*) and pronouns (*she, it*); (ii)

coreference by repetition (*home*); (iii) coreference by synonym (*walk, got* 'movement').

Hoey (1991) pursues this approach further and analyses more challenging texts. He shows that in principle all the cohesive means that we have discussed in section 2.1.3 above (pronouns, determiners, comparison, substitution, ellipsis, lexical cohesion, place relators, time relators and cataphoric reference) can partake in such a network. Hoey (1991: 35) analyses the following piece of popular factual reporting.

(118) **1** A drug known to produce violent reactions in humans has been used for sedating grizzly bears *Ursus arctos* in Montana, USA, according to a report in *The New York Times*. **2** After one bear, known to be a peaceable animal, killed and ate a camper in an unprovoked attack, scientists discovered it had been tranquillized 11 times with phencyclidine, or 'angel dust', which causes hallucinations and sometimes gives the user an irrational feeling of destructive power. **3** Many wild bears have become 'garbage junkies', feeding from dumps around human developments. **4** To avoid potentially dangerous clashes between them and humans, scientists are trying to rehabilitate the animals by drugging them and releasing them in uninhabited areas. **5** Although some biologists deny that the mind-altering drug was responsible for uncharacteristic behaviour of this particular bear, no research has been done into the effects of giving grizzly bears or other animals repeated doses of phencyclidine.

The lexical patterns in this text can be visualized by arrows as before. In order not to make the picture too confusing Hoey shows sentence by sentence how the lexical elements in a current sentence relate to the following sentences. Figure 2.18 shows how lexical elements of sentence 1 relate to following elements in the text by what Hoey calls 'repetition links'. The lexical patterns that have sentence 1 as a starting point are again of diverse types. Besides the repetition of lexemes there is hyponomy between *bear* and *animal*, synonymy between *produce*, *cause* and *responsible for*, morphological relation between *used* and *user* and coreference between *bears* and *them*.

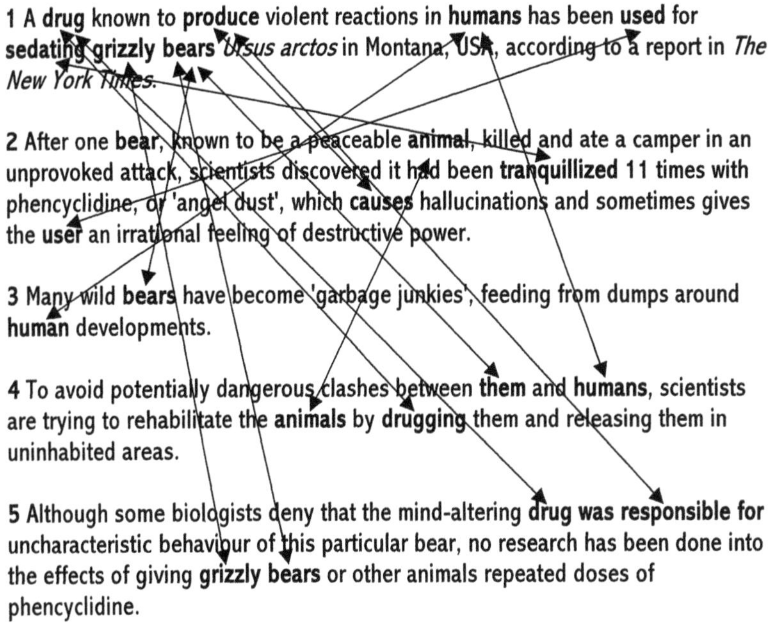

Formal Texture I

1 A drug known to **produce** violent reactions in **humans** has been **used** for sedating **grizzly bears** *ursus arctos* in Montana, USA, according to a report in *The New York Times*.

2 After one **bear**, known to be a peaceable **animal, killed** and ate a camper in an unprovoked attack, scientists discovered it had been **tranquillized 11** times with phencyclidine, or 'angel dust', which **causes** hallucinations and sometimes gives the **user** an irrational feeling of destructive power.

3 Many wild **bears** have become 'garbage junkies', feeding from dumps around **human** developments.

4 To avoid potentially dangerous clashes between **them** and **humans**, scientists are trying to rehabilitate the **animals** by **drugging** them and releasing them in uninhabited areas.

5 Although some biologists deny that the mind-altering **drug was responsible for** uncharacteristic behaviour of this particular bear, no research has been done into the effects of giving **grizzly bears** or other animals repeated doses of phencyclidine.

Figure 2.18:Lexical pattern in example (118)

It is evident that the recurring lexical items tell us something about the topic of this article. This can be easily demonstrated with the help of a word list of the text which ranks the tokens of the text in a frequency hierarchy (cf. Figure 2.19). The function words in Figure 2.19 are aligned to the left, the content words to the right. The ranking shows that the highest ranking content words tell us something about the contents of this article: that it deals with bears, drugs, humans and scientists.

Rank	Word-token	Freq.
1	in	5
2	the	5
3	to	5
4	a	4
5	and	4
6	of	4
7	bears	3
8	been	3
9	them	3
10	an	2
11	animals	2
12	bear	2
13	drug	2
14	for	2
15	grizzly	2
16	has	2
17	humans	2
18	known	2
19	or	2
20	phencyclidine	2
21	scientists	2
22	times	2

Figure 2.19: Word frequency above 1 in example (118)

Sinclair (1990: 30) describes a method by which it is possible to get clues about the topic of a text and changes of topics in a text. It is obvious that lexical repetitions reflect the topic of a text and that frequency lists like that in Figure 2.19 are useful. Sinclair's idea is a 'first order word list', which is a list of the word-forms of a text in the order of the first occurrence. Sinclair (1990: 30) describes it as follows:

> Each successive word-form is compared with each previous one. If it is a new word-form it is provided with the counter set at 1; if the word-form has occurred before, it is deleted from the text and 1 is added to the counter at the place of first occurrence of the word-form.

Such a list can show topic changes or topic digressions. Sinclair (1990: 139-140) exemplifies a first order word list based on the following text, example (119).

(119) [1] There are many kinds of activity, and communication is only one of them, although often it does not look much like activity. [2] The shelves of a library can look very inactive indeed, and someone sitting with his eyes shut listening to a transistor through earphones may seem fairly static. [3] But in a library we see a stage of communication where the activity is halted in time. [4] If we consider the whole process, the activity is obvious enough. [5] The nervous activity of authors is legendary, and the silent reader in his armchair is making continuous, fast, and precise eye movements. [6] And, like the radio listener, his brain is highly active if he is taking anything in.
[7] There are many kinds of communication, too, and human communication through language is only a small sub-section, although it is very important. [8] Attempts to set out the special characteristics of human language have become quite sophisticated. [9] But research workers have now created most aspects of human verbal communication in animals and machines. [10] Perhaps mankind's only remaining boast is that we thought of it first! [11] It is certainly an intricate and distinctive kind of activity.

An excerpt from the first order word list of this text is given in Figure 2.20. Note that the first twenty word-tokens in this list (*there – like*) correspond roughly to the first sentence in example (119). The list is truncated: it disregards the orthographic sentences [3] to [5] (indicated by the broken line in Figure 2.20) and [8] to [11]. The word-forms marked by broken underlining are the nouns and adjectives that recur in the text, i.e. have a counter larger than 1. The list shows that the repeated lexical items *activity*, *communication* and *library* occur fairly early in the text and that, after about two thirds of the text, the lexical items *human* and *language* enter the text as new items with repetition chains.

Word-token	Counter	Word-token	Counter
there	2	sitting	1
are	2	with	1
many	2	his	3
kinds	2	eyes	1
of	10	shut	1
activity	6	listening	1
and	8	to	2
communication	5	transistor	1
is	11	through	2
only	3	earphones	1
one	1	may	1
them	1	seem	1
although	2	fairly	1
often	1	static	1
it	4	---------------	-------
does	1	radio	1
not	1	listener	1
look	2	brain	1
much	1	highly	1
like	2	active	1
the	8	he	1
shelves	1	taking	1
a	5	anything	1
library	2	too	1
can	1	human	3
very	2	language	2
inactive	1	small	1
indeed	1	subsection	1
someone	1	important	1

Figure 2.20:Truncated first order word list of example (119)

Similar observations can be made in almost any text. A very clear example can be seen in the British National Corpus (BNC) document ABC from the book *Dolphins: Their Life and Survival*. Since there are not many alternative ways to refer to dolphins, the word-forms *dolphin* and *dolphins* can be found in almost every sentence of the text. However, there is a digression in sentences 746 to 754 (already prepared in 744-745), which make up two paragraphs only about porpoises, consisting altogether of 255 words.

(120) [Excerpt from BNC document ABC, 744-756] Between 1977 and 1981, the season for hunting Dall's porpoise increased from 4 months to 10 months, and in 1987 the number of boats hunting the dolphins and porpoises in the area increased from 200 to 350. By 1988, it had almost doubled again to 600, and boats based on Iwate took over 90 per cent of the total reported Japanese dolphin and porpoise catch.

[746] Kasuya's fears proved to be well founded, and he dropped a bombshell at the 1989 meeting of the IWC's Scientific Committee, when he revealed to the Small Cetaceans Subcommittee the staggering increase in the number of Dall's porpoise killed in the harpoon fishery based on Iwate Prefecture. In 1988, according to Kasuya, over 39,000 Dall's porpoise were killed in the harpoon fishery, not including porpoises that were struck but escaped, possibly mortally wounded. At the same IWC meeting, Kasuya tabled a paper which estimated the abundance of Dall's porpoise in the harpoon fishery area to be no greater than 105,000. In a single year the unregulated Japanese hunt had killed almost half the local porpoise population.

The Scientific Committee had in previous years expressed concern about the Dall's porpoise harpoon fishery, fearing that even the much smaller annual catch may not have been sustainable, since Japanese scientists had calculated a replacement rate of only about 5000 porpoises each year. However, the scientists' attitudes towards the current catch level were clear. At the 1989 meeting, the subcommittee concluded that the take was clearly not sustainable and that, depending on the stock composition of the catch, the situation could be even worse than was immediately apparent. For example, the incidental take from squid gill-net fisheries by Taiwan and Korea was unreported and therefore an unknown quantity. The subcommittee said it was a matter of urgency to ensure the catch was reduced to at least the levels of previous years (which themselves had possibly been too high).

[755] Concerned at the rapid expansion of the hunt, and the declining stocks of small cetaceans around the coastline, the Iwate Prefecture in January 1989 instituted a licensing system, so that for the first time ever, the hunt could be regulated. No new applications for dolphin hunting will

be accepted, and the number of licensed vessels is to be reduced from 600 to 540.

This excerpt from the book on dolphins nicely shows how lexical patterns of repetition links mirror the content structure of a text.

2.2.2 Collocation and naturalness

After dealing with small-scale textual analyses of corpora in terms of lexical patterns in single texts, we now turn to large-scale analyses of text collections that are frequency-based. As was noted above, the frequency-based corpus-linguistic study of words in texts is not interested in the syntagmatic relations of concrete items in one specific text, but rather in the likelihood that a given word-form co-occurs with another word-form in a larger collection of texts, i.e. in a computerized corpus which may be considered as representative of a language as a whole or of a defined part of it, e.g. spoken or written or technical language.

This is where the notion of 'collocation' becomes relevant. Vaguely, it has to do with the company that a word keeps, i.e. with characteristic word combinations (cf. Firth 1957). More technically, "collocation is a relation of *probable* co-occurrence of items" (McCarthy 2002: 343). The emphasis on *probable* makes it clear that collocation is not a grammatical concept of syntactic arrangement, but rather a probabilistic and semantic concept.

The horizontal, syntagmatic and the vertical, paradigmatic viewpoints are now not applied to the syntactic classification of concrete items (cf. Figures 2.12 and 2.15) but rather to the results of statistical corpus analyses. Statistical analysis tells us something about the probability of the co-occurrence of two items. It can be between one hundred per cent, as in *to and [fro]*, or zero per cent, as in *to and [back]*. That is, in its adverbial function the slot after *to and* is always filled with *fro* but never with *back*.

It should be noted that immediately neighbouring collocates must be distinguished from 'coherence collocates'. These are words that we associate as related in meaning, e.g. *letter* and *stamp*, which do not have to be neighbours in texts. This topic will be taken up again in section 4.3.

The probability of co-occurrence is established between two units which can be word-forms or morphologically related lexical items. For example, it is not only the word-forms *strong* and *argument* that co-occur but also morphologically related word-forms, for example *he argued strongly against ...* and *the strength of his argument* (cf. Halliday 1966: 151). This means that the units of collocating items can be viewed as concrete word-forms or more abstractly by grouping together inflectionally or derivationally related word-forms (cf. McCarthy 2002: 343). It must also be noted that the order of elements and intervening elements is not crucial in this perspective, which goes to show as well that we are dealing with a lexical, semantic phenomenon and not with a syntactic one.

The preceding or following collocates of one unit form sets which comprise all the co-occurring units that can be found in the respective positions in a corpus. Leaving the extreme cases of one hundred per cent and zero per cent of co-occurrence out of consideration, the set of units that precede or follow as collocates a given unit can be arranged according to their 'probability rank'. This can be represented schematically as in Figure 2.21.

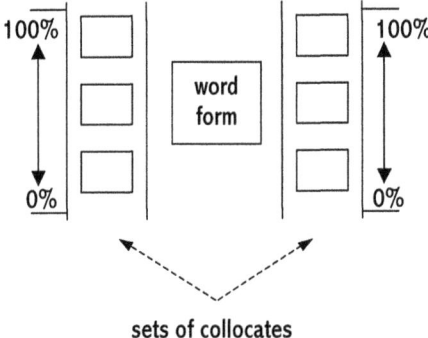

Figure 2.21:Probability rank of preceding and following collocates

In practice the probability rank can be established by looking up in a corpus which elements precede or follow a given word-form as collocates and how often they do so. In the BNC, for example, the adjectives *strong, good, powerful, convincing* and *robust* are among the left-hand collocates of *argument* in the frequencies displayed in Figure 2.22. The results show that in the BNC the sequence *strong argument* is significantly more frequent than the other sequences. If one takes the BNC as representative of present-day English, one can conclude that *argument* prefers *strong* over the other items in Figure 2.22 as preceding collocates. To put it differently, as language users we are likely to have heard or read *strong argument* more often than the other combinations. Therefore we are more familiar with this combination. In the words of Hoey (2006: 6), we can refer to *strong argument* as a 'normal collocation' and to *robust argument* as an 'unusual collocation'. This conceptual distinction plays a role in the explanation of the somewhat diffuse concepts of 'naturalness' and 'clumsiness'.

Freq.	Set of collocates	Word-form
55	*strong*	
31	*good*	
24	*powerful*	*argument*
20	*convincing*	
1	*robust*	

Figure 2.22:Some left-hand collocates of >argument< *in the BNC*

The notion of 'naturalness' was introduced by Sinclair (1984). He suggests that the syntactic variable well-formed/ill-formed should be supplemented by the variable 'natural/non-natural'. He describes the latter as "the concept of well-formedness of sentences *in text*" (p. 213). We should note that he does not speak of "*in a text*" but "*in text*". As we have seen in section 1.1 above, the sense of this generic use of the word *text* is that of a corpus. Carter/Malmkjaer (2002: 550) write:

> In text linguistics, then, the links between clauses are observed across sentence boundaries, and these links can be seen to form larger patterns of text organization. In addition, however, reference to the text surrounding a given sentence may be seen to cast light on the *naturalness* of the sentence in question. [...] Some of the determinants for the fulfilment of the criteria of naturalness are situated in the surrounding discourse, while those for well-formedness are all within the sentence itself.

That is, texts (singular or as a corpus) are not studied for their text-building features but rather as the context for naturally occurring (and not concocted) sentences.

There are several factors that contribute to naturalness, for example the use of pronouns and deictic expressions. But perhaps the most important factor is collocation. Therefore Sinclair (1984: 204) writes: "The textual evidence for naturalness is probabilistic to begin with". And we should add that probability in terms of corpus statistics has expectation as its psycholinguistic correlate on the part of the language user, cf. section 4.1 below.

The following example from Sinclair (1984: 203) is often quoted to demonstrate how normal collocations influence our expectations.

(121) Prince Charles is now a husband.

The oddness of (121) is explained by Sinclair (1984: 207) as follows:

> Note that a supporter such as *good* modifying husband would immediately improve the naturalness of the sentence. [...] There is a conflict between the mutual expectations of the equative structure, the indefinite article, and the word *husband*. Words denoting occupations (eg *sailor*) would not cause this conflict.

In an article on "Clumsy English" Hoey (2006) shows that unusual collocations may contribute to the clumsiness of texts written by non-native students of English. Here is an example from the texts he examines (p. 49):

(122) ... but if the writer wants to convince the reader about something in an ad, it has to have enough information.

The problematic strings are *convince the reader about something* and *have enough information*. In the corpora that Hoey consulted he found 238 instances of the string *convince [somebody] of [something]* and only 9 of *convince [somebody] about [something]*. He concludes: "So the most natural expression would appear to be convince the reader of something" (p. 49-50). The second expression is problematic for at least three reasons. Firstly, it is associated with denial like in *don't have enough information*. Secondly, *have information* is biased towards occurring with a postmodification, for example *have information about x*. The third reason is explained as follows:

> Finally, there is an implicit receiver of the information in the example before us (*enough information for the reader*); *have information* is not however associated with receivers, *have* being a more static verb. In a sample of 200 instances of *have ... information*, there is an implied interaction in only 20% of cases. On the other hand *provide ... information*, which occurs with some expression of receiver of the message 59% of the time in a sample of 200 instances. (Hoey 2006: 50)

As a last point in our discussion of naturalness I want to report on a study of collocations in which Hoey (2005: 33-35) describes the collocates of the two morphologically related word-forms *consequence* and *consequences*. I will concentrate on the left-hand collocates that are adjectives and give the main results in Figures 2.23 and 2.24.

Freq.	Set of collocates	Word-form
82	*inevitable*	
47	*direct*	
23	*little*	
21	*another*	
17	*natural*	
15	*logical*	
11	*immediate*	
8	*serious*	*consequence*
8	*possible*	
8	*only*	
7	*likely*	
6	*political*	
6	*necessary*	
6	*important*	
5	*great*	

Figure 2.23: Adjectival left-hand collocates of >consequence<

The probability ranks of the left-hand collocates of the word-forms *consequence* and *consequences* show quite different sets of collocates. In fact, they only share the items *serious*, *possible* and *political*. This shows that the collocational meaning is not necessarily a matter of the lexeme or lemma but of the individual word-forms. (Some linguists use 'lemma' and 'lexeme' synonymously, others make a difference: While 'lexeme' unites word-forms of the same lexical meaning, 'lemma' does not neccessarily so. Therefore $BANK_1$ 'money institution' and $BANK_2$ 'raised area of a river' can be regarded as two lexemes but only one lemma.) Hoey (2005: 35) summarizes these findings as follows:

> The collocational behaviours of grammatically different instances of a lemma may overlap very little; we might therefore expect to see the same lack of overlap in semantic association.

Freq.	Set of collocates	Word-form
122	*serious*	
87	*political*	
79	*disastrous*	
70	*social*	
70	*dire*	
64	*economic*	
43	*financial*	consequences
34	*environmental*	
28	*negative*	
27	*devastating*	
26	*grave*	
22	*possible*	
22	*practical*	
21	*terrible*	

Figure 2.24: Adjectival left-hand collocates of >consequences<

After dealing with corpus-linguistic approaches to the study of words in individual texts and in text collections, we now turn to corpus-linguistic approaches to the classification of texts.

2.3 Corpus-linguistic approaches to the classification of texts

The corpus-linguistic approaches to the classification of texts must be seen in the context of other approaches. Therefore it is useful to consider the corpus-linguistic approaches in an overall framework. What follows is first of all not a classification of texts, i.e. of text-types, but an overview of the most important criteria for text classification. This overview is given in Figure 2.25.

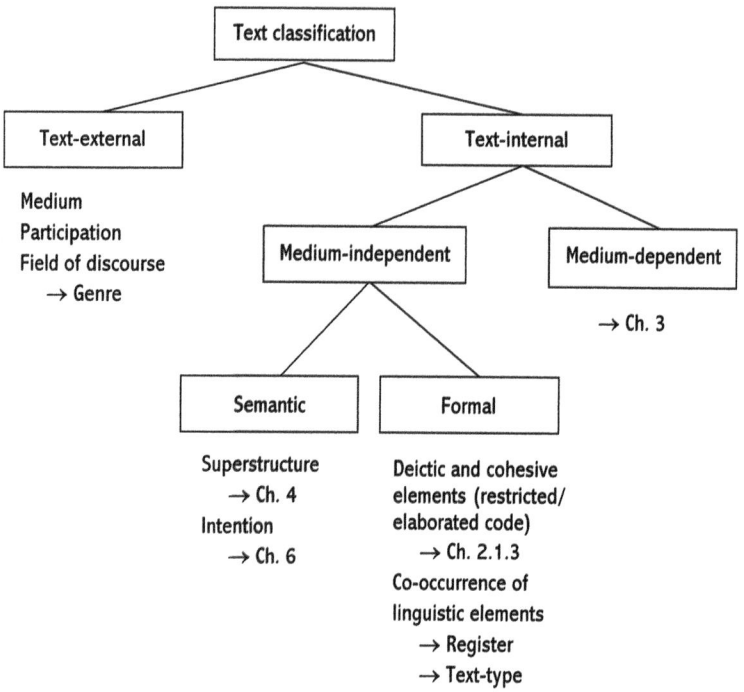

Figure 2.25: Criteria for text classification

The first distinction that must be made is that between text-external and text-internal approaches. Text-external approaches are based on distinctions that are not intrinsically linguistic in nature but which can be made, for example, by laymen or librarians. These distinctions will be addressed later in this chapter under the topic of 'genres' (cf. section 2.3.1.1).

Text-internal approaches can be either medium-independent or medium-dependent. This is a distinction that is already reflected in the overall structure of the present book. The medium-independent lexicogrammatical structure of texts can be studied in terms of semantic approaches and of formal approaches. Among the semantic approaches two research lines will be given special consideration in later chapters of this book, namely the study of superstructures in chapter 4 and the study of intentions in chapter 6.

Among the medium-independent formal approaches to text classification two research trends can be distinguished. On the one hand, there is the study of deictic and cohesive elements. This research line was addressed above in chapter

2.1.3 when we discussed the distinction between 'restricted' and 'elaborated code'. On the other hand, there are studies in the co-occurrence of linguistic elements which are studied with corpus-linguistic methods. These research lines will be discussed in the present chapter under the topics of 'registers' and 'text-types' (cf. sections 2.3.1.2 and 2.3.1.3).

Lastly, there are text-internal medium-dependent approaches where the written, graphic presentation or the spoken, oral presentation constitute decisive factors for the assignment of a text-type, e.g. a death notice or a pop song. We will deal with these factors of text-typology in chapter 3.

2.3.1 Genres, registers and text-types

2.3.1.1 Genres

Like many notions in linguistics, the concepts 'genre', 'register' and 'text-type' are bound to specific theories and must be explained with more basic concepts. Following Enkvist (1973: 14-15), we classed such terms as "notational terms" (cf. section 1.1 above). In the framework developed here, the meanings of 'genre', 'register' and 'text-type' are interrelated and, as we will see, there is a progress of sophistication from genre to register to text-type. This is not to deny that other definitions of these concepts do exist. In fact, several authors have changed their terminology and definitions over the years. These differences, however, are not relevant for the purpose at hand.

We understand 'genre' as a text-external notion. It is used to classify texts mainly according to the criteria 'medium', 'participation' and 'field of discourse' (cf. Figure 2.25 above). The criterion 'medium' refers to the origin of a text, namely whether it originated in speech or in writing. The criterion 'participation' refers to the distinction between monologue and dialogue (or polylogue, i.e. discourse between more than two individuals). The criterion 'field of discourse' has to do with the subject matter or topic of a text. We can regard these three criteria as basic guidelines for the collection of texts in corpora, with possible further, more delicate distinctions.

The basic distinctions made in one of the oldest corpora, the Survey of English Usage, are as shown in Figure 2.26 (cf. Quirk/Svartvik 1979 and Greenbaum/Svartvik 1990). The distinction between 'origin in writing' and 'origin in speech' is made according to the criterion 'medium', and the distinction between 'monologue' and 'dialogue' according to the criterion 'participation'. Non-printed material consists of personal journals, correspondence, examination essays, minutes of meetings and handwritten notices. The material for spoken delivery comprises talks, news broadcasts, stories, scripted speeches and plays.

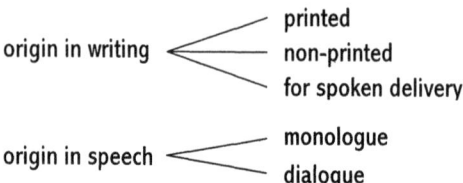

Figure 2.26:Basic components of the Survey of English Usage

The printed material is classified according to the criterion 'field of discourse'. Its subdivisions are shown in Figure 2.27. Note that the components of printed material reflect major categories as we would expect them in a public library. It is obvious that such classifications have inspired the choice of text categories in many corpora. Therefore we find similar text categories in other corpora, for example, in the Brown Corpus, the Lancaster-Oslo/Bergen (LOB) Corpus and the British National Corpus (BNC).

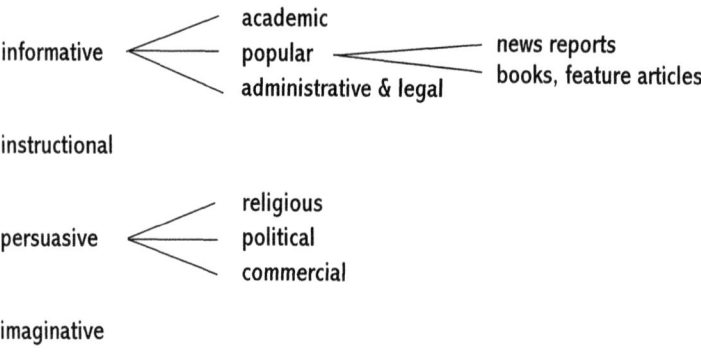

Figure 2.27:Components of printed material in the Survey of English Usage

For corpus-linguistic studies it is imperative to distinguish between the description of texts that are analysed and the description of the corpus-linguistic statistical results. Therefore, Biber (1988: 70) introduces a distinction between text-external 'genre' and text-internal 'text-type':

> In the present study I use the term 'genre' for the general categories distinguished in the LOB and London-Lund corpora [the latter being

the spoken component of the Survey of English Usage, JE]. [...] As noted above, I use the term 'genre' to refer to categorizations assigned on the basis of external criteria. I use the term 'text-type', on the other hand, to refer to the groupings of texts that are similar with respect to their linguistic form, irrespective of genre categories. [...] In a fully developed typology of texts, genres and text-types must be distinguished, and the relations among them identified and explained.

Before we move on to 'text-types', we have to look at the older concept of 'register'.

2.3.1.2 Registers

The idea to relate text-external distinctions with "groupings of texts that are similar with respect to their linguistic form" had been formulated more than 20 years earlier – before the general availability of computers – by Halliday et al. (1964: 89):

> If two samples of language activity from what, on non-linguistic grounds, could be considered different situation-types show no differences in grammar or lexis, they are assigned to one and the same register.

The formulation "no difference in grammar or lexis" does of course not mean that the two samples have exactly the same wording. It can only be understood as referring to an abstraction in the sense that the samples show the same statistical features, for example many past tense forms, few present tense forms, many third person pronouns and few adjectives. It was impossible to calculate the statistical features in the early sixties when no machine-readable spoken and written corpora were available. Therefore Halliday et al. (1964: 90) add:

> We are not yet in a position to talk accurately about registers; there is much work to be done before the concept is capable of detailed application.

The notion of 'register' must be seen in the context of the discussions about linguistic variation in the 1960s which centred around the question of how one could relate extralinguistic factors to the choices of linguistic form. In this context Halliday et al. (1964: 77) made an important distinction, namely that between 'user' and 'use': "The variety according to user is a DIALECT; the variety according to use is a REGISTER."

The dimensions of linguistic variation according to 'user' are relatively permanent; among them are 'time', 'region', 'social group', 'intelligibility' (standard/non-standard) and 'individuality' (idiolect), cf. Esser (1993: 11). As for 'register', Halliday et al. (1964: 90) propose three major dimensions:

> There is enough evidence for us to be able to recognize the major situation types to which formally distinct registers correspond; [...] It seems most useful to introduce a classification along three dimensions, each representing an aspect of the situations in which language operates and the part played by language in them. Registers, in this view, may be distinguished according to *field of discourse*, *mode of discourse* and *style of discourse*. [emphasis added]

The dimension 'field of discourse' was identified above as one of the major criteria of text-external text classification (cf. Figure 2.25). It can often be understood as 'subject matter', as Halliday et al. (ibid.) explain:

> In the type of situation in which the language activity accounts for practically the whole of the relevant activity, such as an essay, a discussion or an academic seminar, the field of discourse is the subject matter.

It will be recalled, for example, that the subject matters of texts (118) to (120) in section 2.2.1 above were 'grizzly bears', 'communication' and 'porpoises' respectively.

The dimension 'mode of discourse' corresponds to the text-external criterion 'medium' in Figure 2.25.:

> This refers to the medium or mode of the language activity, and it is this that determines, or rather correlates with, the role played by the language activity in the situation. The primary distinction on this dimension is that into spoken and written language, the two having, by and large, different situational roles. (ibid.)

The notion 'style of discourse' is sometimes also referred to as 'tenor of discourse', 'attitude' or 'formality' (cf. Esser 1993: 41). It refers to the social relations between the speaker/writer and the listener/reader. Halliday et al. (1964: 93) characterize this dimension as follows:

> It is best treated as a cline, and various more delicate cuts have been suggested with categories such as 'casual', 'intimate' and 'deferential'.

Registers are sometimes understood as one-dimensional varieties, for example 'spoken English' according to the one factor 'medium', 'legal English' according to the factor 'field of discourse/subject matter', and 'formal English' according to the factor 'style of discourse/attitude/formality'. We have already taken this view into account in the quotation from Halliday et al. above (1964: 90): "Registers, in this view, may be distinguished according to field of discourse, mode of discourse and style of discourse."

On the other hand, 'register' is also taken as a product of these three dimensions of linguistic variation. Halliday et al. (ibid.: 93) write: "It is as the product of these three dimensions of classification that we can best define and identify register."

The idea of a 'product' is not only relevant for the combination of the factors of external text classification of field of discourse (subject matter), mode of discourse (medium) and style of discourse (formality), but it is also relevant for the text-internal co-occurrence of linguistic items, which is at the heart of the definitions of 'register' by Halliday et al. ("no differences in grammar or lexis") and of 'text-type' by Biber ("the groupings of texts that are similar with respect to their linguistic form") that were quoted above.

It is common to both conceptions that they refer to an abstracted statistical norm that can be used to define 'register' or 'text-type'. Such an 'abstracted corpus norm' can be used as a point of reference for comparisons of registers or text-types and for comparisons of individual texts with these norms. A special concern in this respect are investigations into the question of how far external genres correlate with internal text-types.

2.3.1.3 Text-types

The extraction of abstracted corpus norms on the basis of genres was first attempted by Gibson (1966). From a linguo-stylistic point of view, his "Appendix 1: Styles and Statistics" is most interesting. Here, he starts from a collection of short prose texts and divides them into three groups according to how he imagines the writer of the passage. In order to describe the three impressionistic genres linguistically, he develops a check-list of sixteen questions on the lexis and grammar of the texts. For example: What is the proportion of monosyllables in the pasage? How many first-person and second-person pronouns does the passage contain? What proportion of verbs are in the passive voice? The recorded values for each of the three genres are the basis of algebraic limits for each question and each genre. The ensemble of these limits is called a 'style machine'. The characteristic correlations of linguistic items are not only understood as descriptions of the original input texts, but also as an abstract frame of reference which allows any analyst to classify further texts into the three genres. Gibson thus established, in the pre-computer era, the methods of an 'abstracted corpus norm' (cf. Esser 1993) which can be used for any externally defined groups of texts. He can therefore be regarded as a forerunner of more advanced and sophisticated work to which we turn now.

The methodology of establishing text-internal text-types on the basis of corpora that are composed of externally defined genres is described in various publications by Biber and Finegan. The most relevant ones for us are Biber/Finegan (1986), Biber (1988) and Biber (1989). They vary according to the number of genres, texts, linguistic features and terminology without affecting the principal methodology; the differences are pointed out in Esser (1993: 50-53).

In the 1986 publication Biber/Finegan choose 545 texts from 16 genres which comprise about one million words. The written texts are taken from the Lancaster-Oslo/Bergen (LOB) Corpus, supplemented by a collection of professional letters. The spoken texts are from the London-Lund Corpus, the spoken component of the Survey of English Usage. The written texts are from 1961, the spoken texts are largely from the 1960s and 1970s. The genres are: press, editorials, skills and hobbies, popular lore, government documents, academic prose, belles lettres, general fiction, romantic fiction, professional letters; face-to-face conversation, telephone conversation, interviews, broadcasts, spontaneous speeches, planned speeches. As explained above, Biber/Finegan distinguish between 'genre' (the components of the corpora) and 'text-type' (a statistically derived notion). They write (1986: 20):

> While genre categories (such as Adventure Fiction, Press Reviews, Prepared Speeches) are used to characterize texts on the basis of external criteria, we define 'text types' in terms of linguistic characteristics of texts themselves.

The corpus was analysed according to 41 morpho-syntactic features (in other studies 67). Then the co-occurrences of the linguistic features in the corpus were established with the help of 'factor analysis'. This was done by means of multivariate statistical computer programmes which identify those linguistic features that co-occur with high frequency in the texts. The co-occurring features are listed under factors according to their weight for a given factor. They are summarized in Figure 2.28. Features with positive weights occur together frequently, features with negative weights are markedly less frequent if the positive features occur.

Factor 1		Factor 2	
.79	questions	.74	nominalizations
.76	*that*-clauses	.61	prepositions
.68	final prepositions	.61	specific conjuncts (e.g. *in conclusion*)
.67	proverb *do*	.60	agentless passives
.67	contractions	.47	*by*-passives
.62	I/you	.45	*it*-clefts
.61	general hedges (e.g. *nearly*)	.42	split auxiliaries
.56	*if*-clauses	.40	word length
.52	WH-questions	.35	attitudinal disjuncts (e.g. *admittedly*)
.49	pronoun *it*		
.48	other subordinators (e.g. *because, if*)	-.57	place adverbs
.46	specific emphatics (e.g. *just, really*)	-.55	time adverbs
.42	demonstrative BE	-.50	relative pronoun deletion
.42	present tense	-.42	*that* deletion
.41	WH-clauses	-.35	third person pronouns
.41	general emphatics (e.g. *completely*)		
.35	infinitives		Factor 3
		.89	past tense
-.71	word length (longer words)	.61	third person pronouns
-.65	type/token ratio (varied vocabulary)	.47	perfect aspect
		-.62	present tense
		-.40	adjectives

Figure 2.28: Co-occurring features of Factors 1-3 in Biber/Finegan (1986)

On the assumption that co-occurrence of linguistic forms is an indication of shared communicative function, the factors are then functionally interpreted as 'textual dimensions'. Factor 1 is interpreted as relevant for the dimension 'interactive vs. edited text', Factor 2 for the dimension 'abstract vs. situated content', and Factor 3 for the dimension 'reported vs. immediate style'. These three dimensions are summarized in Figure 2.29.

Dimension 1 (Factor 1)	Dimension 2 (Factor 2)	Dimension 3 (Factor 3)
interactive text	abstracted content	reported style
↑↓	↑↓	↑↓
edited text	situated content	immediate style

Figure 2.29:Dimensions 1-3

See the dialogue from a telephone conversation in (125) on pp. 89-90 below for an example of an interactive text with situated content. On the other hand, the piece of academic prose in (123) exemplifies abstracted content presented in immediate (not reported) style.

In a next step, the salient features for each factor (or textual dimension) were counted for each text. For example, a text analysed according to Factor 3 might have shown 156 past tense forms, 117 third person pronouns, 24 perfect aspect forms, 46 present tense forms and 88 adjectives. With the help of these figures the 'factor score' of that text can be calculated:

$$(156 + 117 + 24) - (46 + 88) = 163$$

Figure 2.30:Calculation of a factor score for Factor 3

The factor scores of the individual texts can be used to calculate the 'mean factor score' for each genre. With these results it is possible to order the genres along each dimension according to the 'rank of their mean factor score'. Figures 2.31 to 2.33 illustrate the plots of the mean factor scores along Dimensions 1-3.

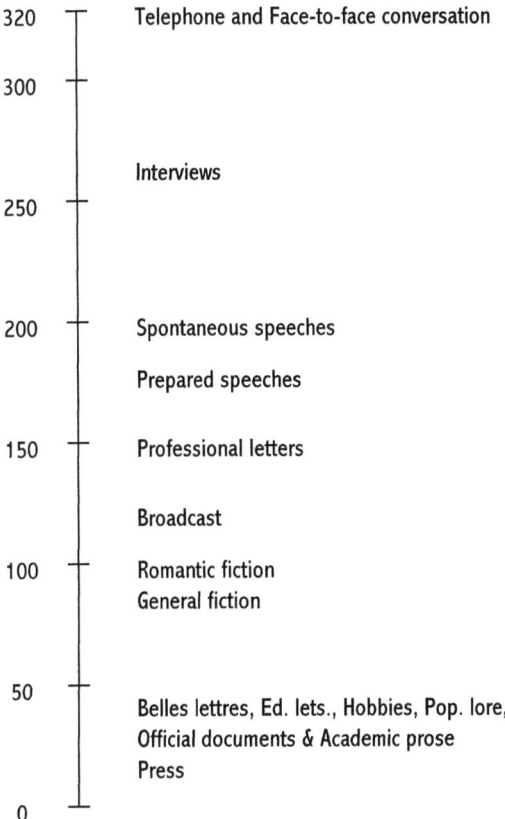

Figure 2.31: Genres along Dimension 1 (interactive vs. edited text) according to the rank of their mean factor score in Biber/Finegan (1986)

Such results show, for example, that the genre 'telephone conversation' can be characterized by co-occurring linguistic features which are interpreted as 'interactive', 'situated' and 'immediate'. Therefore, 'telephone conversation' scores high on Dimension 1, low on Dimension 2, and low on Dimension 3.

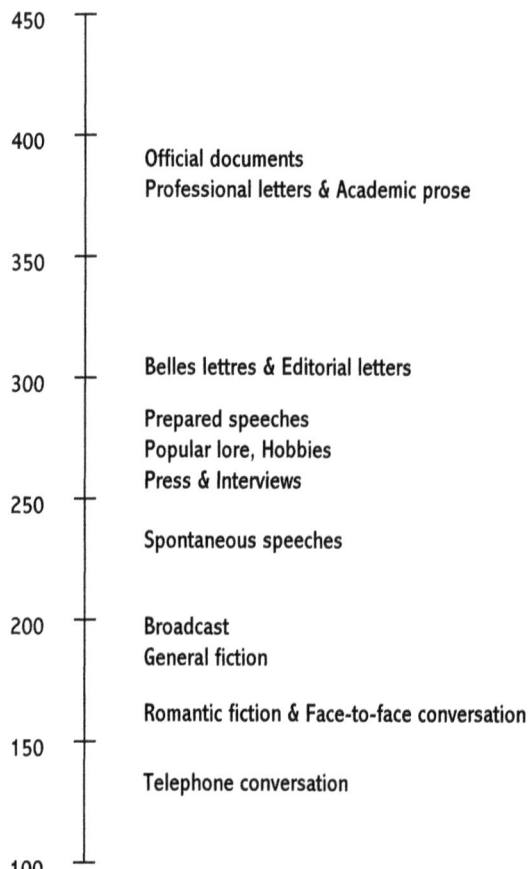

Figure 2.32:*Genres along Dimension 2 (abstracted vs. situated content) according to the rank of their mean factor score in Biber/Finegan (1986)*

Formal Texture I

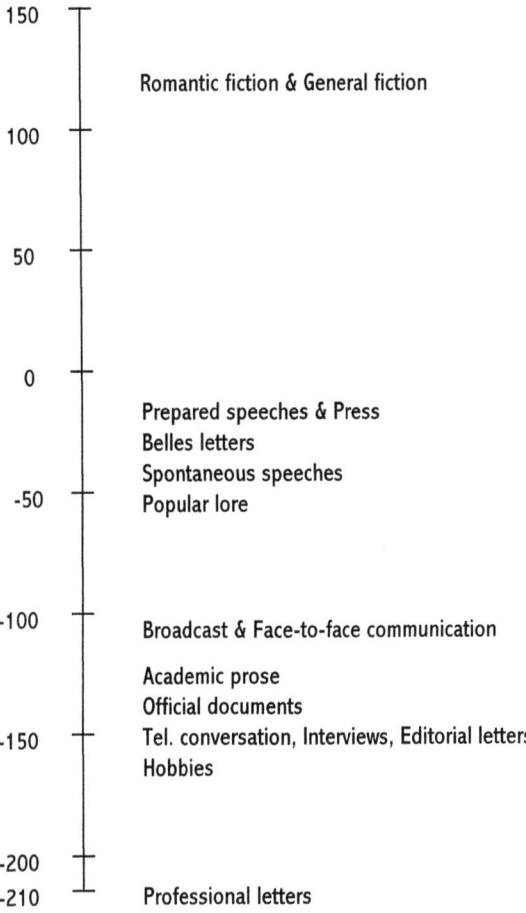

Figure 2.33: Genres along Dimension 3 (reported vs. immediate style) according to the rank of their mean factor score in Biber/Finegan (1986)

A similar procedure is used for 'cluster analysis'. For this purpose, those texts with the most similar factor scores (not mean scores as just before) in the three dimensions are grouped in clusters. This means that texts are grouped in such a way "that the texts within each cluster are maximally similar to each other in their exploitation of the textual dimensions" (Biber/Finegan 1986: 32-33). The statistical threshold levels between clusters are arbitrary and can be manipulated according to delicacy. Biber/Finegan demonstrate the results of a 3-

cluster solution and a 9-cluster soulution. (Biber 1988 offers a 6-cluster solution.)

The results for a 3-cluster solution are shown in Figure 2.34. The clusters are "groupings of texts that are in fact similar in their linguistic form regardless of external criteria" (p. 33). They are interpreted as 'text-types' as Biber/Finegan (1986: 34) explain:

> Figure [2.34] summarizes the distinguishing characteristics of each of the three clusters in the 3-cluster solution, plotting the mean dimension score for each cluster. That is, in the same way that we can compute a mean dimension score for each genre (by adding the frequencies of the linguistic features grouped on each dimension and averaging across all texts [...]) it is also possible to compute and plot the mean dimension score for each cluster. [...] In the 3-cluster solution (Figure [2.34]), the clusters correspond to three general text types, which can be characterized in terms of the dimension labels as 1) Edited, Abstract, and Immediate; 2) Edited, Situated, and Reported; and 3) Interactive, Situated, and Immediate. An overview of the texts grouped in each cluster indicates that they generally correspond to 1) argumentative/expository, 2) narrative, and 3) conversational/interactional styles.

Formal Texture I

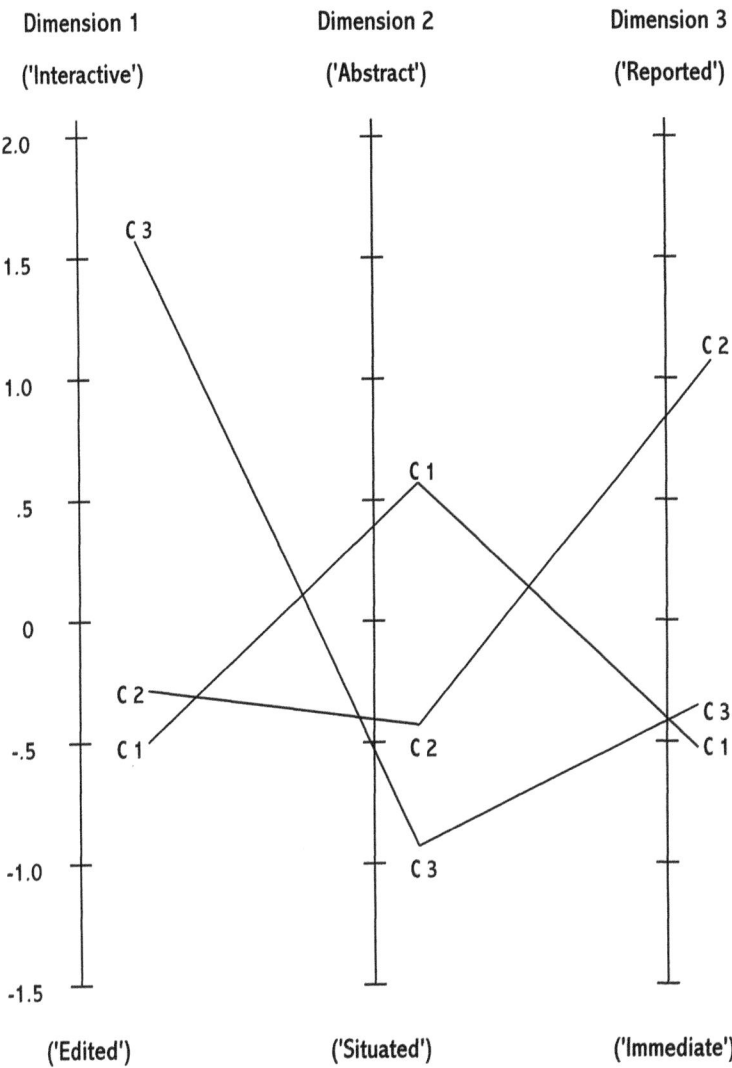

Figure 2.34:Plot of the mean dimension scores for each clustered text-type: 3-cluster solution

The general text-types according to the 3-cluster solution are summarized in Figure 2.35.

(C1) edited, abstract, immediate: argumentative/expository text-type
(C2) edited, situated, reported: narrative text-type
(C3) interactive, situated, immediate: conversational/interactional text-type

Figure 2.35: General text-types according to the 3-cluster solution

If one compares the mean factor scores in Figures 2.31 to 2.33 with clusters 1-3 one can see that the genres 'academic prose', 'belles lettres' and 'telephone conversation' are typical of the texts in clusters 1-3 respectively. Examples (123) to (125) are more or less typical examples of the three corresponding text-types.

(123) It follows that the performance of down-draught systems can be improved by the influence of cross draughts only if the thermal currents are blown into exhaust air streams moving at higher velocities than the cross draughts, so that the resultant direction of all dust-bearing air streams is towards the grid. If the grid is unduly blocked on the down-wind side of the cross draughts, the thermal currents will be blown into a zone of reduced exhaust air velocities, and control of the dust-bearing air streams can be impaired, particularly if the speed of the cross draughts is high in relation to the exhaust air movement. The important conclusion is that the performance of correctly designed and operated down-draught systems for the knock-out of hot moulds is not unduly affected by cross draughts of the order usually present in foundries. Obviously, high velocity cross draughts, such as may be found when the knock-out is situated near large open doors, will seriously impair their performance. (LOB J75: Academic prose)

It is only of limited conclusiveness to count the features in the factor scales of Figure 2.28 in a single text. However, some existing and missing features can be identified. Example (123) does not show questions, final prepositions, contractions, first and second pronouns and hedges; on the other hand, the words are fairly long (cf. Factor 1). There are nominalizations, prepositions, passives, but no place and time adverbs (cf. Factor 2). There are neither past tense forms, third person pronouns nor perfect aspect forms (cf. Factor 3). All these three features contribute to the impression that (123) is an example of an argumentative/expository text-type.

(124) A postman named Giancarlo Peppino Dante Tagliabue had been delivering letters for thirty years in a rural district near Aquila, it seemed, and was proud of never having missed a day. Heavy snowfalls had

covered the rugged district with a deep, thick mantle, interspersed with
occasional drifts. Giancarlo strapped on his skis nevertheless, and set off
on his round. At seven-thirty in the morning he was seen by a shepherd,
gamely negotiating a particularly tricky section of the mountain road to
San Doloroso. At about ten o'clock, linesmen working on a power cable
four kilometres from Monte Callifugo thought they heard howls and a
deep-throated baying. At four, when it was already growing dark, a patrol
of carabinieri found Tagliabue's official cap halfway down a snow-
covered hillside. On the road above, half-buried in drifts, were scattered
twenty or thirty letters, five copies of the Corriere dell' Aquila and an
official receipt-book for registered mail. Of Giancarlo nothing was left....
Several papers ran banner headlines: DEVOTED POSTMAN EATEN BY
WOLVES. A left-wing organ recalled that only the previous year
Tagliabue had received a scroll from the Postal Workers' Union. Two
agencies circulated smudgy photographs of his unattractive wife and
seven children. The Voce di Trastevere opened a nation-wide subscription
fund. It was not until several weeks later that Tagliabue was detained by
the Foggia police for simulating an offence. He had been sweating up that
snow-covered hillside, he explained, reflecting that he would not be
pensioned for another fifteen years. He thought of his nagging wife and
appalling brats, and it was just too much for him. He threw down his
letters and his hat into the snow and took the first train to Foggia. He had
been living there ever since with a waitress from a local trattoria. The only
wolf he had ever seen, he said, was in a travelling zoo. (LOB G54: Belles
lettres)

Example (124) is similar to (123) along Dimensions 1 and 2 and according to
the feature scales of Factors 1 and 2. It differs, however, along Dimension 3
because there are many past tense forms and third person pronouns. In all, the
text shows narrative, reporting features which make it a moderately typical
example of a narrative text-type.

(125) *B* anyway
how did you get on skiing

A skiing
skiing was good fun actually

B oh

A m
I I I enjoyed actually skiing
and it was really quite funny

        being with thrust together with
        sort of sixteen other people for a
        fortnight and
        and

    B   oh
        I'd love a fortnight's holiday where you can
        relax

    A   well it's it's fantastic
        because it's so completely different from
        anything that you you know
        would ever get yourself to do otherwise

    B   yes
        yes

    A   I think

    B   yes   (LLC 7,3f)

The excerpt from a telephone conversation in (125) is an example of a conversational/interactional text-type. As a help for the reader it is not presented in medium-independent run-on lines. Each line corresponds to one (medium-dependent) tone unit. Along Dimension 1 this text is characterized by contractions, first and second person pronouns, hedges (*actually*, *quite*), short words and many repetitions (cf. Factor 1). Along Dimension 2 there are no nominalizations (cf. Factor 2).

The 9-cluster analysis offers finer distinctions. They are basically modifications of the categories identified in the 3-cluster solution: exposition, narration, interaction. The nine text-types at which Biber/Finegan (1986) arrive are given in Figure 2.36. There are in fact few text-types (clusters) which coincide with the majority of the texts of a genre. Text-type 9, imaginative narrative, comprises 97% of the texts belonging to the genre romance fiction and 83% of the genre general fiction; the participation of six other genres in this cluster is low and very low. This means that the genres romance fiction and general fiction can be classed together statistically under the label imaginative narrative. But this quasi-match of genres with cluster text-types is in fact an exception.

1) Immediate interaction
2) Formal exposition
3) Informational-interactional text
4) Present reportage
5) Informal informational narrative
6) Informal exposition
7) Interactional narrative
8) Formal exposition with narration
9) Imaginative narrative

Figure 2.36:Text-types of a 9-cluster solution

Almost all the genres (with the exception just mentioned) are spread over several text-types and all the text-types contain texts from several genres. This may appear at first sight disappointing, but it pays tribute to the fact that text-types have to be viewed as prototypes which allow for variation and less central exemplars. For example, prepared speeches have more in common with academic prose than with telephone conversations although both genres are spoken.

In all, one has to say that the results of Biber's method are artefacts that depend highly on the manipulation of various factors: choice and groupings of genres, the delicacy of threshold levels of factors and clusters. Biber's approach to the study of text-types is restricted because many of the determinants that play a role in a wider understanding of text-types are excluded, for example the study of superstructures and the study of intentions in terms of speech acts. We will address these topics in chapters 4 and 6. Further limitations of this approach are the restriction to machine-readable features, the exclusion of semantic features (for example metaphor) and of layout features. Still, Biber's method makes it possible to describe formally distinct registers, something that was only theoretically, but not practically feasible for Halliday 20 years earlier (cf. section 2.3.1.2 above).

2.3.2 Styles

The method of extracting statistical corpus norms can be used not only to discover text-types in a language, but also to describe the styles of genres and their stylistic shifts across time. If a general corpus with many genres is used for analysis, the idea is that the corpus represents the language activities of a speech community in a more or less valid way. Similarly, this method can be used to describe the statistical corpus norm of a corpus that is only representative of a genre, but not of the language as a whole. There are several studies by Biber und Finegan which show how genres have developed over the centuries. Biber/Finegan (1988: 96) report, for example, about stylistic shifts in narratives and letters from the 18th century to modern times:

> 18th-century narratives are extremely explicit and elaborated in reference; 19th-century narratives are moderately so; and modern narratives and contemporary fiction are markedly situation-dependent and non-elaborated in reference. [...] The shift from 19th-century to modern letters is as dramatic as that for narratives. 19th-century letters are relatively elaborated in reference, while modern and contemporary letters are markedly situated and non-elaborated.

As a last field of application of Biber's method, it must be pointed out that extracted corpus norms can also be used to determine the style of a single text. The comparison of the features of the norm with the features found in a text can tell us something about the question of how prototypical a given text is for a text-type or genre. This complies with our notion of prototypicality of 'text' (cf. section 1.1 above).

2.4 Questions and exercises

1. What is the difference between a 'clause pattern' and an 'allo-sentence'? Give illustrative examples.

2. Indicate the 'lexical patterns' in text example (123).

3. Indicate the 'time relators' and 'place relators' in text example (124).

4. With the help of online corpora or the world wide web, work out the probability ranks of *strong* and *powerful* as left-hand collocates of *tea* and *coffee*.

5. "Dialects tend to differ primarily, and always to some extent, in substance. Registers, on the other hand, differ primarily in form." (Halliday et al. 1964: 88) Discuss this quotation.

6. Compare the following text with the abstracted corpus norms of the three general text-types discussed in section 2.3.1.3 and try to assign it to one of them. Take the co-occurring features in Figure 2.28 as a starting point.

A book is arranged to start at the beginning of the first chapter and to finish at the end of the last chapter. This seems natural enough but in fact it is purely an arrangement to suit authors, printers and booksellers. It does not at all correspond to the needs of the reader's mind. For a piece of understood knowledge is not a mere succession of ideas. It is a pattern of connected ideas. Some of the ideas in a book, though connected, may occur on pages which are widely separated. If books were designed to meet the needs of the reader they would be printed on one side of the paper only and not bound. They would be loose-leaf books. And the reader should have a large table on which he could spread out the leaves and see the connections of meaning. Of course there are many practical objections to such a method of printing but we must ask how can the reader overcome the handicaps which the present design of books imposes on him? (LOB F1)

2.5 Further reading

Halliday/Hasan (1976) have written a classic work on cohesion. The book by Hoey (1991) explores in detail lexical patterns in texts. The grammar by Quirk et al. (1985) is a standard work of reference with special emphasis on clause structure and the realization of clauses in texts. Sinclair (1991) is a valuable introduction to corpus linguistics with many illustrative analyses especially of concordances and collocations. Kennedy (1998) is a more recent and comprehensive survey of corpus linguistics. Esser (1993) gives a systematic overview of the field of English linguistic stylistics, which nowadays takes into account also text-linguistics, pragmatics and corpus linguistics.

3 Formal Texture II: Medium-dependent Presentation

So far we have dealt with textual properties that are based on the linguistic abstractions of grammar, namely the units 'clause complex', 'clause', 'phrase', 'word' and 'morpheme' (cf. Figure 2.1 above). Indeed, when we discussed the order and realization of elements, their cohesive properties and their statistical co-occurrences in collocations and text-types, we abstracted from the medium-bound, physical properties of graphic and phonic presentation. Therefore, when we discussed word-forms in texts, we disregarded these presentational properties and only dealt with the distribution and the meaning of medium-independent word-forms. This is common practice in linguistics although it is not common to realize that the written word-forms in linguistic examples are in fact tacitly understood as medium-independent unless stated otherwise. As we have seen in chapter 2 above, the written forms <Your> and <your> and the spoken forms [jɔː] and [jʊər] are all instantiations of the medium-independent word-form >your<, which we usually render just in italics (*your*) to mark it as object language.

In this chapter we shall reduce our level of abstraction and also deal with the medium-bound properties of texts, for example graphic layout and intonation. Very often the medium-bound properties of texts are not considered and in fact most of the research in text-linguistics is happy to ignore these aspects. But in a more comprehensive approach to text-linguistics, medium-dependent presentation must have its place, as for example in the first chapter of Halliday's (1985) *Introduction to Functional Grammar*. Also, in the wake of an increased awareness of the media, of more presentational possibilities with computers, electronic hypertexts and the Internet, questions of medium-bound presentation have become an issue in text-linguistics. The medium-dependent units that will be discussed are shown in Figure 3.1, which is inspired by a similar comparison in Halliday et al. (1964: 51).

The 'orthographic word-form' is an uninterrupted sequence of characters which is bounded on either side by spaces. 'Punctuation units' are those written stretches of text that are separated by punctuation marks like comma, semicolon or dash; Halliday (1985: 3), for example, speaks of the 'comma unit' and the 'colon unit'. The 'orthographic sentence' is a sequence of word-forms that begins with a written word-form with an initial capital letter (at the beginning of a text or after a final punctuation mark) and ends with final punctuation marks like a full stop or a question mark. The 'orthographic paragraph' comprises a sequence of lines that are set off by additional spacing or indenting. The 'page' is the maximal medium-dependent constitutive unit of a written text; it is the unit at which the major layout features become relevant.

Medium-dependent units	
Written	Spoken
Orthographic word-form	Phonological word-form
Punctuation unit	Tone unit
Orthographic sentence	Tone unit sequence
Orthographic paragraph	
Page	

Figure 3.1: Medium-dependent units

It must be noted that 'page' is understood here as a non-electronic page. It is true that the screens of browsers and e-mail programmes may change the intended shape of a page due to the properties of the software or to the manipulation by the recipient. Therefore, the shape of electronic pages is frequently not that intended by the author.

The medium-dependent units are subject to considerable variation. There are two major types of variation for written word-forms. One type of variation has to do with the 'choice of characters' in a word-form, which is fixed by national orthographic standards (for example, British English <colour> vs. American English <color>) and also for variation within these standards and deviations from orthodox orthography. A second type of variation, leaving more room for personal choice, is 'variation of character' in terms of font, typeface and typesize. The features of all medium-dependent written units and their relevance for texts will be discussed in section 3.1.

In spoken texts 'phonological word-forms' are usually not set off by pauses, comparable to spaces surrounding orthographic word-forms. Rather, phonological word-forms are normally integrated into 'tone units' and thus differentiated from their isolated use as in quotations. Spoken word-forms notoriously vary geographically. But the main distinction that is interesting from the point of view of text-linguistics is that between 'citation forms' and 'contextualized word-forms'. We will deal with these concepts and other features of medium-dependent spoken units in section 3.2.

3.1 Written presentation

3.1.1 Orthography and punctuation

Compared to spoken presentation, orthography (as an important element of written presentation) is highly standardized and codified. Orthography is relevant for most written text-types. That is, we expect the realizations of most text-types to conform to some standard orthography of written word-forms.

Such expectations are not met in the following text (1) from a brochure on mental fitness distributed in German pharmacies (*Kopf fit* 6/2007, p. 24). Text (2) is the equivalent in standard orthography.

(1) HocH AuFd eMg ElBenW agen sitz ichb EiMS chwAgerv orN.
    VorwäR Tsd ieRo sseTrab en,l uStig SchMett ertD asHorn.
    Ber GeTäl erundH ügel, leUchteNdesÄ hRengold.
    Ichmö Chtes oGernen ochsch Auen,
    ABER DER WAGEN, DER ROLLT.

(2) Hoch auf dem gelben Wagen sitz ich beim Schwager vorn.
    Vorwärts die Rosse traben, lustig schmettert das Horn.
    Berge, Täler und Hügel, leuchtendes Ährengold.
    Ich möchte so gerne noch schauen,
    ABER DER WAGEN, DER ROLLT.

At the medium-independent level, texts (1) and (2) are the first stanza of the folk song *Hoch auf dem gelben Wagen*. The written presentation of (1), however, is highly distorted. With the exception of the last line, the refrain, the lines contain all the characters that are needed to express the written word-forms. However, the spacing between the word-forms and the use of capital letters (which are used in German to indicate nouns, proper names and the beginnings of orthographic sentences) are radically different.

More specifically, the medium-dependent 'characters', for example <A> (binary code 01000001) and <a> (binary code 01100001), are not assigned according to standard orthography. Therefore, a reader of the text must abstract from this kind of variation and read the text at the abstract level of medium-independent 'letter-type', which in our case would be >a<. This kind of abstraction is equivalent to the processing of characters that are keyed in a non-case-sensitive format, which only concentrates on the last five digits, which are the same, and disregards the first three digits, which are different (cf. Esser 2006: 92). The effect for the human reader of (1) is that the written word-forms are not recognized easily, which makes reading the text a task slightly or very difficult, depending on their mental fitness.

We can observe milder forms of orthographic deviation in printed material when we consider the national orthographic standards of American English and British English. Due to modest spelling reforms there are well-known American spellings like <color>, <defense>, <traveler>, <fulfill> and <encyclopedia>, which differ from their British English equivalents <colour>, <defence>, <traveller>, <fulfil> and <encyclopaedia>. It is mainly such spellings that would reveal to a reader whether a given text was published in England or America. However, since these words are not very common and have a low frequency, it is almost impossible or pure chance to assign the national standard of a text as an exponent of the one-dimensional variable 'region' on the basis of this kind of medium-dependent presentation (cf. section 2.3.1.2 above).

After the last spelling reform in Germany, which affected more words and especially highly frequent function words, notably the conjunction <dass>, which is no longer spelled <daß>, the one-dimensional variable 'time' is much easier to detect. Almost any text will give away very soon whether it was produced before or after the spelling reform.

Without special mention we have already observed earlier a kind of orthographic variability that was not addressed as a case of medium-dependent variation: contractions that were counted in Biber's corpus-linguistic analysis (cf. Figure 2.28 above). Strictly speaking, the variation between <he is> and <he's> should not be considered a medium-independent linguistic feature (like all the others in Biber's list), but as a kind of medium-dependent variation in written presentation. The same holds for merged word-forms like <wanna> and <gimme>. They all should be analysed as in the sample analysis in Figure 3.2 (cf. Esser 2006: 55).

Medium-independent word-forms	>he is<	>they are<	>do not know<
Spoken form	/hiːz/	/ðeə/	/dənˈəʊ/
Written form	<he's>	<they're>	<dunno>

Figure 3.2   Contracted and merged word-forms

Deviant orthographic word-forms can occur as individual style markers that create a local stylistic effect or occur in distribution to create a global stylistic pattern that contributes to the assignment of a text-type (cf. Esser 1993: 92). This is not only true for contracted and merged word-forms, but also for orthographic variants that are associated with modern technology and pop culture (cf. Mukherjee 2000). Thomas (2007: 24) reports on the case of a teenage schoolgirl who had handed in a written essay that was presented completely in the style of 'text language' (SMS language). The beginning of this school essay is quoted as (3), the translation into standard orthography is given in (4).

(3) My smmr hols wr CWOT. B4, we used 2go2 NY...

(4) My summer holidays were a complete waste of time. Before, we used to go to New York...

We have to note that at a medium-independent level these two excerpts are completely equivalent. The only difference is that the presentation of (3) is appropriate for sending messages between mobile phones, whereas (4) conforms to standard orthography on paper.

The special orthography for text messages draws mainly on various kinds of reduction and on homophony between words and numbers. Here are some further well-known examples:

(5) WAN2   want to
    L8r   later
    CW2CU   can't wait to see you
    HAGT   have a great time
    JJ   just joking
    THNQ   thank you
    B4N   bye for now
    T4LMK   thanks for letting me know
    ASAP   as soon as possible

Sometimes such abbreviations are also used in situations of paper communication and have gained the status of new words, e.g. <asap> ~ /'eisæp/.

There are similar techniques of deviant spelling that are used in pop song lyrics as written attention-seeking devices that have become an attribute of the written presentation of the text-type 'pop song'. Kreyer/Mukherjee (2007: 40) quote from their Giessen-Bonn Corpus of Popular Music (GBoP):

(6) He was a sk8er boi
    He was a sk8er boi
    She said see you later boi (GBoP Let 03)

While the deviant written presentation of (6) does not suggest a deviant spoken presentation, the situation is different in (7).

(7) bwoy ce'cile, I see it clear yuh know, mi need ya yuh know
    please!!! I got a man ok

yeah but mi neva hear yuh seh nuttin bout him, mi Talk bout mi and you now
well he's there so I gotta let ya know yuh know
well let's go kick it then we can chill
anyway yuh caan do nuttin (GBoP Dut 12)

This excerpt exemplifies a kind of 'eye-dialect'. This is a graphic presentational device of authors to characterize a non-standard accent for the spoken delivery. As Kreyer/Mukherjee (2007: 41) explain:

> Sean Paul sings with a thick *patois* accent. It is the deviation from General American English pronunciation (and sometimes grammar, of course) that is encoded in the lyrics of his songs. As pointed out by Mair (2003, 256), the use of Caribbean Creoles in Jamaican diaspora communities (also on the Internet) helps to create a specific group-identity, constituting "an additional ethnic 'we'-code" in in-group communication and a "semiotic resource used to perform ethnicity and to negotiate community boundaries" in communication with out-groups.

In other words, the medium-dependent orthographic presentation of (7) fulfils a social role and contributes to classifying the text as a special text-type.

It is not only the written presentation of word-forms, namely the 'orthographic word', but also the 'orthographic sentence' that is highly standardized. We expect an orthographic sentence to be coextensive with a clause complex. That is, the cohesive function of syntactic units is complemented by a corresponding visual orthographic unit. The orthographic sentence can be regarded as a metalingual comment that facilitates the decoding process at the syntactic level. Hence the general stylistic rule taught at schools: "We write in complete sentences."

Again, as with the presentation of deviant orthographic word-forms, the deviation from the rule that clause complexes are presented in orthographic sentences, can frustrate the reader's expectations and lead to a more laborious decoding of the syntactic structure. This is a device that can be used artistically by an author, as the following passage (8) illustrates. It is taken from *A Winter Book* by Tove Jansson (2006: 41), which on the whole is presented in standard orthography.

(8) Through endless forest dark and drear no comfort near a little girl alone did roam so far from home the way was long the night was cold the thunder rolled the girl did weep no more I'll find my mother kind for in this lonely haunted spot my awful lot will be beneath this tree to lie and slowly die.

It takes very careful reading to understand (8) and a main help is the segmentation of this unusual orthographic sentence into a sequence of orthographic sentences that indicate the boundaries of clause complexes. Two possible 'translations' could be (9a) and (9b).

(9a) Through endless forest dark and drear, no comfort near, a little girl alone did roam so far from home. The way was long. The night was cold. The thunder rolled. The girl did weep no more. I'll find my mother kind, for in this lonely haunted spot my awful lot will be beneath this tree to lie and slowly die.

(9b) Through endless forest dark and drear, no comfort near, a little girl alone did roam so far from home. The way was long. The night was cold. The thunder rolled. The girl did weep: No more I'll find my mother kind, for in this lonely haunted spot my awful lot will be beneath this tree to lie and slowly die.

The difference between (9a) and (9b) concerns the syntactic status of *no more*. The punctuation in (9a) suggests that it belongs to the preceding clause *the girl did weep* whereas (9b) suggests that it belongs to the following clause *I'll find my mother kind*. In any case, it is difficult to indicate with the means of standard orthography the shift from introduced direct thought (*weep: 'no more I'll find my mother kind'*) to unintroduced free direct thought ([Ø:] *for in this lonely haunted spot my awful lot will be beneath this tree to lie and slowly die*).

In example (8) we witnessed that an orthographic sentence can be larger than a clause complex. The reverse situation, that the orthographic sentence is smaller, can also be observed as a medium-dependent stylistic device by an author. The following examples (10) to (12) are taken from the novel *Snobs* by Julian Fellowes (2005: 61, 219, 277).

(10) I was watching Edith as she gazed at Charles with a kind of fresh-faced, open adoration that reminded me of Elizabeth Taylor in *National Velvet*. When she's given the horse.

(11) As for his wife and children, I think it would be wrong to say he didn't worry about them. He did. As much as he was able.

(12) I suppose the point was it had come. The End of Her Marriage.

In (10) and (11) the adjuncts *When she's given the horse* and *As much as he was able* are presented for emphasis as independent orthographic sentences. These kinds of medium-dependent segmentation can be viewed as hints by the author of how the reader should segment the wordings in his reading process. The situation is similar in (12) with the difference that the punctuation is triggered off by a medium-independent syntactic structure, 'right dislocation', that is typically found in speech and less so in writing (but there may indeed be an ongoing change). In example (12) the subject pronoun *it* is co-referential with the dislocated noun phrase *The End of Her Marriage*. Note that in this case emphasis is expressed at three levels of description: (i) medium-independent structure, (ii) orthographic sentence and (iii) deviant spelling by use of capital letters, as in a heading.

The interaction of cohesion by clause complex and cohesion by orthographic sentence can be demonstrated with the following quotation from p. 95 of the present text:

(13) The 'page' is the maximal medium-dependent constitutive unit of a written text; it is the unit at which the major layout features become relevant.

As it stands, the cohesive tie between the two clauses is expressed (i) medium-independently by the backward-pointing, co-referential pronoun *it* and (ii) by the bracing function of the orthographic sentence, which joins the two main clauses by a semicolon and lower-case *it*. A less cohesive version would be (14), where both main clauses are presented as independent orthographic sentences.

(14) The 'page' is the maximal medium-dependent constitutive unit of a written text. It is the unit at which the major layout features become relevant.

A further alternative would be (15), where at the medium-independent level *it is* is replaced by the coordinator *and*, which signals that the following is part of a larger syntactic structure of two co-ordinated clauses sharing one subject and verb, with the second subject and verb elided.

(15) The 'page' is the maximal medium-dependent constitutive unit of a written text and the unit at which the major layout features become relevant.

The three presentational possibilities are summarized in (16).

(16) (a)   ... a written text; it is the unit ...

   (b)   ... a written text. It is the unit ...

   (c)   ... a written text and Ø the unit ...

The situation in (16a) is called 'asyndetic coordination', i.e. coordination without a linking word, and the situation in (16c) is called 'syndetic coordination', i.e. with a linking word (cf. Quirk et al. 1985: 1425, 1429).

In order to deal systematically with the cohesive functions of medium-independent syntactic structure, medium-dependent orthographic presentation structure and their interaction, a new concept is needed. This is the 'script unit', to which we will turn now.

3.1.2 Script unit

The possible and sometimes systematically exploited incongruence between the clause or clause complex on the one hand and the orthographic sentence on the other was studied in depth by Hoffbauer (2003). She distinguishes conceptually (though not terminologically) between medium-independent syntactic structure and medium-dependent graphic presentation in terms of punctuation, which she calls 'text-constructional unit'. It is defined as follows:

> To capture both the syntactic structure and the structuring function of punctuation, a unit of analysis must be chosen which is potentially larger than the syntactic unit, and potentially larger than the orthographic sentence. [...] In the simplest case, the text-constructional unit is a unit in which one syntactic sentence coincides with one orthographic sentence. Beyond that, a text-constructional unit may consist of several independent syntactic units included in one orthographic sentence, or it may consist of one syntactic sentence which is divided into several orthographic sentences. (Hoffbauer 2003: 86)

I propose to call the unit in question a 'script unit'. This term underlines the medium-bound nature and avoids confusion about the medium-independent or medium-dependent status of the notion 'text'. The script unit may be visualized as in Figure 3.3. The left-hand brace, i.e. script unit, refers to the "simplest case" in the quotation from Hoffbauer. The right-hand brace / script unit refers to the situation that "several independent syntactic units [are] included in one orthographic sentence". The brace / script unit in the middle refers to the situation that "one syntactic sentence [...] is divided into several orthographic sentences".

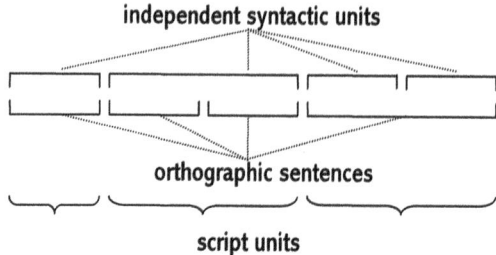

Figure 3.3: Script units

Disregarding the default "simplest case", where an independent syntactic unit is coextensive with an orthographic sentence, one can distinguish three types of complex script units: (i) those that contain combinations of syntactically unrelated clauses in one orthographic sentence, cf. (8); this type of script unit is also used in legal documents (cf. Crystal/Davy 1969: 193-194); (ii) those in which one syntactic unit is divided into several orthographic sentences, cf. (10) and (11); (iii) those that contain multiple fillings of syntactic slots, cf. (12) with the first subject *it* and the dislocated, co-referential subject *The End of Their Marriage*.

3.1.3 Layout

Beyond the 'script unit', in which medium-dependent 'orthographic sentence' and medium-independent 'clause complex' interact, there are the 'orthographic paragraph' and the 'page' as larger medium-dependent units (cf. Figure 3.1). For Krause (2000: 51) these constitute external macrostructures as opposed to semantic macrostructures. The branch of text-linguistics that is concerned with external macrostructures he calls "Architektonik" whereas "Komposition" is concerned with semantic macrostructures (cf. section 4.5 below). *Architektonik*, which is perhaps best rendered into English as 'layout', deals with the physical arrangement of the text components, i.e. the presentation of medium-dependent units. Krause (ibid.) points out that although layout may appear less important in comparison with composition, it is nevertheless important for the acceptability of a text, which can also be important in intralingual comparisons:

> Diese architektonische Gestaltung erscheint gegenüber der inhaltlichen Seite des Textes zunächst sekundär, dennoch sollte sie im Hinblick auf ihre praktische Bedeutung (auch beim interlingualen

Vergleich von Texten) nicht unterschätzt werden. Die Akzeptanz von Texten hängt nicht zuletzt auch von ihrer äußeren Gestaltung ab.

Basically, layout has to do with the arrangement of letters on a page. For our purpose three layout features should be distinguished: (i) type-area, (ii) spacing and (iii) lineation.

The layout feature 'type-area' describes the position of the printed text on a page and the margins. These variables are influenced by aesthetic, practical and economic considerations, but also by cultural conventions. The latter state, for instance, where to place in a letter the address of sender and recipient. The *Oxford Advanced Learner's Dictionary* (Hornby 1995: 1340), for example, gives the following advice for writing English letters:

> In a letter to a friend, you write your address, or a short form of it, at the top right of the letter, and then the date. You do not need to put the name and address of the person you are writing to. In a formal letter, you put your own address in the top right-hand corner, and then the date. You put the name and address of the person you are writing to below and to the left of this.

These suggestions are exemplified in the dictionary by the two layout examples quoted in Figures 3.4 and 3.5 (ibid.).

Besides such detailed conventions, the text in the type-area may be presented, quite generally, in one column as in most books (but not, for example, in dictionaries) or in more than one column as in newspapers or journals. This means that we can recognize from the purely external medium-dependent layout feature 'type-area' whether a page is from a book or from a newspaper. These expectations are not met if we read newspaper articles that are distributed not on paper but in an electronic format like an archive-CD or an online version. These formats offer little more information than the pure ASCII-code and they are in the main a medium-independent presentation. At this level there is no medium-dependent difference between newspaper article and book. It is true, however, that a screen-page on a browser has its own characteristics for navigation, advertisements and other electronic hypertext features (cf. section 3.1.4 below). The cohesiveness of the various possibilities of type-area are based on the togetherness of strings of word-forms and the graphic boundedness of lines for the human reader's eye-span.

> 26 Windmill Road
> Bromley
> Kent BR2 6DP
>
> 22 March
>
> Dear Barbara
>
> How are you and Tom? It seems ages since we saw you. I hope your new job is going well. David and I are both fine, and Lizzie is getting on well at her new school.
>
> I'm writing because I'm coming to Oxford next Tuesday for a meeting, and I wondered if we could meet for a pizza or something afterwards. Alternatively, I could just call round at your house for a little while on my way home. The meeting should be over by 5.30 at the latest.
>
> Let me know what suits you. It would be lovely to see you if you have time.
>
> > Love from
> >
> > Rachel

Figure 3.4: Layout of a letter to a friend

Formal Texture II

> 26 Windmill Road
> Bromley
> Kent BR2 6DP
>
> 22 January 1995
>
> The Information Officer
> Welsh Tourist Board
> Brunel House
> 2 Fitzalan
> Cardiff CF2 1UY
>
> Dear Sir
>
> I hope to have a holiday in North Wales this summer with my family.
>
> Could you please send me a list of camp-sites in the area, and information about the facilities they offer?
>
> My son and daughter would like to go pony-trekking; could you therefore also send me a list of riding centres that cater for children aged between 11 and 14?
>
> Thank you very much.
>
> Yours faithfully
>
> *Rachel Watts*
> Rachel Watts

Figure 3.5: Layout of a formal letter

This brings us to the layout feature of 'spacing'. There are various ways to mark an 'orthographic paragraph'. One method is to use larger vertical spaces between the lines at orthographic paragraph boundaries. A better, unequivocal method is to indent the first line of a paragraph, i.e. to give more horizontal space. The orthographic paragraph can be found as a medium-dependent cohesive device on almost any hand-written, printed or electronically displayed page.

The orthographic paragraph is an obtrusive presentational unit, but it stands only in a loosely systematic relation to the 'notional paragraph', which is a conceptual unit of text-linguistics, as Longacre (1979: 115-116) explains:

> 'Paragraph' is taken here to designate a structural rather than an orthographic unit. The paragraph indentations of a given writer are often partially dictated by eye appeal; that is, it may be deemed inelegant or heavy to go along too far on a page or a series of pages without an indentation or section break. A writer may, therefore, indent at the beginning of a subparagraph to provide such a break. Conversely, a writer may put together several paragraphs as an indentation unit in order to show the unity of a comparatively short embedded discourse.

Basic for the recognition of a 'notional paragraph' is the chain of medium-independent word-forms, usually comprising more than only one clause or clause complex. The clauses and clause complexes in a notional paragraph are linked by lexical or grammatical cohesion. The notional paragraph is intermediate in size between the clause complex and the whole text and will be discussed in section 4.5 below.

As indicated in the quotation from Longacre above, the medium-dependent graphic presentation of medium-independent sequences of words and clause complexes as a cohesive 'orthographic paragraph' leaves room for personal interpretation, style and emphasis. But ideally, an orthographic paragraph should be coextensive with a notional paragraph.

The last layout feature to be discussed is 'lineation'. If we examine the graphic structure of a printed orthographic paragraph, we notice that the lines can be of even length, the so-called 'justified setting', and of uneven length, 'unjustified setting'. Unjustified setting is normal for handwritten documents (cf. Figure 3.4) and sometimes used in printing besides justified setting to indicate that a text portion is of a different kind, for example, in a newspaper to set off typographically a commentary from the news articles. Justified setting is the default case for books. However, due to the possibilities offered by personal computers justified setting has become popular also in ephemeral writing, e.g. in letters and reports.

What is common to both typological practices, i.e. justified and unjustified setting, is that the cohesive function of the typological arrangement pertains to the paragraph as a whole and not to subsections such as clauses or phrases.

Contrary to these conventions, the potential of unjustified setting can be used to indicate cohesive relations below the paragraph. Crystal/Davy (1969) discuss layout possibilities for liturgical texts that are read in unison by the whole congregation. They say that for this functional purpose "instructions to the reader must be introduced" (p. 156). One of the examples they quote (ibid.: 154-155) is the *Gloria* from *The Rite of Low Mass*:

(17) *The celebrant begins*:
Glory be to God on high ... *and the people continue with him*:
and on earth peace to men of good will.
We praise thee.
We bless thee.
We adore thee.
We glorify thee.
We give thee thanks for thy great glory.
Lord God, heavenly King, God Father almighty.
Lord Jesus Christ, the only-begotten Son.
Lord God, Lamb of God, Son of the Father.
Thou who takest away the sins of the world,
 have mercy on us.
Thou who takest away the sins of the world,
 receive our prayer.
Thou who sittest at the right hand of the Father,
 have mercy on us.
For Thou alone art holy.
For Thou only art the Lord.
Thou alone art most high, O Jesus Christ.
With the Holy Ghost, in the glory of
 God the Father. Amen.

The effect of lineation and other graphic features in (17) is described as follows:

> The main graphological devices one can make use of are paragraphing, spacing, and capitalisation, alongside the normal range of other punctuation marks, some of which tend to be used idiosyncratically for this variety. The central feature is the combination of all these factors to split the text as a whole into clearly demarcated graphic units, which are sometimes sentences, sometimes not. The initial letter of each of these rhythm-cum-sense units is always a capital; they always end in a period; in all cases [...] they begin on a separate line; and when they contain more than one line, all lines except the first are set a little way in from the margin. The

consequence of this clear demarcation of sense units is that the reader is guided through the text in a series of jumps, and not in a smooth, continuous flow; this facilitates his speaking in unison, and also reduces the likelihood of losing the pace.

Another factor facilitating unison speech is that the punctuation on the whole is very simple, and is given a clear phonetic value. [...] There is an almost complete coincidence of periods with major pauses, and commas with brief pauses; and there is little variation in the length of pauses of both types throughout any given text. (Crystal/Davy 1969: 156-157)

While example (17) consists of many short orthographic sentences (and script units), the following two examples in Figure 3.6 from Stiff (1996: 134) consist each of only one orthographic sentence. The (slightly differing) wordings are presented in two typographical lineations, namely justified setting and 'sense-lining'. We note that sense-lining in the second version is not accompanied by unusual punctuation and capitalization. There is more information for the reader in the second version because here the lines are coextensive with grammatical units. It is therefore easier for a reader to survey the text and organize his spoken presentation in advance. Line breaking has a similar metalingual function as we noted earlier for orthographic sentences, although now the line units correspond to smaller syntactic units, mainly phrases and clauses.

> ALMIGHTY God, give us grace that we may cast away the works of darkness, and put upon us the armour of light, now in the time of this mortal life, in which thy Son Jesus Christ came to visit us in great humility: that in the last day, when he shall come again in his glorious Majesty, to judge both the quick and the dead, we may rise to the life immortal; through him who liveth and reigneth with thee and the Holy Ghost, now and ever.
>
> Almighty God,
> give us grace to cast away the works of darkness
> and to put on the armour of light,
> now in the time of this mortal life,
> in which your Son Jesus Christ
>   came to us in great humility:
> so that on the last day,
> when he shall come again in his glorious majesty
>   to judge the living and the dead,
> we may rise to the life immortal;
> through him who is alive and reigns
>   with you and the Holy Spirit,
> one God, now and forever.

Figure 3.6: Justified setting vs. sense-lining

3.1.4 Classification of texts

In section 3.1.3 we considered the medium-bound layout features 'type area', 'spacing' and 'lineation', which are constitutive for the presentation of orthographic paragraphs on a page. The concomitance of some of these layout features and certain text-types has become so conventionalized that the recognition of some text-types is possible if we consider just the layout and not the actual wording. As a consequence, the acceptability of a text as belonging to a certain text-type depends on such layout features. It is therefore part of the competence of a text producer and a reader to know about the presentational conventions that help to classify texts.

One of the most salient features of external macrostructure concerns the length of a text. A letter, for example, will always be shorter than a novel. But also within the shorter text-types, we can clearly distinguish exclusively on external grounds, for example, a letter from a diary entry even if they occur in a novel, as Figures 3.7 and 3.8 show.

> Dear Morris,
> Oddly enough I do believe you about this Mary Makepeace, though the kosher reference was despicable as only you know how to be. But don't blame Philip Swallow for the leak. It was your Irish colleen, the toothless Bernadette, if orthography is any clue, who betrayed you and your 'yaller-hared whoor' in a smudged, greasy and tear-stained epistle which I received the other day, unsigned.
> Have you ever heard of Women's Liberation, Morris? I've just discovered it. I mean I read about the way they busted up the Miss America competition last November, but I thought they were just a bunch of screwballs. Not at all. They've just started up a discussion group in Plotinus, and I went along the other night. I was fascinated. Boy, have they got *your* number!
> Désirée

Figure 3.7: Letter in a novel

Figure 3.7 is a letter within the novel *Changing Places* by David Lodge (1978: 151), and Figure 3.8 is a diary entry from the novel *The Secret Diary of Adrian Mole Aged 13 3/4* by Sue Townsend (1983: 45). Although the main body of the orthographic paragraphs is similar, there is an opening address in the letter where there is a date in the diary, and the letter ends with a signature but the diary does not so.

> Thursday   March 12th
>
> Woke up this morning to find my face covered in huge red spots. My mother said they were caused by nerves but I am still convinced that my diet is inadequate. We have been eating a lot of boil-in-the-bag stuff lately. Perhaps I am allergic to plastic. My mother rang Dr Gray's receptionist to make an appointment, but the earliest he can see me is next Monday! For all he knows I could have lassa fever and be spreading it all around the district! I told my mother to say that I was an emergency case but she said I was 'over-reacting as usual'. She said a few spots didn't mean I was dying. I couldn't believe it when she said she was going to work as usual. Surely her child should come before her job?
>   I rang my grandma and she came round in a taxi and took me to her house and put me to bed. I am there now. It is very clean and peaceful. I am wearing my dead grandpa's pyjamas. I have just had a bowl of barley and beef soup. It is my first proper nourishment for weeks.
>   I expect there will be a row when my mother comes home and finds that I have gone. But frankly, my dear diary, I don't give a damn.

Figure 3.8: Diary entry in a novel

There is an interesting interrelation between medium-independent structure and medium-dependent layout that can be observed in electronic texts. Peters (2002: 88) calls this the 'stretched sentence'. She quotes the example in Figure 3.9, which is the entry "Colon" from the website of the Online Writing Laboratory at Purdue University (http://owl.english.purdue.edu/handouts/grammar/g_overvw.html), and describes the features of this stretched sentence as follows:

Use a colon ...

in the following situations:	for example:
after a complete statement in order to introduce one or more directly related ideas, such as a series of directions, a list, or a quotation or other comment illustrating or explaining the statement.	The daily newspaper contains four sections: news, sports, entertainment, and classified ads. The strategies of corporatist industrial unionism have proven ineffective: compromises and concessions have left labor in a weakened position in the new "flexible" economy.
in a business letter greeting.	Dear Ms. Winstead:
between the hour and minutes in time notation.	5:30 p.m.
between chapter and verse in biblical references.	Genesis 1:18

Figure 3.9: Example of a stretched sentence

The stretched sentence is marked by a colon to show that more is to come. In Figure [3.9] the connection with the introductory sentence is all the more stretched, because the two columns of the table present lists of (phrasal) alternatives, and so the column heads, which are constituents of the stretched sentence, have to be read recursively. The column headings are marked with colons to show that what follows will complete the sentence, and use of lower case in both column heads and the points in the left column allows them to be read as parts of the stretched sentence. [...] The use of lists entails the need for parallelism in the wording of points, so that reliable connections can be made with the stretched sentence, even in the vertical domain. [...] The stretched sentence is itself a phenomenon that will need to be recognized in the grammar of written English. (Peters 2002: 88)

Other text-types that depend heavily on the medium-dependent presentation of layout are the dictionary and the telephone directory. In these cases, too, it is possible to name the text-type without recognizing the medium-independent word-forms.

An interesting case of culture-specific difference has been noted by Fries (1990), who compares German and English death notices. Whereas the German text-type requires a more or less defined layout, the presentation of an English death notice is hardly distinguishable from small advertisements, because it is presented in plain text. Here is a likely adaptation of an English death notice to a Swiss-German newspaper and the corresponding version in an English newspaper provided by Fries (1990: 59):

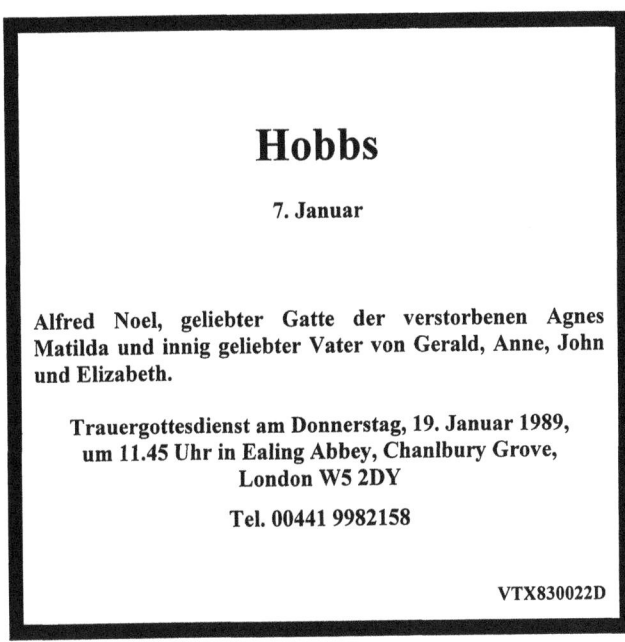

Figure 3.10:Death notice in Swiss-German style

HOBBS – on January 7th, Alfred Noel, beloved husband of the late Agnes Matilda and dearly beloved father of Gerald, Anne, John, and Elizabeth.

Figure 3.11:English-style equivalent

It is clear that death notices follow culture-specific templates and these have to be described also in terms of medium-independent presentation, for example as different superstructures which conventionalize the contents and sequence of textual elements, as shown by Fries (1990) and Reis (1978).

There is another, extreme case where the graphic presentation is decisive for the text-type, namely a poem, even if there are no phonological regularities. In such a case the author simply declares via graphic line breaks that the text should be regarded as a poem (cf. Plett 1975: 86-87). Here are the first four stanzas from Michael Hulse's (2002: 32) poem "Heathrow":

Heathrow

This might be the kind of place you'd pause for a while,
    as Auden visited the grave of Freud
    or Larkin on his bike stopped at a church,
        a place to chill the head

with transit, fraughtness, fear, the ache of departure –
    keeping one eye on the board and one on
    the bag you mustn't leave unattended.
        Whatever you thought you

believed translates as a traffic in hope. Chanel.
    Gucci leather. Hermès silk. Gordon's gin. Love.
    From here you can go anywhere. Because.
        Because you can. Because

the commerce of futures and regeneration
    demands your flight. Because there's a census
    that summons you home to your native parts.
        Home to be crucified.

Figure 3.12: Four stanzas from Michael Hulse

If the wording in Figure 3.12 is stripped of the medium-dependent presentation of layout and reduced to a near-equivalent of the ASCII-code, the text looks as in (18):

(18) This might be the kind of place you'd pause for a while, as Auden visited the grave of Freud or Larkin on his bike stopped at a church, a place to chill the head with transit, fraughtness, fear, the ache of departure - keeping one eye on the board and one on the bag you mustn't leave unattended. Whatever you thought you believed translates as a traffic in hope. Chanel.

Gucci leather. Hermès silk. Gordon's gin. Love. From here you can go anywhere. Because. Because you can. Because the commerce of futures and regeneration demands your flight. Because there's a census that summons you home to your native parts. Home to be crucified.

Presented without the layout features used in Figure 3.12, the text is still impressive but it would be hard to recognize it as a poem and not just a flood of thoughts. If people were given version (18) and asked to present the text in stanzas, one would get many differing solutions, not necessarily the one in Figure 3.12, where the lining and the punctuation structure as well as the syntactic structure do not relate to each other in systematic ways. Also, the spoken delivery, i.e. the transcoding written → spoken → written, would give no clue for a non-arbitrary layout presentation. This shows, then, that in some cases it is the medium-dependent presentation and not the wording that classifies a poem as a poem.

3.2 Spoken Presentation

3.2.1 Phonological word-forms in tone units

As was noted above in connection with the discussion of Figure 3.1, the medium-dependent units for the spoken presentation of word-forms are 'phonological word-form', 'tone unit' and 'tone unit sequence'. In this section we will see what the properties of these three units are and how they relate to each other and to the more abstract medium-independent units to form cohesive ties.

Perhaps the most salient feature of phonological word-forms is that they are usually not set off by pauses that could be compared to the spaces surrounding orthographic word-forms. In contrast to orthographic word-forms, phonological word-forms give no systematic clues for the recognition of individual medium-independent word-forms. On the contrary, the phonetic amalgamation of spoken word-forms in connected speech disguises the divisions between word-forms in English, as Robins (1980: 115) explains:

> In English the phonetic marking of word divisions is often potential rather than actual; that is, the phonetic features that serve to mark them are such as may occur rather than such as invariably do occur.

This observation accommodates the fact that words in connected speech are presented not in isolation but rather in what are called 'tone groups' or 'tone units'. The tone unit is a chunk of speech in which words are presented without interruption in one larger unit, which is sometimes called a 'contour': they are, so to speak, squeezed together and further characterized by one prominent syllable, the nucleus. Take for example the following contribution in a conversation from the London-Lund Corpus (01: 974-5):

(19) (a)   >and she was sort of pretty and bright<

    (b)   and she was sort of <u>pretty</u> / and <u>bright</u> \

    (c)   ənʃɪwəsɔːtəfprˈɪtɪ / əmbrˈaɪt \

    (d)   ænd ʃiː wɒz sɔːt ɒv prˈɪtɪ ænd braɪt

The sequence of medium-independent word-forms is given in (a), the chunking into tone units is represented in (b) using standard orthography and underlining for easy reading. This line further specifies that the nuclear (accented) word in the first tone unit is *pretty* and in the second tone unit *bright*. Furthermore, there is a rising tone (marked /) at the end of the first tone unit and a falling tone (marked \) at the end of the second. Line (c) gives a possible transcription of the phonic segments in the two tone units. This representation indicates that there are no boundaries between the phonic representations of medium-independent word-forms and that the first syllable in *pretty* and the whole of *bright* are the prominent syllables in the two respective tone units. Furthermore, the word-forms of connected speech that are used in (c) differ from the word-forms that are given in line (d). The latter indicate the spoken citation forms of the respective medium-independent word-forms. The distinction between the representations in (c) and (d) is commonly known as that between '(special) context form' and 'citation form'. Here is what Gimson (1980: 283) has to say about this distinction:

> If [...] the word is admitted as an abstracted linguistic unit, it is important to note the differences which may exist between its concrete realization when said (often artificially) in isolation and those which it has when, in connected speech, it is subject to the pressures of its sound environment or of the accentual or rhythmic group of which it forms part. Those word forms which are typical of connected speech are often known as *special context forms*. The variations involved may affect the word as a whole, e.g. weak forms in an unaccented situation or word accentual patterns within the larger rhythmic pattern of the complete utterance; or may affect more particularly the sounds used at word boundaries, such changes involving a consideration of the features of morpheme and word junctures, junctural assimilations, elision, and liaison forms. In addition, it will be seen that the extent of variation depends largely upon the speed of utterance, the slower and

more carefully the delivery the greater the tendency to preserve a form nearer to that of the isolated word.

The description of special context forms has been largely a topic of phonetics and foreign language teaching, but less so of lexicology and morphology. A notable exception is Obendorfer (1998: 14), who distinguishes between 'phonological word' corresponding roughly to 'citation form' and 'phonological word-form' corresponding roughly to 'context form'.

The notion 'phonological word' is used for descriptions completely out of context as they are applied, for example, in minimal pairs, e.g. <and> /ænd/ vs. <end> /end/. Such use of citation forms in minimal pairs is paradigmatic. On the other hand, the notion 'phonological word-form' is used for context forms, e.g. the weak form of <and>, /ənd/, and the strong form /ænd/ that is used if the word carries the intonational nucleus of a tone unit. This use is called "syntagmatic citation form" by Obendorfer (ibid.)

The distinction between context form and citation form is particularly relevant for the so-called function words (grammatical words), which very often have both types of pronunciation given in dictionary entries, namely weak/reduced and strong/unreduced forms. The *Longman Dictionary of Contemporary English* (Summers 1995), for example, gives the following phonological word-forms for *and*: /ənd, nd, ən, n, *strong* ænd/. Such variations of the spoken morphological shape are called 'allomorphs of connected speech'. To these we may add the assimilated form /əm/ that occurred in (19c) above. It is important to note that in the medium-dependent presentation of (19c) the two medium-independent word-forms >and< and >bright< are fused and presented cohesively in one tone unit /əmbr'aɪt/ and that there is no presentational hint that indicates that we are dealing with two medium-independent word-forms.

Gimson (1980: 283), in the quotation given above, mentions assimilation, elision and liaison as types of special context features. Assimilation and elision were already exemplified in example (19c) above. Liaison describes mainly the linking /r/, e.g. >near it< /nɪərɪt/, and the intrusive /r/, e.g. >idea of< /aɪdɪərəv/ (cf. ibid.: 208, 294). To these may be added reduced context forms. Reduced forms can be found both in function words and lexical words.

Reduced forms in function words are mostly weak forms involving a vowel reduction. Quite generally, reduction in function words very often involves other processes besides vowel reduction. There are lists in handbooks of phonology, especially for learners of English as a foreign language, for example Gimson (1980: 261-263) and Arnold/Hansen (1996: 196-200).

Reduction in lexical words involves 'compression' of two syllables into one:

Sometimes a sequence of sounds in English has two possible pronunciations: either as two separate syllables, or **compressed** into a single syllable. [...]

Generally the uncompressed version is more usual
• in rarer words
• in slow or deliberate speech
• the first time a word occurs in a discourse.

The compressed pronunciation is more usual
• in frequently used words
• in fast or casual speech
• if the word has already been used in discourse. (Wells 1990: 152)

For the word-form *lenient*, for example, "two pronunciations are possible: a slower one /ˈliːn i ənt/ and a faster one /ˈliːn jənt/" (ibid.). That is, one word-form is presented in three syllables and one with only two. Also note that in these examples spaces are used to indicate syllable boundaries.

Besides the default cases of context forms discussed so far, there are also cases where the allomorphs of connected speech are deliberately not used in order to mark an open juncture, e.g. in the disambiguation of minimal pairs as in (20), where the cohesion of adjacent word-forms in a tone unit is interrupted:

(20) <a name> vs. <an aim> /əneɪm/ vs. /ənʔeɪm/

Normally, the word sequences that are disambiguated in (20) are homophonous, namely /əneɪm/. In contrast, the open juncture cancels the effects of the allomorphs of connected speech, i.e. there is no liaison and instead there are segmental separation features like the glottal stop /ʔ/ in front of a word beginning with a vowel. Knowles (1991: 153) calls such cancelling processes "segmental discontinuity".

3.2.2 Tone units and tone unit sequences

The tone unit was defined above as a chunk of speech in which words are presented without interruption ("squeezed together") in one larger unit (contour) with one prominent syllable, the nucleus. If we consider the position of the nucleus in a tone unit, there are four structural types. They all can be derived from the formula $(X)\underline{X}(X)$ (cf. Esser 1988: 6):

(21) (i)   proclitic word(s) + nuclear word + enclitic word(s)

(ii) proclitic word(s) + nuclear word

(iii) nuclear word + enclitic word(s)

(iv) nuclear word

(A proclitic word is an unaccented word that is pronounced with a following nuclear word as a single unit of sound. An enclitic word is a word that is pronounced with a preceding nuclear word as a single unit of sound.) The structural type (i) can be seen in the second tone unit of (22a) and in (22b). The dialogue in (22) is a corny joke taken from Lewis (1977: 36) in an adapted notation:

(22) (a) *Diner*: waiter\ there's a fly in my soup\

(b) *Waiter*: then perhaps you'd prefer a red wine sir\

The structural type (ii) is very common and can be witnessed in the two tone units of example (19b) where the nucleus is placed at the end of each tone unit. This situation is conventionally called 'end-focus'. But since 'focus' is a medium-independent semantic notion, we should rather speak of 'end-nucleus' (or 'final nucleus'), which is medium-bound, i.e. cannot be transferred unequivocally to or from the written medium. The nucleus is an encoding device for the benefit of the listener that points out to him what is important in a message, namely the focus. Its function in the other structural types will be exemplified below. The structural type (iii) is given in (23) taken from the ICE-GB (S1A-040 085) and type (iv) is exemplified in the first tone unit of (22a).

(23) that's it\

Quite generally, non-final nucleus indicates that enclitic elements following the nucleus in a tone unit are presented as 'given' or 'understood'. The non-final nucleus in (22a) expresses urgency and indignation, in (22b) possibly contrast, assuming that the diner had ordered white wine before. A more controlled and less urgent presentation of the propositional content of (22a) would be (24), although less effective for presenting a joke:

(24) waiter\ in my soup/ there's a fly\

At the level of the clause or clause complex, the presentational difference between end-nucleus and non-final nucleus can be explained with the theory of Functional Sentence Perspective and its two basic notions of 'theme' and 'rheme'; 'theme' being what is non-focal and 'rheme' what is focal. Our presentational type (ii), in which proclitic words precede the nuclear word, signals that the theme precedes the rheme. The arrangement of the elements of theme and rheme, and hence the position of the focus and additionally of the nucleus in spoken presentation, is described by Mathesius (1975 [1961]: 156) in the following, repeated quotation (cf. section 2.1.2):

> The usual position of the theme of an utterance is the beginning of the sentence, whereas the rheme occupies a later position, i.e. we proceed from what is already known to what is being made known. We have called this order o b j e c t i v e, since it pays regard to the hearer. The reversed order, in which the rheme of the utterance comes first and the theme follows, is s u b j e c t i v e. In normal speech this order occurs only in emotionally coloured utterances in which the speaker pays no regard to the hearer, starting with what is most important for himself.

According to these distinctions, (22a) exemplifies a subjective order and (24) an objective one.

The function of the second tone unit in (24) is similar to that of the enclitic segment in (22a) because it marks off intonationally the given, thematic part of the proposition. Quite generally, given elements (represented as 'X' below) can be marked intonationally in three ways:

(25) (i) X/Y

 (ii) XY

 (iii) YX

Given elements can be intonationally set off (i) by a tone unit boundary with a rising tone, (ii) by a non-final position in a tone unit preceding a final nucleus or (iii) by following the nucleus in a tone unit (enclitic position).

Intonational marking is less clear for the rhematic elements. The semantic interpretation of what elements are focal besides the nucleus can vary and is not signalled intonationally. This is shown by the following example with end-nucleus from Quirk et al. (1985: 1364), which can be used in different contexts:

(26) we're going to the races\

As an answer to the question *What's on today?* the whole clause is new or rhematic and we can speak of a 'broad focus'. As an answer to the question *What are we doing today?* only the section *going to the races* is new, focal or rhematic. Answering the question *Where are we going today?* only *to the races* is in 'narrow focus'.

The relative communicative weight of word-forms that is expressed through intonation pertains not only to the internal structure of the tone unit but also to the sequences of tone units, cf. (19b) and (25i). For the arrangement of clauses in clause complexes and their presentation in reading, Quirk et al. (1985) have introduced the notion of 'principle of resolution', which refers both to the medium-independent chain of words and to the medium-dependent intonation pattern of a sequence of tone units with rising tones, terminated by a tone unit with a falling tone:

> One of the factors which determine the order in which the constituent clauses of a sentence are arranged is the principle of RESOLUTION, the principle that states that the final clause should be the point of maximum emphasis [...]. In reading aloud, the resolutory effect of the final clause is often pointed by intonation. A typical reading [of a clause complex] would put rising or falling-rising tones on all points of information focus [of each clause] except the last. [...] As rising and falling-rising tones have implications of non-finality, the effect of this pattern is to build up a continuing sense of anticipation, which is at last resolved by the finality of the falling tone. This principle of resolution is the counterpart, on the sentence level, of the principle of end-focus [...] in the tone unit. (Quirk et al. 1985: 1036)

The intonation pattern associated with the principle of resolution can be observed not only with tone units that are coextensive with clauses, but with any sequence of words within a clause or clause complex, cf. e.g. (19b) and (24).

The principle of resolution leads to the question of the relative weight of neighbouring tone units. A falling tone unit has greater informational weight than a rising tone unit. This can also be seen in sequences where a tone unit with a falling tone precedes the one with a rising tone (cf. ibid.: 1360):

(27) (a)   I went to France\ last week/

   (b)   last week/ I went to France\

In both cases *France* is the element that receives most intonational prominence.

An early description of the relative informational weight of neighbouring tone units was given by Palmer (1922: 88, 91):

> The English tone-sequences may be grouped into two classes, which for want of better terms we may respectively call co-ordinating and subordinating. The co-ordinating sequences are those in which the successive Tone-Groups are *identical.* [...] The subordinating

sequences are those in which the successive Tone-Groups are *dissimilar*.

[The subordinating sequences] are used in sentences containing two prominent elements, the one expressing the more important, and the other the less important fact. The one expressing the more important has the falling, and the one expressing the less important has the rising or falling-rising nucleus.

This means that at a purely abstract yet medium-dependent level the principle of resolution signals coordination in the sequence of rising tone units, which are subordinate with respect to the last, falling tone unit. This may be rendered in an abstract notation, for example:

(28) _/ _/ _/ _\

If we apply the distinction described by Palmer to example (27a) we must state that the first tone unit is more important than the second, whereas in (27b) the first tone unit is subordinated to the second.

According to the linguistic model proposed in this book, medium-independent syntactic information is in principle independent of its accompanying spoken or written presentation. The independence of medium-independent syntactic structure and medium-dependent intonation structure was aptly characterized by Bolinger (1958: 37) at the very beginning of the often futile discussions about intonation and grammar: "The encounters between intonation and grammar are casual, not causal." However, the independence of syntactic structure and intonation structure does not rule out certain principles or conventions to establish (textual) cohesion by means of intonation structure. This means that the relations between intonational units, especially tone units, and syntactic units, especially clauses and phrases, are correlational but not implicational. There are numerous lists of correlations in scholarly literature, e.g. Wode (1966), Crystal (1969: ch. 6), Quirk et al. (1985: 1357-1360), Leech/Svartvik (1994: 194) and Tench (1996: 39-49).

Here are some of the recurring syntactic units that are recommended in literature to be given separate tone units in clause complexes (cf. Leech/Svartvik 1994: 194, 266 and Quirk et al. 1985: 1358):

(29) last year/ the warfare grew\
 [initial adverbial phrase]

(30) what we want/ is plenty of rain\
 [clausal subject]

Formal Texture II

(31) the tall lady by the door/ spoke to John\
    [long noun phrase subject]

(32) I would like a ham sandwich/ an ice-cream/ and a cup of tea\
    [coordinated phrase]

(33) doctor\ I'm very anxious\
    [initial vocative]

(34) the Smiths/ as you probably know/ are going to America\
    [medial adverbial phrases or clauses]

(35) the emergency services were hampered by thick smoke\ which spread quickly through the station\
    [non-restrictive postmodifier]

(36) he opened the door/ and walked straight in\
    [coordinated clause]

(37) her writing/ I find unintelligible\
    [fronted object]

(38) my mother/ she has gone shopping\
    [left dislocation]

Such correlations between syntactic structure and tonality are sometimes called 'normal intonation' (cf. Wode 1966) or 'neutral tonality' (Tench 1996: 33); or it is said that intonation "fulfils a grammatical function" (ibid.: 39). I would, however, prefer to say that intonation merely characterizes or corroborates medium-independent syntactic information with medium-dependent means. Intonation certainly does not establish syntactic relations or segments.

3.2.3 Talk unit

It will be remembered that in section 3.1.2 we introduced the 'script unit' as a unit within which the completion of medium-independent syntactic structure and the completion of medium-dependent orthographic sentence coincide. In our discussion of the relations that operate between medium-independent syntactic structure and medium-dependent intonation structure, we can draw on a similar concept, which was developed earlier than the script unit: The 'talk unit' was first introduced by Euler (1991) and Halford (1996). Halford (1996: 33-34) defines the 'talk unit' as follows (cf. Euler 1991: 84):

The talk unit is the maximal unit defined by syntax plus intonation. Neither may a single prosodic presentation unit ever be analysed as more than one talk unit nor may a single self-contained syntagm form the base of more than one talk unit. In other words: several syntactically unrelated phrases can be linked by prosodic features, and two or more independent prosodic presentation units may be linked by virtue of spanning one syntagm.

Notwithstanding minimal definitional differences, we can define the talk unit, quite generally, as comprising those stretches of speech in which syntactic completeness (in terms of clauses and clause complexes) and prosodic completeness coincide. This can be visualized as follows:

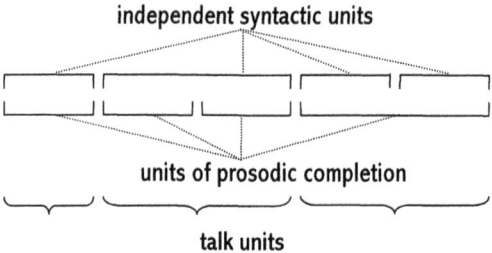

Figure 3.13: Talk units

For our purposes, units of prosodic completion can be regarded as tone units with a falling tone; see, for example, Mukherjee (2001: 21-22) for a more detailed discussion.

The left-hand brace in Figure 3.13 depicts the situation in which an independent syntactic unit, e.g. a clause, is coextensive with a unit of prosodic completion. This can be (i) a clause that is coextensive with a tone unit ending with a falling tone, called a 'minimal talk unit', cf. example (26), or (ii) the situation where one independent syntactic unit is presented in more than one tone unit, the last one ending with a falling tone, i.e. cases where the principle of resolution is chosen for a medium-dependent presentation, cf. example (34).

The brace in the middle of Figure 3.13 typifies cases where prosodic completion occurs in a larger syntactic unit. In other words, prosodic completion coincides with syntactic incompletion. This can be found, for example, in the clause complex in example (40).

The right-hand brace represents the case in which more than one independent syntactic unit is presented in a sequence of tone units with rising tones, except the last one, which has a falling tone. This type can be briefly exemplified in (39).

(39) he came/ he saw/ he conquered\

Here we are dealing with asyndetic coordination which is achieved through intonation, or more specifically, through the presentation of the three clauses according to the principle of resolution.

Talk units make it possible to conjoin by means of intonation parts of a text that are syntactically unrelated; conversely, syntax may conjoin tone units that are unrelated. Some special cases deserve particular mentioning.

First, there are 'minor talk units', which end at points where prosodic and syntactic closure is achieved, but where a sentence introduced with a co-ordinator follows to form a larger talk unit. A minor talk unit is exemplified in the first line of (40).

Second, there are 'major talk units', which end at points where prosodic and syntactic closure are achieved and where there is no structural indicator for a larger unit neither to the left nor to the right. Example (40) from the London Lund Corpus (11.3f, 888-891) is given in a functionally simplified notation. Note that here, for the listener, there are potential terminations of the current structure at the end of each line.

(40) it was vaguely vase shaped\
and they had a lot of seashells\
stuck all over it\
forming the word mother\

Third, there are cases in which there is a contradiction of prosodic and syntactic closure information. This can be shown at the end of the first line in the talk unit in example (41), taken again from the London Lund Corpus (11.3d, 475-478), where there is a prosodically closed status combined with syntactic incompletion. (We disregard the possibility of treating *it happened* as an answer or confirmation, as in a dialogue, since this talk unit is part of a longer contribution.)

(41) it happened\
at a small hotel in Sussex\
where I happened to be staying/
after dinner\

Fourth, there are cases of misleading prosodic information, in which case there is temporary syntactic completeness only with regard to the language material to the left, but not to the right. This can be seen in the second line of (41), where a prosodically closed status is combined with syntactic completion to the left, but stranded elements to the right.

Fifth, it is obvious that the ends of talk units mark the places of polite turn taking in conversation (cf. Mukherjee 2001: 126-129). If neither a syntactic structure is left open by a current speaker nor does the intonation signal that the speaker has not finished, the contribution of another speaker will not be felt as an interruption. In contrast, impolite turn taking takes place in the middle of a current talk unit. This can be demonstrated in the following example from the London Lund Corpus (LLC-5.3, 335-344), where there is also an overlap (marked * ... *) of the last two tone units of speaker A and the first three of speaker B.

(42) *A*: yes it is perfectly true\
that it includes those marginal cases/
that you've referred to\
but\
*these these wait/
let me just finish/*

B: *excuse me\
your point\
your your case*
is an example of the cases of the marginal ones\

Besides its application in conversation analysis, the talk unit also reflects stylistic differences. Mukherjee (2001: 68) found out, for example, that the mean value for the length of talk units is roughly eight tone units in monologues but only roughly three tone units in dialogues. Mukherjee also shows that the frequency of minimal talk units, i.e. talk units that consist of only one tone unit, increases in conversations with intimates, but decreases with strangers (ibid.: 78).

3.3 Questions and exercises

1. With reference to the orthographic word-forms that are used for text messages under (5), explain the phonological and morphological reasons for choosing these abbreviated word-forms.

2. With reference to example (8), find more possible ways to present the wording in orthographic sentences.

3. Find instances of 'sense-lining' in printed advertisements and discuss their function.

4. Apart from the text-types mentioned in section 3.1.4, find more text-types where the medium-bound layout features give away the text-type.

5. Give examples of 'syntagmatic citation forms' making use of prosodic notation and phonetic transcription.

6. Take a passage from the book *A Corpus of English Conversation* by Svartvik/ Quirk (1980) and

(i) determine the structural types as shown under (21),
(ii) identify cases of 'objective order' and 'subjective order'.

7. Take a passage from a conventional novel and indicate by underlining and slashes (forward and backward) how a possible presentation according to 'normal intonation' could be achieved. Make use of the suggestions made in (29) to (38).

8. Take a passage from the book *A Corpus of English Conversation* by Svartvik/ Quirk (1980) and

(i) identify 'talk units',
(ii) identify cases of polite and impolite turn taking.

3.4 Further reading

On medium-dependent structures and their relation to medium-independent structures see chapters 5 and 6 in Esser (2006). Crystal (1990: chs 4 and 5) gives a short, yet informative overview of pronunciation and spelling in present-day English. The article by Mukherjee (2000) deals with deviant spelling in popular culture. Crystal/Davy (1969) offer insightful analyses of medium-independent and medium-dependent expression systems. Mukherjee (2001) is a detailed study of the stylistic potential of talk unit variation. Monschau (2004) describes the interaction of medium-independent syntax and medium-bound intonation in oral reading.

4 Semantic Texture: Psycholinguistic and Cognitive Aspects of Text Constitution

In the preceding chapters 2 and 3 we have dealt with different aspects of formal texture, i.e. formal constituents and their material presentation in written or spoken substance. In the sections that follow now, we will consider textlinguistic aspects that rely not only on the wording of texts but also on the human language user and his psychological and cognitive disposition. These extensions of textlinguistic research are described, for example, by Beaugrande (1994: 4574) and House (1994: 4582) as follows:

> Yet accruing research revealed that the text lies 'beyond the sentence' not merely in length, i.e. in space or time, but in its close integration with factors not relating to formal constituency and dependency, but to human activities of communication and cognition.

> Over and above being a set of structures, texts are realized as outcomes of problem-solving 'cognitive procedures'.

Basic human activities that can be regarded as problem-solving are understanding and formulating texts. Among others, both aspects deal with the question: "Have I heard or read this or something similar before?" This question relates to the language user's expectations which are in turn based on previous encounters of language use. Previous encounters of language use are systematically explored in corpus linguistic studies of collocation, which were a topic of section 2.2.2 above. Now we have to return to collocation and discuss this phenomenon from a psycholinguistic point of view in section 4.1.

4.1 Lexical priming

The language user's expectations, which are based on previous encounters of language use, help him to understand and to formulate new texts. However, there is the practical descriptive problem that the encounters of language use of individuals are not recorded as such and are therefore not empirically verifiable. There exist two theoretical models that try to approach previous encounters of language use. One model is to approximate an average language user by consulting a corpus that aims at representing language use, as for example the British National Corpus (cf. Burnard 1995). The other model is to give a psychological explanation for why some wordings are preferred to others. This model is known as 'priming'. The study of collocations and the study of priming can be viewed as working in a complementary fashion in order to account for the repeated co-occurrence of words. While collocations are based on recorded frequencies in corpora, priming deals with unrecorded frequencies of individual language users.

In recent linguistic literature it is Hoey who has brought together the corpus linguistic concept of collocation and the psychological concept of priming. This is how he sees the connection:

> We can only account for collocation if we assume that every word is mentally **primed** for collocational use. As a word is acquired through encounters with it in speech and writing, it becomes cumulatively loaded with the contexts and co-texts in which it is encountered, and our knowledge of it includes the fact that it co-occurs with certain other words in certain kinds of context. (Hoey 2005: 8)

The plausibility of the contribution of corpus collocation for priming, and eventually also for naturalness (cf. section 2.2.2 above), is convincingly demonstrated by Hoey (2005: 5) with the help of the following examples (1) and (2). Example (1) is the first sentence from a travel book, example (2) is a purposeful attempt to reformulate (1) maintaining the meaning of the original sentence and many of its words.

(1) In winter Hammerfest is a thirty-hour ride by bus from Oslo, though why anyone would want to go there in winter is a question worth considering.

(2) Through winter, rides between Oslo and Hammerfest use thirty hours up in a bus, though why travellers would select to ride there then might be pondered.

Why is it that (2), although grammatically correct, is clumsy? Hoey explains the difference between (1) and (2) with the concepts 'normal collocation' and 'unusual collocation'. Without going into concrete figures one can say that in a corpus unusual collocations are less frequent than normal collocations. Some of the striking differences that Hoey (2005: 6-7) describes are shown in Figure 4.1. Note that the collocations described here can be of two kinds: the word-forms in question may be directly neighbouring or in the vicinity of the text.

Semantic Texture

Normal collocations in (1)	Unusual collocations in (2)
in–winter	*through–winter*
[number]–hour	*use–[number]–hours–up*
ride–from	*rides–between*
by–bus	*in–a–bus*
anyone–would	*travellers–would*
would–want	*would–select*

Figure 4.1: Normal and unusual collocations

The unnaturalness and clumsiness of example (2) is not only due to its unusual collocations but also due to the fact that the collocations in (2) are not interconnected as they are indeed in (1). This is shown in Figure 4.2, where one collocation evokes a next one; the 'joints' are printed in bold.

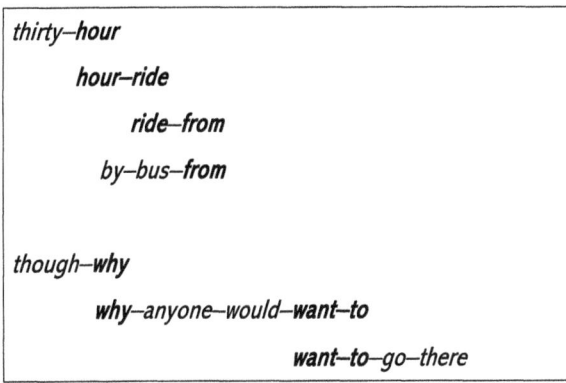

Figure 4.2: Interconnected collocations in example (1)

Hoey (2005: 7) sums up his findings as follows:

> It is worth noting that even my rewritten version still makes use of existing collocations; it is hard to construct a meaningful sentence

without calling upon them. My version has fewer of them, though, and those it does have are weaker and do not interconnect.

This means, then, that normal collocations give a text texture beyond grammatical categories. This texture relies heavily on the frequencies of collocations. These frequencies can be established in corpora and they are an indirect way to account for lexical priming in individual speakers.

Hoey (2006: 16-17) further shows that priming is not exclusively connected with specific word-forms but that it also operates at a more abstract semantic level. He argues:

> We can say that for most speakers of English the word *hour* is likely to be primed for semantic association with NUMBER and JOURNEY. Thus *thirty-hour ride* belongs to a pattern that (in my corpus) also includes:
>
> *half*-hour *drive*
> *four*-hour *flight*
> *two*-hour *trip*
> *three*-hour *journey*
> *two*-hour *hop*
> *three*-hour *slog*

Hoey (2005: 17) suggests the term 'semantic association' to describe the fact that priming does not only concern concrete word-forms but also abstract meanings that are not bound to particular word-forms. This can be exploited creatively by transferring the primed meaning to a new element, e.g. *a 27-hour meander* meaning 'meandering journey'.

Hoey (2005: 22) also uses the term 'semantic association' for what Louw (1993) and Stubbs (1996) call 'semantic prosody'. Among other associations, the term is used to indicate positive or negative connotations. It would explain, for example, that the verb *happen* is associated with words expressing unpleasant things or circumstances like accident, cancer, concern, damage, death, disease, pain, problem, trouble.

The cases we have discussed so far can be regarded as 'local priming'. Besides this type of priming, Hoey (2005) also introduces 'textual priming' as an important category. It describes, for example, the fact that some word-forms are primed for typically appearing at the beginning of a sentence as the 'theme' ("any textual material in a clause up to and including the Subject where the Subject precedes the main verb of the clause", p. 49), as with *consequence*, cf. examples (3) and (4), or in the end-of-sentence position as with *reason*, cf. examples (5) and (6); all these examples are taken from Hoey (2005: 50, 98):

(3) In *consequence*, the draw proved all-important.

(4) One *consequence* of this will be less flexibility in the choice of text.

(5) And along with their arrogance, their fees swelled beyond any *reason*.

(6) There is also considerable speculation as to whether the Iraqi leader shows any *reason* at all.

It should be noted that with regard to these and other examples it is the individual word-forms and not the more abstract lemmas (the union of morphologically related word-forms) that enter textual priming. Hoey (2005: 130) summarizes some of his results as follows:

> Just as a word may be primed to occur (or to avoid occurring) in first or last position in a sentence, so it may also be primed to occur (or avoid occurring) in the first or last position in a paragraph, a section or a text. So, for example, *consequence* is not only primed to favour Theme, it is also primed to avoid paragraph-initial and text-initial position. The plural *consequences*, on the other hand, which is less strongly primed to occur as Theme, is positively primed to be paragraph-initial, though it shares the aversion of *consequence* for being text-initial.

This means, then, that some word-forms typically occur at the beginnings or ends of sentences, paragraphs and texts. This appears to be a promising new line of research in corpus-based text-linguistics.

4.2 Scenes and frame semantics

The importance of previous encounters of language use for a proper understanding and the felicitous production of texts is not only relevant for co-occurring word-forms but also for communication situations and world knowledge. This echoes the following passage from Hoey (2005: 8) that was already quoted above in section 4.1, "co-occurring word-forms" relating to "co-texts" and "communication situations" to "contexts":

> As a word is acquired through encounters with it in speech and writing, it becomes cumulatively loaded with the contexts and co-texts in which it is encountered.

The important point is recurrence that is recognized in a new situation. Words evoke certain situations and certain situations evoke certain words. This has already been described by Fillmore (1977: 57) as follows:

> The process of using a word in another situation involves comparing current experiences with past experiences and judging whether they are similar enough to call for the same linguistic encoding.

There are two conceptual spheres that are separate and yet related: on the one hand the mental representations of situations and world knowledge, and on the other the linguistic encodings of such mental representations in terms of word-forms and constructions. Fillmore (1977: 63) uses the terms 'scene' and 'frame' to designate these two spheres.

> I want to say that people, in learning a language, come to associate certain scenes with certain linguistic frames. I intend to use the word **scene** [...] in a maximally general sense, to include not only visual scenes but familiar kinds of interpersonal transactions, standard scenarios, familiar layouts, institutional structures, enactive experiences, body image; and, in general, any kind of coherent segment, large or small, of human beliefs, actions, experiences, or imaginings. I intend to use the word **frame** for referring to any system of linguistic choices [...] that can get associated with prototypical instances of scenes. [emphasis supplied]

Prototypical instances of scenes are such that are typical and recurring. As Fillmore (1977: 57) puts it: "prototypes are essentially experiential."

Fillmore (1977: 59) considers the commercial transaction as an example of a prototypical scene. It involves, in the main, goods, money, human participants and transfers of ownership. Such a scenario can be described from various perspectives:

(7) John bought a sandwich from Henry for three dollars

(8) Henry sold John the sandwich for three dollars

(9) John paid Henry three dollars for the sandwich

(10) The sandwich cost John three dollars

Fillmore concludes (ibid.): "There happens not to be any simple one-clause way of representing all the aspects of an entire commercial event."

In the context of text-linguistics this means that a text decoder draws on previous knowledge (textual or of the world) for a proper understanding of the text. Fillmore (1977: 61) describes the task of a text interpreter as follows:

> What happens when one comprehends a text is that one mentally creates a kind of world; the properties of this world may depend quite a bit on the individual interpreter's own private experiences -- a reality which should account for part of the fact that different people construct different interpretations of the same text. As one continues with the text, the details of this world get filled in, expectations get set up which are later fulfilled or thwarted or left hanging, and there are such experiences as surprise, suspense, disappointment, and so on, experiences which can be at least partly explained by a description of the temporal development of the interpretation experience.

Fillmore's (1977) situation model of 'scene' must be complemented by a model of the 'background knowledge' that language users must have for a proper understanding of texts and for the felicitous producion of texts, which take care of potential readers' reasonable background knowledge. One theoretical attempt is 'script theory' as developed by Schank/Abelson (1977: 41). They define 'script' as follows:

> A script is a structure that describes appropriate sequences of events in a particular context. A script is made up of slots and requirements about what can fill those slots. The structure is an interconnected whole, and what is in one slot affects what can be in another. Scripts handle stylized everyday situations. They are not subject to much change, nor do they provide the apparatus for handling totally novel situations. Thus, a script is a predetermined, stereotyped sequence of actions that defines a well-known situation. Scripts allow for new references to objects within them just as if these objects had been previously mentioned; objects within a script may take 'the' without explicit introduction because the script itself has already implicitly introduced them.

One of Schank/Abelson's examples is the following (ibid.: 40):

(11) John went into the restaurant. John ordered a Big Mac. He paid for it and found a nice park to eat in.

They explain the coherence of this sequence as follows (ibid.: 41):

This story is understandable precisely because it calls up the track of the restaurant script that states that you don't have to be inside a fast food restaurant to eat there. However, if the reader does not understand that 'Big Mac' calls up the fast food track, he will have difficulty understanding the story. That is, the same story with 'coq au vin' substituted for 'Big Mac', would seem rather odd. A story with this substitution would in principle be understandable, but the lack of applicability of available scripts would make it harder (and take more time) for a hearer to understand.

Other scripts that Schank/Abelson discuss besides the script for eating in a restaurant are 'riding a bus', 'watching and playing a football game', and 'participating in a birthday party'.

There are often-quoted examples in literature which all show that two sentences which are not linked overtly by cohesive devices are nevertheless related by an understanding decoder, who fills the open slot in a script or adds a missing link. The following examples are taken from Brown/Yule (1983: 257). The (a) and (b) sentences are linked by background knowledge that is expressed in the (c) sentences.

(12) (a) I bought a bicycle yesterday.

(b) The frame is extra large.

(c) The bicycle has a frame.

(13) (a) Mary dressed the baby.

(b) The clothes were made of pink wool.

(c) Dressing involves clothes.

As the definite article in the (b) sentences makes it clear, the writer assumes that the reader will have the necessary background information in terms of the world knowledge expressed in the (c) sentences in order to understand the coherence between the (a) and the (b) sentences.

A more recent model to explain background understanding is the 'profile-base' model in cognitive linguistics. Croft/Cruse (2004: 15), for example, define 'profile' and 'base' as follows:

> The profile refers to the concept symbolized by the word in question. The base is that knowledge or conceptual structure that is presupposed by a profiled concept.

Standard examples of the profile-base relation are the part-whole relations that are given as part of word definitions in dictionaries, as for example in Figure 4.3.

Profile	Base
arm	part of a body attached to the shoulder
daughter	female child of parents
trunk	main stem of a tree
radius	distance from the center of a circle to its outside edge
circle	a curved line enclosing an area

Figure 4.3: Profile-base relations

Thus, using the concepts of profile and base, we can say that in example (12) the *frame* is a profile against the base *bicycle*. It is this conceptual relation that is at work when background information is supplied by the interpreter of a text.

The examples in Figure 4.3 also show that one concept can serve as a base for another concept. For example, 'circle' as part of the base description to the profile radius, is itself a profile and hence presupposes yet another concept as its base. It is also evident that different profiles can have the same base. Croft/Cruse (2004: 15) point out: "The fact that a base supports multiple concept profiles is what makes the base a **domain**." And finally, they come to the following conclusion:

> In fact, no concept exists autonomously: all are understood to fit into our general knowledge of the world in one way or another. What matters for semantic analysis is the profile-base relation, and the relationships between bases and domains. (ibid.: 16)

For a better understanding of the literature (not necessarily of the concepts used here) one should point out that there is little terminological consistency, sometimes even in writings by the same author. Contrary to his earlier definition, but in congruence with Minsky (1975), Fillmore (1985), for example, also uses the term 'frame' much in the same sense as 'base' and 'domain' just described by Croft/Cruse. And the term 'script' is often used for a sequence of events in a frame/base/domain (cf. Croft/Cruse 2004: 17).

4.3 Coherence

Our discussion of scenes and frames has shown the importance of the text interpreter's background knowledge, which he supplies for a full understanding of a text. In a more general way one could say that the human decoder compensates for conceptual gaps that cannot be recovered from the surface structure of a text. The research direction that will be presented next has similar concerns, the main difference being that the focus is not only on 'concepts' but also on 'relations'. It will be recalled that the two notions were central for the notion of 'coherence' as propagated by Beaugrande/Dressler. They define coherence as follows:

> The second standard will be called COHERENCE and concerns the ways in which the components of the TEXTUAL WORLD, i.e. the configuration of CONCEPTS and RELATIONS which *underlie* the surface text, are *mututally accessible* and *relevant*. (Beaugrande/Dressler 1981: 4)

Before we discuss coherence in detail, some terminological remarks are in order. As we have already seen in section 1.3, Beaugrande/Dressler make a terminological distinction between 'cohesion' and 'coherence', which is now widely accepted. While 'cohesion' relates to components of the surface text, 'coherence' deals with cognitive models that help the text interpreter to understand a text if there is no overt cohesive relation between two sentences. This terminological distinction was not made in the early days of text-linguistics. The word-forms *cohesion* and *coherence* were often used synonymously. Halliday/Hasan (1976: 23), for example, only use 'cohesion' as a technical term and seem to use *coherent* and *cohesive* as stylistic variants, which therefore do not show in the detailed index of their book. According to Beaugrande/Dressler's distinction, *cohesion* refers to surface phenomena even though Halliday/Hasan (1976: 2, 7) insist that 'text' is a "semantic unit" and that 'cohesion' refers to "semantic relations". On the other hand, van Dijk (1977: 126) uses the word-form *coherence* synonymously with *cohesion*. He writes in his chapter 4, titled "Coherence":

> Other terms are used to denote similar concepts. Halliday and Hasan (1976) use the term COHESION, though sometimes in a broader way than we use the term 'coherence'.

But it is also important to note that, after the terminological distinction introduced by Beaugrande/Dressler and after more detailed studies in the areas of cohesion and coherence were made, it turned out that 'coherence' was understood in different ways and thus became polysemous.

For instance, referring to the word-forms of connected speech that are used in a tone unit one could speak of 'phonetic coherence', as illustrated in example (14); referring to the principle of resolution, one could speak of 'prosodic coherence' as illustrated in example (15); and in cases of syntactic parallelism one could speak of 'syntactic coherence' as illustrated in example (16). All examples are repeated from section 3.2.

(14) ənʃɪwəsɔːtəfpr'ɪtɪ / əmbr'aɪt \

(15) the Smiths/ as you probably know/ are going to America\

(16) >he came he saw he conquered<

Van Dijk/Kintsch (1983: 149) also introduce 'stylistic coherence' which they describe as follows:

> *Stylistic coherence* would mean that the speaker or discourse makes use of the same style register, in lexical choice, sentence complexity and length, etc. This notion seems necessary to account for the phenomenon of stylistic breaks.

And lastly, there is 'semantic and pragmatic coherence' (which I do not wish to differentiate). This will be the main topic of the rest of this section. In particular, we will be dealing with various kinds of non-overt conceptual 'relations' that exist between sentences. The point is that the awareness was growing in the Seventies of the last century that non-overt relations also play an important role in the understanding and writing of texts. Notwithstanding terminological differences and changes, 'coherence' will be understood here, quite generally, as that part of conceptual knowledge that is supplied if a sentence is not formally, i.e. overtly, linked to a preceding sentence.

The effects of cohesion and coherence can be shown in the limiting case in examples like (17) and (18) from Mani (2001: 106-107):

(17) Wash and core six apples. Use them to cut out the material for your new suit. They tend to add a lot to the color and texture of clothing. Actually, maybe you should use five of them instead of six, since they are quite large.

(18) John can open Bill's safe. He knows the combination.

Example (17) is cohesive because there are overt relations between *six apples* in the first sentence and *them* in the second, *they* in the third, and *them* and *they* in the fourth sentence. However, (17) is not coherent. There is no frame that could make the sequence in (17) plausible. On the other hand, (18) is only in a limited way cohesive because the referent of *he* is unclear without world knowledge. It is true that *he* refers to *John*, but if the second sentence was *He has given away the number*, it would relate to Bill. Only the knowledge of the SAFE script, which stores the information that safes often have number locks, can make the reading clear and thus fully coherent.

Besides the formal, cohesive contribution of the pronoun reference and of the semantic script there is more to add to the coherence of the two sentences in example (18). It is the relation of 'elaboration' that helps the reader to fully understand the implications of the first sentence. And it is to coherence relations that we will turn next.

Beaugrande/Dressler have not elaborated the notion of 'relation' in detail, but it is elaborated in other work, some of which we will discuss. A general distinction is made by Halliday/Hasan (1976: 241) in their discussion of types of conjunction. They distinguish between two "planes of conjunctive relation, the external and the internal". 'External' refers to world organisation, i.e. to "relations that are inherent in the phenomena that language is used to talk about" (ibid.), whereas 'internal' refers to text organization, i.e. to the relations "that are inherent in the communication process" (ibid.) and can be regarded as a comment to the benefit of the decoder; they are not coherent in the strict sense. For example, the conjunction *next* can be understood externally as in (19) or internally as in (20), cf. Halliday/Hasan (ibid.: 239):

(19) <Next he inserted the key into the lock.>

(20) <Next, he was incapable of inserting the key into the lock.>

In example (19) *next* refers to the time sequence in the content of what is stated, i.e in the outside world, and in (20) *next* refers to "the time sequence in the speaker's organization of his discourse" (ibid.). But often, both functions can be fulfilled at the same time and it is impossible to draw a clear-cut line. Therefore, the following relations will not be classified according to Halliday/Hasan's two "planes".

It will be remembered that the part-whole relation was already mentioned above in connection with the definition of 'profile' and 'base' (cf. Figure 4.3). This important relation is also included in van Dijk's (1977: 106) list of relations that hold "between individuals or properties denoted by the subsequent sentences." The following examples illustrate van Dijk's seven relations (ibid.: 106-107):

(21) Peter always comes later. He won't be in time tonight either.
    [general – particular]

(22) She could see Harry Duke. She could see his powerful shoulders ...
[whole – part/component]

(23) Many girls had applied for the job. Some of them were invited to a meeting with the staff. But only one got the job.
[set – subset – element]

(24) There was a large glass on the table. In it was a pinkish juice.
[including – included]

(25) Peter climbed upon the hill, which was covered with pine trees. Under the trees were thick bushes.
[large – small]

(26) We came to an isolated inn. The lights were already on.
[outside – inside]

(27) Peter was shabbily dressed. His jeans had large holes in them.
[possessor – possessed]

A different, only slighty overlapping inventory of coherence relations is offered by Hobbs (1985), who himself is inspired by Grimes (1975: ch. 14) and his 'rhetorical predicates'. The following relations and illustrative examples are all taken from Hobbs' 1985 paper unless stated otherwise.

It will be remembered from our discussion in section 1.2 that a linear textual sequence of two clauses can be interpreted as temporal sequence in the text world and additionally as a relation of cause and effect. To illustrate this, I repeat example (3) from section 1.2 above as example (28):

(28) The policeman held up his hand. The car stopped.

The situation is different in example (29), which is taken from section 3.2:

(29) He came. He saw. He conquered.

The sequence in example (29) demonstrates that the clauses describe not just temporal succession, this would not be enough; but neither does the sequence describe cause-effect relations, this would be too strong. Hobbs argues that the coherence relation in cases like (29) is best described as 'occasion'. It is a relation in which a previous event sets up the occasion for a following event.

In the 'evaluation' relation one clause tells the recipient why a clause preceding or following a story was said or written, cf. (30) to (32).

(30) Did you bring your car today? My car is at the garage.

(31) The funniest thing happened to me.
[a story]

(32) [a story]
It was funny at the time.

The second clause in example (30) explains why the preceding question is put, probably with the aim of getting a lift from work.
    The 'background' relation relates a text segment to the listener's/reader's prior knowledge, for example:

(33) [1] And one Sunday morning about ohhhh five o'clock in the morning I set down in the Grand -- no no, not in the Grand Central, in the Penn Station, [2] and while I was sitting there a young cat came up to me, ...

Hobbs (1985: 13) describes the background relation in example (33) as follows:

> The first segment [...] seems to furnish background information for the second segment. It provides the "geography" against which the events of the second segment take place, or the "ground" against which the second segment places a "figure".

The following five relations to be discussed form a class which Hobbs calls 'expansion' relations. They are characterized as follows:

> These are relations that, in a sense, expand the discourse in place, rather than carrying it forward or filling in background. They all involve inferential relations between segments of the text and can probably be thought of as easing the listener's inference processes. (ibid.: 14)

    First, the 'parallel' relation holds when two text segments share some reasonably specific property or properties. The example that Hobbs (ibid.: 16) gives is from a medical textbook on hepatitis:

(34) Blood probably contains the highest concentration of hepatitis B virus of any tissue except liver. Semen, vaginal secretions, and menstrual blood contain the agent and are infective. Saliva has lower concentrations than blood, and even hepatitis B surface antigen may be detectable in no more than half of infected individuals. Urine contains low concentrations at any given time.

The parallel properties that relate the four sentences are BODY MATERIAL (cf. blood; semen, vaginal secretions, menstrual blood; saliva; urine), CONTAINS (cf. contains; contain; has; in; contains), CONCENTRATION (cf. highest concentration; lower concentrations; detectable ... no more than half; low concentrations), AGENT (cf. hepatitis B virus; agent; hepatitis B surface antigen).

Second, the 'elaboration' relation is given if the same proposition can be inferred from a preceding and a following text segment. This is shown by example (35) that was quoted as example (18) above from Mani, who took it from Hobbs.

(35) John can open Bill's safe. He knows the combination.

Hobbs (1985: 19) describes the inference that links the two clauses in (35) as 'elaboration':

> From the first sentence and from what we know about "can", we can infer that John knows some action that will cause the safe to be open. From the second sentence and from what we know about combinations and knowledge, we can infer that *he*, whoever *he* is, knows that dialing the combination on whatever it is the combination of will cause it to be open. By assuming that "he" refers to John and that the combination is the combination of Bill's safe, we have the same proposition *P* and have thus established the *elaboration* relation (and solved some coreference problems as a by-product [...]).

Third, the 'exemplification' relation arranges text segments from general to specific, as in example (36), and the 'generalization' relation arranges text segments from specific to general, as in example (37).

(36) This algorithm reverses a list. If its input is "A B C", its output is "C B A".

(37) If its input is "A B C", its output is "C B A". This algorithm reverses a list.

Hobbs (1985: 21) notes: "The *generalization* coherence relation is simply *exemplification* with S_0 and S_1 reversed." [S stands for text segment.]

Fourth, in a 'contrast' relation two entities have a contrasting property, for example:

(38) Research proper brings into play clockwork-like mechanisms; discovery has a magical essence.

While the concepts 'research' and 'discovery' are viewed as similar elements, 'mechanism' and 'magical' are contrary. Hence, 'research' and 'discovery' are contrasted.

Fifth, in the 'violated expectation' relation, a proposition P can be inferred from one text segment and not-P from another:

(39) John is a lawyer, but he's honest.

(40) This paper is weak, but interesting.

Hobbs (1985: 22) gives a culture-specific explanation of example (39):

> Here one would draw the inference from the first clause that John is dishonest since he is a lawyer, but that is directly contradicted and thus overridden by the second clause.

In example (40), from a referee's review, "one can infer from the first clause that the paper should be rejected, but from the second clause that it should be accepted" (ibid.).

4.4 Rhetorical structures

Like the model of coherence relations by Hobbs that was portrayed in the preceding section, the model to be discussed now is also inspired by Grimes' (1975) rhetorical predicates. The name is Rhetorical Structure Theory and the most relevant publications are by Thompson/Mann (1987), Mann/Thompson (1988), Matthiessen/Thompson (1988) and Mann/Matthiessen/Thompson (1992). Rhetorical Structure Theory (RST) seeks to describe the semantic relations between text components. Its descriptive elements are semantic and not directly related to linguistic forms:

> All of RST is pre-realizational, since it makes statements about how such meanings and intentions are structured and combined, but not about how they are realized. (Mann/Matthiessen/Thompson 1992: 45)

A rhetorical structure can be conceived of as a structure that can serve as a plan of how to formulate (or generate) a text but also as a tool to describe the meanings and intentions of a given text. In other words, rhetorical structures can be used deductively for text production and inductively for text comprehension. The inductive approach will be presented here for two reasons. Firstly, it describes partially the method of how the researchers arrived at their model. (They analysed more than 400 short texts from a wide variety of genres.)

Secondly, it is a useful tool to describe the meanings and intentions of given texts.
Although rhetorical structures exist independently of syntactic structure, the category 'clause' plays an important role in this model. The text components entering rhetorical relations are called (rhetorical) units (cf. Matthiessen/Thompson 1988: 287). A textual analysis begins with the identification of its (rhetorical) units. These are

> what most grammarians would call 'clauses', except that clausal subjects and complement and restrictive relative clauses represent units that are part of their matrix unit rather than separate units.

This means that, by and large, clause complexes which have subject clauses, complement clauses and restrictive relative clauses as part of a larger structure are regarded as only one (matrix) unit. On the other hand, adverbial clauses and non-restrictive relative clauses are regarded as separate units which relate to other units. The reason for this proviso is that the components of the first type are necessary in a clause complex whereas those of the second type are optional. But it may be noted that in the reception of the theory this proviso is often ignored (cf. for example Butler 2003: 366 and Mani 2001: 110). More important is the fact that clause combining as described in Rhetorical Structure Theory shows the relations between clauses within a clause complex and beyond, such that all clauses of a text become part of one big structure.

The analysis aims at describing the hierarchical organization of the units in terms of two kinds of relation: 'nucleus-satellite' and 'list'. Nucleus-satellite relations rest on the general assumption that most rhetorical relations are asymmetric, i.e. that of two text segments one is more essential than the other. This echoes at the text-semantic level the traditional endocentric relation. While the nucleus is more essential, the satellite has a supportive function. List relations, on the other hand, are best understood as a kind of coordination of equally ranking elements.

Matthiessen/Thompson (1988: 291-292) explain the two nucleus-satellite relations 'enablement' and 'elaboration' and the 'list' relation in the following example (41), and offer an analysis of rhetorical structure as depicted in Figure 4.4:

(41) 1. The University Press of Kentucky has announced the establishment of the Kentucky Foreign Language Conference Award to be given annually for the best manuscript dealing with some aspect of foreign language and/or literatures.

2. The Award, $500 and acceptance of the manuscript for publication, is offered in conjunction with the Kentucky Foreign Language Conference.

3. The deadline for submission of manuscripts for the 1972 Award is December 1, 1971.

4. For further information write: KFLCA, The University Press of Kentucky, 104 Lafferty Hall, Lexington, Kentucky 40506.

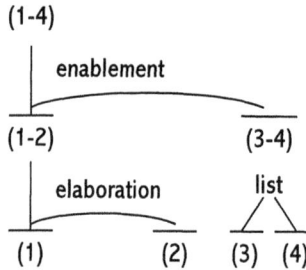

Figure 4.4: Rhetorical structure of example (41)

The figure claims the following: unit 2 is in an elaboration (satellite) relation to unit 1, the nucleus; units 3-4 are in an enablement (satellite) relation – typical of directives and offers – to units 1-2; units 3-4 are in a list relation; unit 1 is the nucleus, not only for its own satellite, but also for the text as a whole. That is, unit 1 is the nucleus which is expanded by the satellite and the list relations. This last aspect is derived from tracing the vertical nuclear lines from the top to the bottom. The theory claims:

> In any multi-unit text, certain portions realize the *central goals* of the writer, while others realize *goals which are supplementary* or ancillary to the central goals. That is, the nuclear part is the one whose function most nearly represents the function of the text span 'covered' by that relation. (Matthiessen/Thompson 1988: 289-290)

Detailed explanations and justifications of the various relations are explained in the articles mentioned above. The researchers have worked with some twenty relations. Quite generally, it is claimed that

> the set of text structuring relations is in principle open, so that additional previously unused relations can arise. However, the frequency of creation of new relations is extremely low, and for all but a kernel set the frequency use of rare or unknown relations is also extremely low, so that text in a culture can be analyzed virtually

entirely in terms of a small set of highly recurrent relations, the knowledge of which is shared in the culture. (Mann/Matthiessen/ Thompson 1992: 46)

The following text and its analysis in Figure 4.5 demonstrate further nucleus-satellite relations (cf. Matthiessen/Thompson 1988: 295-296):

(42) 1. Thumbs began to be troublesome about 4 months ago

2. and I made an appointment with the best hand surgeon in the Valley

3. to see if my working activities were the problem.

4. Using thumbs is not the problem

5. but heredity is

6. and the end result is no use of thumbs

7. if I don't do something now.

It should be noted that the rhetorical units in (42) are not coextensive with orthographic sentences, as was the case in (41). The model can make explicit how different readers understand a text. Therefore, Rhetorical Structure Theory "sometimes yields multiple analysis for a text" (Mann/Matthiessen/Thompson 1992: 52). The analysis in Figure 4.5 claims that unit 6 expresses the main idea. It also shows that a lot of background information is given before the central idea is expressed.

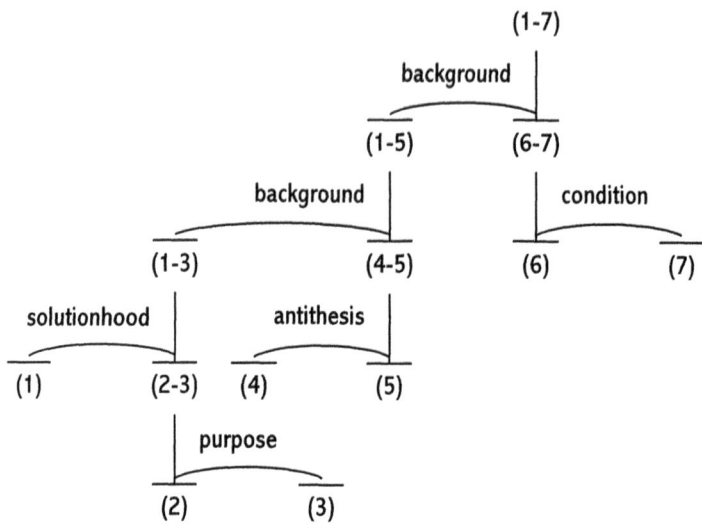

Figure 4.5: Rhetorical structure of example (42)

As a stylistic variant, the author could also have started with her main idea and then supplied the background information:

(43) 1. I may not be able to use my thumbs any more
[corresponding to unit 6 above]

2. if I don't do something now.
[corresponding to unit 7 above]

3. Thumbs began to be troublesome about 4 months ago
[corresponding to unit 1 above]

etc.

These few examples show that Rhetorical Structure Theory is also suitable for registering discourse organization in terms of textual variation; it helps to identify received semantic relations of discourse organization.

A somewhat broader approach is suggested by Nash (1980) and taken up by Quirk et al. (1985). The authors describe four discourse strategies which make implicit use of some of the major relational structures of Rhetorical Structure Theory. The four strategies are 'step', 'chain', 'stack' and 'balance'.

The 'step' realizes a "'step by step' procedure" (cf. Quirk et al. 1985: 1435 and Nash 1980: 9). It corresponds to the list relation and must enter into a larger structure such as background or elaboration. It is often used in descriptive, narrative and instructional texts. For example (Quirk et al. 1985: 1435):

(44) The 100-metre race was run immediately after lunch. This was followed by the 400-metre relay. After a brief interlude with an acrobatic display, spectators spread around the track to watch the first cycling event.

Contrasting with the idea of rhetorical structures, the 'chain' is defined in terms of explicit surface elements (cf. ibid.); these were described in section 2.1.3 above. Nash (1980: 14) writes: "It presents a series of items each of which is related to its predecessor by means of explicit verbal links." An analysis of the examples given by Nash and Quirk et al. shows that the (semantic) elaboration relation is very typical of this kind of discourse organization. Example (45) is the first part of a text sample by Nash (ibid.), rewritten in terms of rhetorical units and analysed in terms of rhetorical structure:

(45) 1. Our Labrador bitch, Candy, was the greediest animal I have ever known, myself not excluded.

2. She combined the vice of greed with the virtue of patience,

3. and would sit for hours with her nose pointing unswervingly at the larder door.

4. Behind the door, as well she knew, there stood a large paper bag full of biscuits allegedly shaped like bones and called (not surprisingly) Bonios.

5. Bonios were to her what chocolates are to portly matrons.

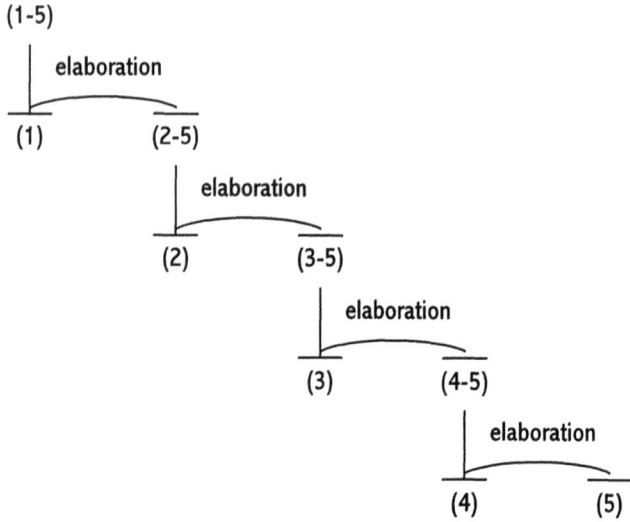

Figure 4.6: Rhetorical structure of example (45)

The 'stack' is characterized as a passage

> in which a thematic or 'topic' sentence is followed by a stack of amplifying comments which may possibly be rounded off by some kind of summary formulation. (Nash 1980: 12)

And Quirk et al. (1985: 1436) say: "we have something more like a vertical structure". This can be exemplified with the analysis of Nash's (1980: 12) example (46) in terms of Rhetorical Structure Theory:

(46) 1. There is something wrong with the morality of a saying like 'Honesty is the best policy'.

2. The wrongness lies in equating virtue with profit.

3. Any tolerably observant person must see that the equation is false.

4. There are countless occurrences in life when doing what we believe to be right does not bring us material rewards.

5. Indeed we may sometimes suffer for it.

6. To offer sound policy as an excitement of good morals is therefore in itself dishonest.

7a. Honesty,

8. if it requires a motive,

7b. must be valued for reasons other than politic.

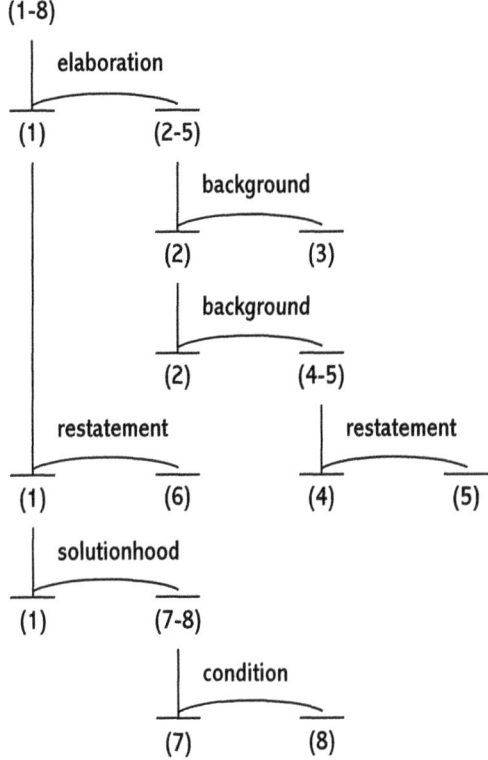

Figure 4.7: Rhetorical structure of example (46)

The 'balance' is a discourse organization which anticipates objections on the part of the reader/hearer by shifting between pros and cons (cf. Quirk et al. 1985: 1436 and Nash 1980: 15). The balance is typical of argumentative texts. In it we typically find the relations of 'concession' and 'antithesis' as the following text example from Quirk et al. (1985: 1436) shows:

(47) For a spring break, Cumbria is hard to beat. There is of course a strong risk of bad weather during the early months of the year. On the other hand, the early tourist is rewarded by empty roads and the feeling that he has the countryside to himself. Not all the hotels are open, it is true, and you may be obliged to drive on to the next village. But this is well offset by the welcome that awaits you in a guest house where you may turn out to be the only resident. Early visitors to Cumbria rarely regret their initiative.

In this text, the relations of concession and antithesis are overtly marked by the expressions *of course, on the other hand, it is true* and *but*. Hünig (1980) has shown that most, if not all, of the relations in a text can be overtly expressed by connective devices. However, too much explicit guidance of the reader may have an overbearing effect.

4.5 Macrostructures and superstructures

We have seen in the preceding section that the global idea of a text can be reduced to one clause or proposition. In the case of Rhetorical Structure Theory this was the outcome (or byproduct) of an assessment of the rhetorical relations between clauses. But there are also approaches with which the idea of reduction is central to capture the meaning of a text. One important contribution in this respect is the work by van Dijk. His idea is that with the help of 'macrorules' sequences of propositions (i.e. clauses) can be rewritten or transformed into more generalizing propositions. They comprise 'deletion', 'generalization' and 'construction' (cf. van Dijk/Kintsch 1983: 190). (Note that the number and terminology vary slightly in different publications.) Macrorules are seen as part of the language users' cognitive competence. Their recursive application yields 'macrostructures' that are "designed to capture the intuitive notion of the 'gist' of a discourse" (ibid.: 52). The 'construction rule', for example, operates on a similar psychological basis as do the 'scenes', 'frames' and 'scripts' that we discussed in section 4.2 above:

> The sequence <'X goes to the airport', 'X checks in', 'X waits for boarding', ...> entails the macroproposition 'X is taking a plane', given the appropriate world knowledge in the form of frames or scripts. (ibid.: 191)

According to van Dijk/Kintsch, many conventional text-types exhibit schematic structures (i.e. macrostructures) that organize the macropropositions in a text (cf. ibid: 16). Such a schematic, conventionalized structure is conceptualized as 'superstructure' in the work by van Dijk (1980) and van Dijk/Kintsch (1983). Van Dijk (1980) begins with the observation that some texts have a

Semantic Texture

'superstructure' which determines the structure and the type of text irrespective of its content or 'macrostructure' (cf. ibid.: 128). For example, the recounting of a burglary can have different shapes: a story told or written to friends, a police report or an assessment of damage for an insurance company. Van Dijk (1980: 131) defines the superstructure as follows:

> Eine Superstruktur ist eine Art abstraktes Schema, das die globale Ordnung eines Textes festlegt und das aus einer Reihe von Kategorien besteht, deren Kombinationsmöglichkeiten auf konventionellen Regeln beruhen.

> [My English translation: "A superstructure is a kind of abstract schema which determines the global organization of a text and which consists of a number of categories whose possible combinations are based on conventional rules."]

Important superstructure categories for the conventional text-type 'narrative' are 'complication' and 'resolution'. Every narrative deals with actions performed by people, and these actions must be somehow interesting in order to be worthwhile telling. The interesting point is usually a kind of complication that has to be resolved by the protagonist. Complication and resolution form the kernel of an everyday narrative; this kernel is termed 'event' (*Ereignis*). Events take place within 'settings' (*Rahmen*); events and settings form 'episodes'. Events and episodes are recursive categories. One or more episodes make up a 'plot'. The plot may be evaluated; thus plot and 'evaluation' constitute a 'story' (*Geschichte*). The story may have a 'moral'; story and moral are the immediate constituents of a 'narrative' (cf. van Dijk 1980: 140-142). The superstructure of a narrative can be represented in the form of a tree diagram or formation rules (like generative syntactic rules). An example was already given in Figure 1.1, which is repeated here for convenience as Figure 4.8. It is important to note that not all of the categories have to be present in a narrative text.

Figure 4.8: Superstructure of a narrative

In a similar vein van Dijk explains the superstructures of the text-types 'argument' (*Argumentation*) and 'examination report' (*Untersuchungsbericht*). We find similar part-whole relations, for example, in Sandig (1986: 173), who states that the text-type 'advertisement' consists of typical action-patterns ("Teilhandlungsmuster") such as 'presenting' the name of the product, 'naming' the referent-class (e.g. beer, cigarettes), 'description' of the product, 'recommendation' of the product and 'invitation' to buy the product.

Van Dijk does not claim that all text-types are definable in terms of superstructures. They are but one factor in a general theory of text-typology. For example, for the text-type 'invitation' the semantic invariable (in van Dijk's terms, the 'macrostructure') is more important than the actual superstructure. Thus an invitation can be informal, e.g. *Come and see me tonight*, or formal with a stated reason, place, time and requested clothing.

We noted earlier that not all of the categories have to be present in a text. Furthermore, some of the categories are not directly relatable to surface clauses (i.e. 'narrative', 'story' and 'plot'), whereas others are. This can be demonstrated with example (48), which we have already discussed in section 1.1 above.

(48) It was late in Portobello and the sky was dark [setting] when I was attacked by a stranger. He demanded my purse [complication]. I defended myself

successfully with my umbrella [resolution]. Therefore I never go without an umbrella on my night walks [moral].

If there are more clauses than one that belong to one category, these may be summarized in a macroproposition, which in turn is related to a superstructure category:

> If the first sentences of a story describe the time, place, participants or, in general, a situation, then the first macroproposition(s) may be assigned to the setting category. Similarly, disruptive events or actions - at the global level - may be assigned to the complication category, whereas reactive actions of some important participant in the story, which are aimed at solving a problem or reestablishing a desired situation, may be assigned to the resolution category. (van Dijk/Kintsch 1983: 240)

The categories of a superstructure form a conventional list from which a speaker or writer chooses certain items, which themselves can be arranged in various ways. The selection and the arrangement of the categories are properties of a particular text and are therefore less conventionalized than the abstract superstructure itself. Van Dijk/Kintsch (ibid.), for example, discuss two possible beginnings of stories:

> Thus, for stories, the strategic hypothesis will simply be that the first episode of a story is information that belongs to the setting. [...] If a story begins with the description of a murder, it may typically be assumed that the episode is not part of the setting, but rather of the complication.

This observation shows that, within a conventionalized superstructure, individual discourse organization is possible. Many modern authors, for example, do not like to begin their novels or short stories with clauses that function as a setting, as would be typical of conventional fairy tales.

An important forerunner of conceptions like 'category' and 'superstructure' is Propp (1990 [1968]). His contribution to narrative grammars is aptly described by Enkvist (1973: 31-32) as follows:

> Propp noted that the plots of Russian folktales could be described in terms of combinations of discrete elements. He listed thirty-one thematic categories such as the theme of absence ('one of the members of the family is absent from home'), departure ('the hero leaves home'), interdiction ('the hero is forbidden something'), provision ('the hero is given a magic agent'), and so on. Thus each folktale is no longer seen

as a unique object *sui generis*, but rather as a selection from, and combination of, these universal themes or "functions".

It must be noted that Propp's categories are purely semantic and that they do not relate directly to all concrete sentences or clauses in a text, i.e. they are not code-centred.

4.6 Thematic progression and hyperthemes

Besides the macrostructure, which captures the content of a text, and the superstructure, which captures the conventionalized components of a text-type irrespective of its content, there are more basic relational structures:

> A text may have one (or more) of an indefinitely large number of purposes: description, persuasion, narrative, etc. [...] But irrespective of the various purposes and general intentions of a text, there are a few relationships within texts that constantly recur [...]. They can be seen as basic relational structures. (Quirk et al. 1985: 1433)

The most important relation is that between 'general' and 'particular'. Quirk et al. (ibid.) write: "It is common for a text to proceed from a general point to a particular." Their example is:

(49) Working in wood calls for great manual skill. The ordinary saw itself is not easy to handle.

On the other hand, the text-producer can also proceed from a particular point to general (cf. ibid.):

(50) The ordinary household saw is not easy to use. In fact, any sort of woodwork calls for great manual skill.

In terms of Rhetorical Structure Theory the progression from 'general' to 'particular' in example (49) can be interpreted as a nucleus-satellite relation of 'elaboration'. On the other hand, the progression from 'particular' to 'general' in example (50) can be interpreted as 'evaluation'.

On a similar general psychological footing there is the analysis of sentences and sequences of sentences in the framework of Functional Sentence Perspective (cf. section 2.1.2.1). The main proponent of this theory, Mathesius (1975 [1961]: 81, 83-84), distinguishes two basic content elements on a general psychological basis:

A closer examination of sentences from the viewpoint of assertiveness shows an overwhelming majority of all sentences to contain two basic content elements: a statement and an element about which the statement is made. [...] The element about which something is stated may be said to be the b a s i s of the utterance or the t h e m e, and what is stated above the basis is the n u c l e u s of the utterance or the r h e m e. [...] In regular two-element sentences that contain the theme (T) and the rheme (R) it is of importance in which order these two elements are arranged. Two arrangements are possible, T – R and R – T, and both are found. When we realize the relation between the speaker and the hearer we find that the order T – R takes into account the hearer. The speaker starts from what is known and proceeds to what is new. This is the so-called o b j e c t i v e order since the speaker takes into account the particular situation and conforms to the usual mental procedure. This order of arrangement is used in unemotional narration: [...] *Once upon a time there was a king. And the king had two sons.* However, it is also possible to use the reverse order, viz. R – T. This is not an unemotional arrangement, but on the contrary, the type of arrangement that is used in excitement. First the speaker impatiently states the new element of the intended statement and only afterwards adds the known elements from which he actually starts. This is the so-called s u b j e c t i v e order.

It must be stressed that the two basic content elements, 'theme' and 'rheme', are semantic concepts which have no unequivocal relation to linguistic forms. However, there are several formal clues, including word order (as just stated in the quotation from Mathesius), the use of indefinite and definite articles, pronouns and ellipsis. In fact, many of the cohesive devices discussed in section 2.1.3 can be interpreted as helping to fulfil the needs of Functional Sentence Perspective.

The catenative function of theme-rheme organisation is already mentioned by Mathesius (1975 [1961]: 81):

In the stream of narration the order of these elements is very simple, the theme of the consecutive sentence being usually the rheme of the preceding one.

This text-building function of theme-rheme organisation was described in more detail by Daneš (1970, 1974). In section 2.1.2.2 above we already discussed two types of linear thematic progression that operate at the level of overt word-forms: 'simple linear progression', which was described in the words of Mathesius just quoted, and 'progression with a continuous theme'. For ease of reference I repeat the examples and the corresponding illustrations from above with new numbering:

(51) The first of the antibiotics was discovered by Sir Alexander Flemming in 1928. He was busy at the time investigating a certain species of germ which is responsible for boils and other troubles.

$$
\begin{array}{lll}
T_1 & \rightarrow & R_1 \\
& & \downarrow \\
& & T_2 (= R_1) \rightarrow R_2 \\
& & \qquad\qquad\quad \downarrow \\
& & \qquad\qquad\quad T_3 (= R_2) \rightarrow R_3
\end{array}
$$

Figure 4.9: Simple linear progression

(52) The Rousseauist especially feels an inner kinship with Prometheus and other Titans. He is fascinated by any form of insurgency... He must show an elementary energy in his explosion against the established order and at the same time a boundless sympathy for the victims of it... Further the Rousseauist is ever ready to discover beauty of soul in anyone who is under the reprobation of society.

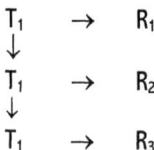

Figure 4.10: Progression with a continuous theme

Besides the two types of thematic progression just mentioned, Daneš also discusses a third type, 'progression with derived theme'. In this case we are not dealing with overt word-forms but rather with a "'hypertheme' (of a paragraph, or other text section)" (Daneš 1974: 120). This is exemplified and illustrated by Daneš as follows:

(53) New Jersey is flat along the coast and southern portion; the north-western region is mountainous. The coastal climate is mild [...]

Semantic Texture

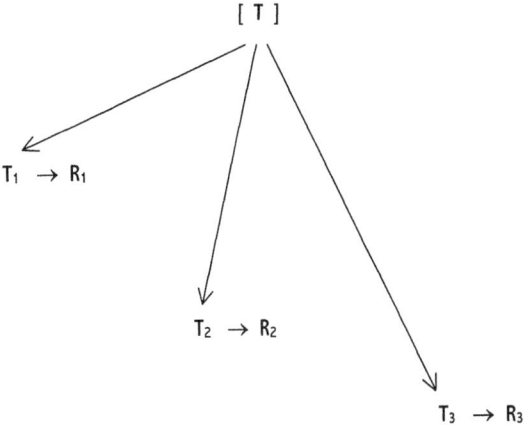

Figure 4.11: Progression with derived theme

The non-overt hypertheme [T] in Figure 4.11 could be dubbed 'geographical data of New Jersey'. New Jersey is the sentence theme in the first clause and can only be related to the hypertheme if one has read the following clauses from which one can derive the notion 'geographical data'.

The special case of progression with derived theme makes it clear that one must distinguish between 'sentence theme' in a theme-rheme arrangement as advocated by Mathesius, and a 'text theme' which is meant by Daneš' notion of abstract 'hypertheme'.

The distinction between 'sentence theme' on the one hand and 'hypertheme', 'paragraph theme' or 'text theme' on the other is also made by Jones (1977: 141-142):

> I wish to contrast theme of sentence and theme of paragraph to reinforce my assertion [...] about the unfeasibility of simply extending sentence models of theme upwards in some fashion to account also for text themes. [...] The theme of a sentence is a constituent of that sentence. [...] The theme of a paragraph is one or more propositions.

One of her examples is (54) (cf. Jones 1977: 6):

(54) First the radiator in the car went bad. Then the starter went out. Next it was a flat tire. Then the brakes wouldn't work well, and after they were fixed, the transmission went out.

The theme of this text segment or paragraph is the poor condition of a car. It results from the list of events which all describe technical faults of a car. The theme expressed in the proposition 'my car became useless and let me down' results from the sum of the individual sentences. It may be noted that the idea of a 'theme of paragraph' is similar to van Dijk's idea of 'macroproposition', although less strictly defined.

Finally, a note on terminology is in order. The expression *theme* is not only used in the two senses described so far, namely 'sentence theme' and 'text theme', but, as will be remembered, also as the first element in a clause, cf. section 4.1 and, for example, Halliday (1967: 212), Halliday (1985: 35) and Hoey (2005: 49).

4.7 Questions and exercises

1. Compare the following two texts A and B taken from Hoey (2006: 49, 53):

A   The strategies for writing a narrative are different from the ones for ads. In ads, the reader is looking for specific information, so it has to be short and precise, but if the writer wants to convince the reader about something in an ad, it has to have enough information.

   In the ad "Why not be a writer?" the purpose is to persuade a reader who hesitates and is very unsure about his/her abilities. Therefore the ad is needed to be written more profoundly to get into the reader's mind – convince the reader and satisfy him from different points of view, until the reader is convinced that it fits his/her needs.

B   The strategies adopted for writing advertisements are different from the ones adopted for a narrative. The reader is looking for specific information, so they have to be short and precise, but if the writer wants to convince the reader of something, they have to provide enough information.

   In the advertisement "Why not be a writer?" the advertiser's purpose is to persuade a reader who wants to be a writer but is hesitant and very unsure about his/her abilities. Therefore the advertisement needs to be written more carefully to get into the reader's mind – to convince the reader and satisfy him/her from different points of view, until the reader is convinced that it meets his/her needs.

(i) Which of the two versions A and B do you regard as more felicitous and why?
(ii) Try to explain the differences in terms of lexical choice and cohesive devices.

2. Make a suggestion of what the superstructure of a letter of complaint could look like. Imagine you have bought an MP3-player on the Internet which does not work properly.

3. Take the instruction manual of your printer and discuss the relation of hyperthemes to orthographic paragraphs.

4.8 Further reading

The book by Hoey (2005) gives many applications of the concept of 'priming'. The article by Hoey (2006) discusses 'priming' in the context of 'clumsiness'. Bellert's (1970) article is a classic on 'coherence'. Schank/Abelson (1977) discuss in their book 'scripts', 'plans' and 'goals' in the framework of artificial intelligence. An overview of the terminological distinctions of 'theme', 'rheme' and related concepts can be found in chapter 2 of Esser (1984). Mann/Thompson (1988) give a modified version of Rhetorical Structure Theory and offer many instructive examples.

5 Decoder-orientation

Having dealt with the semantic aspects of text constitution, we now come to those psycholinguistic and cognitive aspects that centre around the regard that a text producer has for the decoder of his message. The central notion here is 'textual rhetoric', which can be understood as an umbrella term that covers various aspects of decoder-orientation. After a discussion of the main components of textual rhetoric we will look in more detail at two specific issues, namely processibility in section 5.2 and optimizing texts in section 5.3.

5.1 Textual rhetoric

The notion of 'textual rhetoric' was introduced by Leech, who uses the notion 'rhetoric' slightly differently from its traditional meanings. Before you read his definition, please note that in the following quotations the symbol s stands for 'speaker(s) or writer(s)', i.e. encoders, and h for 'hearer(s) or reader(s)', i.e. decoders (cf. Leech 1983: xiii).

> Whereas rhetoric has been understood, in particular historical traditions, as the art of using language skilfully for persuasion, or for literary expression, or for public speaking, I have in mind the effective use of language in its most general sense. [...] The point about the term *rhetoric* [...] is the focus it places on a goal-oriented speech situation, in which s uses language in order to produce a particular effect in the mind of h. [...] I shall also use the term RHETORIC as a countable noun, for a set of conversational principles which are related by their functions. Using a distinction familiar in the work of Halliday, I shall distinguish two rhetorics, the INTERPERSONAL and the TEXTUAL rhetoric. (Leech 1983: 15)

The 'interpersonal rhetoric' comprises in the main two principles: (i) the 'cooperative principle' with the maxims of quantity, quality, relation and manner as proposed by Grice (1975) and (ii) the 'politeness principle' with the maxims of tact, generosity, approbation and modesty as proposed by Leech (1983). These topics are extensively dealt with in the volume *Introduction to English Pragmatics* (Schneider forthcoming) in the TELL Series. Cooperation and politeness are regulative factors which underlie socially acceptable communication. The aim is to establish and foster social relations.

The aim of textual rhetoric, on the other hand, is to facilitate the decoder's task. Leech (1983: 60) speaks in this context of a 'well-behaved' utterance:

The textually 'well-behaved' utterance [is] one which anticipates and facilitates *h*'s task in decoding, or making sense of, the text. [...] To produce a well-behaved text is to coordinate a number of complex skills, and it is not surprising if failure in the performance of these skills often leads to a rhetorically 'unhappy' utterance. For this reason, it is in written language (where planning and final execution can be separated in time) that the operation of Textual Rhetoric can be observed more directly.

The encoding and decoding of verbal messages involves tasks at different functional planes. These tasks are described by Leech (1983: 59) as "transactions" between the encoder and the decoder: (i) interpersonal transaction or 'discourse' to convey the encoder's intention, (ii) ideational transaction or 'message transmission' to convey experience of the world, and (iii) textual transaction or 'text' to convey the actual wording of a text. The ordering of the three transactions is described by Leech with the formula rendered in Figure 5.1.

Figure 5.1: Functional planes and transactions in Leech (1983: 59)

The ordering of the functional planes at which transactions take place in Figure 5.1 can be interpreted with the general cognitive concept of 'instantiation' that was introduced above in section 2.1.1. This means that, for example, in a given situation the discourse 'complaint' can be instantiated by the message 'a fly is in my soup', which in turn can be instantiated, among others, by the allo-sentences, i.e. texts, >there's a fly in my soup< or >in my soup there's a fly<.

In view of the broader perspective taken in this book, namely not to exclude the presentation of texts in the phonic or graphic substance, we have to elaborate on the transaction at the level of 'text' in Figure 5.1 to indicate medium-independent word-forms and ultimately the phonic or graphic substance of the language material that is actually conveyed. This leads, then, to an increase of functional planes as proposed in Figure 5.2.

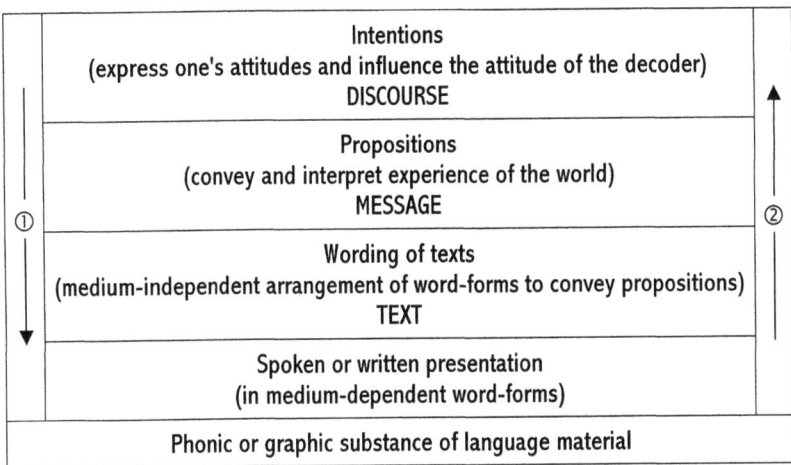

Figure 5.2: Extended functional planes

The arrows in Figure 5.2 symbolize relations in two distinct and only loosely related areas. The first one is that of linguistic models. Here arrow ① indicates relations of instantiation. That is, the entities of lower levels instantiate entities of higher levels until instantiation reaches the actual phonic or graphic substance of language material. Conversely, arrow ② indicates stages of abstraction from concrete language material to abstract intentions.

The second area that is symbolized by the arrows in Figure 5.2 is that of functional processes in encoding and decoding. Thus arrow ① indicates possible functional decisions by the encoder. By this we do not mean that the arrow necessarily represents actual psychological processes, although they can partially occur in this way. Conversely, arrow ② indicates corresponding functional interpretations by the decoder, which again do not represent psychological processes in every detail. As an example of this take the phenomenon of lexical priming and collocates, discussed in section 4.1 above, which can only be explained in terms of frequencies irrespective of the structural properties.

Based on work by Slobin (1975), Leech (1983: 64-70) makes out four pragmatic principles with corresponding maxims as summarized in Figure 5.3.

The processibility principle
 end-focus maxim
  (principle of end-nucleus)
  (principle of resolution)
 end-weight maxim

The clarity principle
 transparency maxim
 ambiguity maxim

The economy principle
 maxim of reduction

The expressivity principle

Figure 5.3: Pragmatic principles of textual rhetoric

Leech (1983: 64) defines the 'processibility principle' as follows:

This principle recommends that the text should be presented in a manner which makes it easy for the hearer to decode in time.

According to the functional planes described above in connection with Figure 5.2 the presentation of a text must be described at two levels, namely (i) the wording in terms of the medium-independent arrangement of word-forms to convey propositions and (ii) the spoken or written presentation in terms of medium-dependent word-forms. The first of these two levels concerns the ordering of constituents in terms of allo-sentences and the second concerns the presentation in terms of tone units or orthographic sentences.

The ordering of constituents is at the heart of the 'end-focus maxim'. The idea of this medium-independent concept was already discussed in section 3.2.2 above as 'principle of end-focus'. According to Leech (1983: 22) the 'maxim of end-focus' is described like this:

[It] recommends that if the rules of the language allow it, the part of a clause which contains new information should be placed at the end.

It will be recalled that the principle/maxim of end-focus derives from the general underlying psychological procedure to start from given information and to move on to new information. This is called the "objective order" by Mathesius (1975

[1961]: 156). In this respect example (1) is more felicitous than example (2); both are notationally adapted from Leech/Short (1981: 214):

(1) >instead of morphine the patient was given opium<

(2) >instead of morphine opium was given to the patient<

The appropriate context and the definite article suggest that the entity *the patient* is 'given' and that the entity *opium* is 'new'. Therefore (1) follows the maxim of end-focus and (2) does not. This does not mean that (2) is impossible or ungrammatical. The point is that version (1) is more suitable for a written presentation, where the encoder should have the decoder in his mind. In (1) the decoder can rely on the automatic assignment of the nucleus according to the principle of end-focus without a detailed analysis of the content in terms of 'given' and 'new'.

Since the decoding of a written text additionally involves (usually) either silent reading or reading aloud, this means that we are actually dealing with a decoding-encoding process that the original encoder must consider. This is where the principle of end-nucleus and the principle of resolution come into play. These two principles describe standard procedures for the presentation of word-forms in speech in terms of tone units or tone unit sequences. The 'principle of end-nucleus' states that the last item in a tone unit receives the intonation nucleus, and the 'principle of resolution' states that the last tone unit in a clause complex receives a falling tone and the preceding tone units receive rising tones which create a sense of anticipation that is fulfilled in the final tone unit with a falling tone. The two principles of end-nucleus and of resolution operate at the medium-dependent level of spoken presentation. They are related to the medium-independent maxim of end-focus and describe the standard procedure for a decoder in a decoding-encoding process. I would not like to call these routines maxims since they are not concerned with choices of primary encoding but only with secondary encoding.

Coming back to our discussion of examples (1) and (2) we can now consider their respective presentations as orthographic sentences and as tone units:

(1') (a) <Instead of morphine, the patient was given opium.>

(b) instead of <u>morphine</u>/ the patient was given <u>opium</u>\

(2') (a) <Instead of morphine, opium was given to the patient.>

(b) instead of <u>morphine</u>/ <u>opium</u> was given to the patient\

By following the principles of end-nucleus and of resolution a reader of (1'a) can give the wording of (1) a felicitous spoken presentation as in (1'b) on an automatized basis. On the other hand, this automatized procedure cannot be applied to the wording (2) presented as (2'a) because *opium* is in focus and should receive the nucleus. However, a spoken presentation as in (2'b) is well possible in an orally originated utterance, where the speaker chooses a "subjective order" (cf. Mathesius 1975 [1961]: 156). In this case the non-final focus is rendered automatically with the non-final nucleus in the first encoding, that is, the non-final focus does not have to be recovered in an ongoing decoding-encoding process.

The second maxim of the 'processibility principle' is that of 'end-weight'. The 'maxim of end-weight' is described by Leech (1983: 65) as follows:

> We may postulate for English a Maxim of End-weight, which (broadly) induces a syntactic structure in which 'light' constituents precede 'heavy' ones. Hence the characteristic English sentence has a predominance of right-branching over left-branching, and many movement transformations (*eg* the rule of extraposition) serve the Maxim of End-weight by helping to ensure that complex constituents are placed at the end of a clause or sentence.

The positioning of complex constituents at the (right-hand) end is supposed to facilitate syntactic processing but Leech is not specific on this point. It will be taken up again in section 5.2 below. The attributes 'light' and 'heavy' should be understood as relative concepts, 'light' meaning 'shorter and less complex' and 'heavy' meaning 'longer and more complex'. In this respect example (3) disregards the maxim of end-weight whereas (4) follows it (cf. Greenbaum 1991: 163):

(3) The rate at which the American people are using up the world's supply of irreplaceable fossil fuels and their refusal to admit that the supply is limited is the real problem.

(4) The real problem is the rate at which the American people are using up the world's supply of irreplaceable fossil fuels and their refusal to admit that the supply is limited.

Since sentence (4) is constructed according to the maxim of end-weight, it is supposed to be easier to process than sentence (3) in which the principle of end-weight is counteracted.

Like all pragmatic principles the processibility principle with its two maxims of end-focus and end-weight also describes pragmatic behaviour and not logical or grammatical rules. Therefore it is quite possible that in certain cases the two maxims contradict each other, for example:

(5) (a) >the eggs were bad that you sold me last week<

(b) the eggs were bad that you sold me last week\

(6) (a) > the eggs that you sold me last week were bad<

(b) the eggs that you sold me last week/ were bad\

The wording in example (5a) follows the maxim of end-weight because here the relative clause is separated from the head noun and placed after the complement which presents new information and therefore the focus. On the other hand, example (6a) follows the maxim of end-focus (with the sub-principles of resolution and end-nucleus) but contradicts the maxim of end-weight.

The 'clarity principle' simply requires of the encoder: "Be clear!" The first maxim of the clarity principle is the 'transparency maxim'. It is described by Leech (1983: 66) as follows:

> Retain a direct and transparent relationship between semantic and phonological structure (*ie* between message and text). [...] For clarity's sake, it is a good idea for semantically adjacent items also to be syntactically adjacent.

Leech gives the example listed as (7) to illustrate a case in which semantically adjacent items are not syntactically adjacent:

(7) The morning came at last when we were due to leave.

Like in example (5) we are again dealing with a relative clause that is separated from its antecedent. However, this time it is not clear whether the *when*-clause is actually a postmodification of *morning* or an adverbial clause of the whole predication.

One further aspect of transparency is 'iconicity'. It means that there should be a correspondence between the characteristics of the realm of experience and the language that represents it. This is particularly true of the linearity of events which should be mirrored in the linearity of language. Thus example (8) would follow the maxim of transparency and, more specifically, of iconicity, but this is not the case with example (9), where the sequence of requested actions does not correspond to the sequence of words:

(8) Close the door and then open the window!

(9) Open the window after you have closed the door!

The second maxim of the clarity principle is the 'ambiguity maxim'. It simply goes: "Avoid ambiguity!" As Leech (1983: 66-67) explains, "ambiguity occurs notoriously with pronoun anaphora" and with so-called "garden path" sentences. Here are his two examples:

(10) If the baby won't drink cold milk, it should be boiled.

(11) Before we started eating the table was absolutely loaded with delicacies.

In example (10) there is an ambiguity at the purely syntactic level as to what noun phrase the pronoun *it* refers to. The disambiguation is based on our world knowledge which only leaves *milk* as a suitable antecedent. The wording of example (11), and the graphic presentation as it stands, may lead a decoder into an intonation trap because we are primed to expect something edible after a word-form of the lexeme EAT which seems to be indicated by the definite article. Examples (10) and (11) have in common that they put extra strain on the decoder, which may effect a slight increase in processing time. As Leech (1983: 67) observes:

> The danger from ambiguity is not so much that it will end by misleading *h*, as that it will confuse and delay *h*'s interpretation of the sentence. In this respect the Clarity Principle might be regarded as subordinate to the Processibility Principle.

The 'economy principle' is summarized in the advice: "Be quick and easy!" It can be related to the general principle of least effort (cf. section 5.3 below). As Leech (ibid.) explains:

> If one can shorten the text while keeping the message unimpaired, this reduces the amount of time and effort involved both in encoding and in decoding.

Leech sees the economy principle at work on the phonological level where "economy favours elisions, assimilations, and other abbreviating and simplifying processes" (ibid.) which are typical of connected speech. On the syntactic level, Leech postulates a 'maxim of reduction' with the enunciation: "Reduce where possible!" A systematic application of this rule was shown above in our treatment of cohesive devices in section 2.1.3, notably the use of pronouns, substitution, and ellipsis.

As we have seen in connection with example (10), the economy principle, which favours the use of the pronoun *it*, and the clarity principle can come into conflict. Less reduction avoids the conflict, and example (10) could be reformulated as (12) by simply repeating the item *milk*:

(12) If the baby won't drink cold milk, the milk should be boiled.

About the last principle of textual rhetoric, the 'expressivity principle', Leech remarks that it "is more diffuse and difficult to define" (ibid.: 68). The examples that Leech gives are cases of what he calls "expressive repetition", for example:

(13) John Brown was guilty of the crime, and John Brown would have to pay for it.

In a similar way, we might explain reduction as also guided by the expressivity principle. We observed this above in section 1.3 when we discussed the informativity of the warning of the Bell Telephone Company, repeated here as (14):

(14) Call us before you dig. You may not be able to afterwards.

We noted above that (14) is more effective, i.e. makes a stronger impression than a corresponding, more explicit version. If impact has something to do with expressivity, then we might regard the expressivity principle also to be at work in example (14).

5.2 Processibility

We have seen in section 5.1 that processibility is only one principle of textual rhetoric besides clarity, economy and expressivity. More specifically, the processibility principle was formulated in two maxims, that of medium-independent end-focus (with the intonational sub-principles of end-nucleus and resolution) and that of end-weight, 'weight' being understood in terms of length and complexity. Thus the maxim of end-weight demands that relatively large and complex constituents should be placed at the end of a clause complex. While the end-focus maxim refers to semantic content of constituents in terms of newness or salience, the end-weight maxim specifically refers to syntactic structure.

There is a psychological basis for the maxim of end-weight in so far as it considers the short-term memory, both of the decoder and of the encoder. Kimball (1973: 33), for example, assumes that no more than two sentences can be parsed at a time because of the limitations of the short-term memory. While Kimball considers the wants of the parsing decoder, Wasow (1997: 350) argues that end-weight also satisfies the needs of the encoder:

> The principal reason speakers postpone the production of complex constituents is that it helps them in planning their utterances.

It was said above that structural weight manifests itself in terms of the length or the complexity of a clause complex. This means that we are dealing with a description at the level of medium-independent word-forms. Several authors have remarked that length correlates with complexity. Clark/Clark (1977: 337) observe, for example: "Long sentences [...] are usually more complex than short ones." Similarly, Smith/Kleeck (1985: 390) find that sentence-length is indexical of surface complexity. And Wasow (1997: 93-94) comes to the same conclusion (Note that 'nodes' are the end points in a tree diagram or the points where there is branching.):

> Long phrases tend to have more complex structures, involving both more phrasal nodes and more nodes altogether and very often having clauses or prepositional phrases following the head. [...] We can conclude [...] that weight can be measured quite well by counting words, nodes, or phrasal nodes.

There is a vast amount of literature on how complexity can be numerically measured, which we need not discuss here for our purposes. As one example of many, I would like to pick out an approach developed by Hawkins over several decades. In its earlier formulation it describes a pragmatic principle which is based on counting medium-independent word-forms and on their hierarchical organisation in phrases. In the 1994 version the basic idea of the so-called principle of Early Immediate Constituents is expressed as follows:

> I believe that words and constituents occur in the orders they do so that syntactic groupings and their immediate constituents (ICs) can be recognized (and produced) as rapidly and efficiently as possible in language performance. Different orderings of elements result in more or less rapid IC recognition. (Hawkins 1994: 57)

Hawkins exemplifies his point with an analysis of the following two strings of word-forms (ibid.):

(15) I gave the valuable book that was extremely difficult to find to Mary

(16) I gave to Mary the valuable book that was extremely difficult to find

In terms of the syntactic framework that is used in this book the two sentences can be analysed as follows in terms of clause elements:

(17) [$_S$ I] [$_V$ gave] [$_O$ the valuable book that was extremely difficult to find] [$_{AP}$ to Mary]

(18) [$_S$ I] [$_V$ gave] [$_{AP}$ to Mary] [$_O$ the valuable book that was extremely difficult to find]

If we compare the constituent structures of (17) and (18), we have to state that in (17) the decoder has to process twelve word-forms before he can recognize the whole structure of the clause, i.e. until he reaches the word *to*. Structurally, we are dealing with an SVOA allo-sentence, which consists of the subject noun phrase (S), the verbal element (V), the direct object noun phrase (O) with relative clause postmodification and an adjunct prepositional phrase (AP). On the other hand, the decoder has to process only five word-forms, i.e. until he reaches the word *the*, in order to recognize the whole structure of (18), in which the adjunct prepositional phrase precedes the direct object phrase. That is, after encountering the clause elements SVA, the definite article indicates the beginning of a noun phrase which functions as the last clause element of the allo-sentence structure SVAO instantiating the clause pattern SVOA. (We are aware of the fact that the relative clause has two verbal elements, *was* and *find*, which could be analysed as two separate clauses. This is of no consequence for the point made here.)

Besides structural weight, the rapid recognition of constituent structure depends also on whether the deepest embedding occurs at the beginning or at the end of a clause complex. The first situation is sometimes called 'left-branching' and the second 'right-branching'. Right-branching structures give away earlier the structural information of a clause complex and are easier to comprehend than left-branching structures, as the following examples from Quirk et al. (1985: 1039) illustrate.

(19) [[That [if you could] you would help me] is of small comfort]

(20) [It is of small comfort [that you would help me [if you could]]]

In his later book Hawkins (2004) extends the principle of Early Immediate Constituents to the more comprehensive principle Minimize Domains. This principle not only accounts for immediate constituents in the classic sense but also for lexical and phrasal combinations. This is exemplified by Hawkins (ibid.: 26, 33) with the phrasal verb *count on*. Kreyer (2008: 128) uses the following two strings to show succinctly the difference between the principles of Early Immediate Constituents and Minimize Domains:

(21) counted on my son in these years

(22) counted in these years on my son

According to the principles of 'end-weight' and of Early Immediate Constituents there is no difference in processing ease between (21) and (22). The verb-form *counted* is followed by two prepositional phrases of three words each. Therefore both the numbers of words and phrases to be processed are equal. On the other hand, the principle of Minimize Domains, covering also multi-word lexemes, would predict that (21) is easier to process since the two word-forms *count* and *on* are adjacent. This is not the case in (22) where *count* and *on* are discontinuous, thus enlarging the domain of the phrasal verb *count on* and making processing more difficult in comparison to (21). In the words of Hawkins:

> The clear intuition that emerges from these examples is that when some property is assigned within a combinatorial or dependency domain [in our example *count on*, JE], the size of that domain should be as small as possible. In other words, parse the fewest possible forms and their associated properties in order to assign the property in question. (Hawkins 2004: 26-27)

The properties to be assigned in (21) and (22) are the combinatorial status of the phrasal verb *count on* and the dependency status of the prepositional phrases *on my son* and *in these years*.

The processing preference of (21) over (22) that is predicted by Hawkins's principle Minimize Domains can also be described with Leech's 'clarity principle' discussed above (p. 171), in particular the transparency maxim, which advises:

> For clarity's sake, it is a good idea for semantically adjacent items also to be syntactically adjacent. (Leech 1983: 66)

We can conclude that Hawkins's principle Minimize Domains covers issues that were already described above in the framework of Leech's textual rhetoric as maxims of end-weight and of transparency.

5.3 Optimizing texts

We assume that it is possible to divide Leech's principles of textual rhetoric into two classes. The first class deals with maxims that are either fulfilled or not. These are the maxims of end-focus, end-weight, transparency and ambiguity. The second class deals with maxims that can only be fulfilled to a larger or lesser degree depending on the context. To these belong the maxims of reduction and expressivity.

The maxim of reduction belongs to a more general economy principle, which was most generally formulated as the Principle of Least Effort by Zipf (1972 [1949]: 19). However, as Leech (1983: 68) points out, there is a trade-off between economy and clarity:

> The pragmatic point about reduction is that it abbreviates the text, and often simplifies its structure, while maintaining the recoverability of the message. It is when, for some reason, the message's recoverability is impaired that reduction comes into conflict with the Clarity Principle.

This means, however, that we cannot give a yes/no answer as to where we can strike a balance between these two conflicting principles.

One aspect, namely clarity, has found special consideration in the work of Rohdenburg (2003: 205), who formulated a 'complexity principle':

> The complexity principle states that in the case of more or less explicit constructional alternatives [...], the more explicit option(s) will tend to be preferred in cognitively more complex environments.

That is, if the writer wants to optimize his text and has two structural alternatives, the more explicit version will be preferred if the decoder's understanding is in question. Such a choice would be, for instance, between (23) and (24) as well as between (25) and (26), cf. Kreyer (2008: 130) and Rohdenburg (2003: 222):

(23) I believe the boy knows the answer

(24) I believe that the boy knows the answer

(25) it is up to them ∅ how they want to go about it

(26) it is up to the people concerned to decide how they want to go about it

Alternative (24) is to be preferred over (23) both according to the clarity principle and the complexity principle. Both principles would seek to avoid a garden-path reading of (23) which would first wrongly assume that the noun phrase *the boy* is an object to the verb *believe*. A comparison of (25) and (26) shows that the full noun phrase *the people concerned* is followed by the explicit verbal element *to decide*, whereas the pronoun *them* is not followed by an explicit verbal element; this ellipsis is marked by the zero sign ∅. Rohdenburg has shown that there is a statistical correlation between a pronoun form like *them* and a zero realization of a *to*-infinitive like *to decide*.

As a last principle of textual rhetoric I would like to mention Kreyer's Principle of Immediate Textual Integration:

> There is a general tendency in clause construction to prefer those structures that allow to integrate the content of the clause as soon as possible into the already existing text structure. (Kreyer 2006: 199)

> This principle emphasizes the importance of considerations of processing with regard to the distribution of information status in the utterance. The progression from given to new information is the most economical way of presenting information considering the recipient's need to integrate new information into the already existing stock of knowledge. (Kreyer 2008: 142)

In the last sentence of example (27) from the BNC (CBR 611 to 614) the inversion and the therefore postponed subject noun phrase demonstrates just this (cf. Kreyer 2006: 200):

(27) A number of implications arise from the model of pragmatic mediation that I have sketched out here. First, the process, as outlined in the diagram, is a scheme for research as well as for teaching conventionally considered: each is seen as a concomitant of the other, and it is this which provides for the professional development of the teacher. The question then arises as to how this pragmatic enterprise differs, if it differs at all, from the kinds of activity which are customarily carried out under the name of research. Related to this question of pedagogic/pragmatic research as an integrated element of classroom practice is the matter of teacher formation.

Here the fronted predication (*Related to ...*) is coherently related to the topics of teaching and research in the preceding sentences. Example (27) demonstrates that the maxim of end-weight (and equally the Principle of Early Immediate Constituents) is overruled by the Principle of Immediate Textual Integration which takes care of coherence needs rather than of needs to recognize the structure of the clause complex.

The text pragmatic principles that we have discussed so far aim at optimizing texts in terms of allo-sentences, that is, in terms of possible alternatives of clause complexes. All principles have in common that they relate to a description of syntactic structure. To complement this set of approaches we finally have to look at readability assessments that are purely based on the number and the length of words in orthographic sentences. In such approaches the orthographic sentence is regarded as a container without any internal hierarchical structure. Such approaches are eventually only based on a superficial assessment of word-forms.

One of the pioneers in this field was Flesch (1948), who wanted to capture with a numerical tool the readability of various text genres in order to classify texts on a scale from easy to difficult. Basically there are two ratios that play a role: On the one hand there is the number of words per sentences, and on the other there is the number of syllables per word. The idea is that longer sentences and longer words are more difficult to read than shorter ones. It is fairly easy to determine the total number of words and the total number of sentences in a given text if by 'word' we understand 'orthographic word-form' and by 'sentence' 'orthographic sentence'. Syllables, on the other hand, are less straightforward to identify and to count because usually this involves reading the text aloud and marking the syllables. Therefore, there are certain limitations to the analysis of the length of a text. For practical and theoretical reasons, which are irrelevant in this context, the formula into which the two ratios enter also contains three constants:

$$\text{readability score} = 206.835 - 1.015 \left(\frac{\text{words}}{\text{sentences}}\right) - 84.6 \left(\frac{\text{syllables}}{\text{words}}\right)$$

Figure 5.3: The Flesch Reading Ease Score

There are two kinds of dependency that are expressed by this and other formulas. If the number of syllables increases (with a constant number of words) the words become longer and the reading score decreases, which means that the text becomes more difficult. If the number of sentences increases (with a constant number of words) the sentences become shorter and the reading score increases, which means that the text becomes easier to read. The absolute maximum of the reading ease score is given if the numbers of syllables, words and sentences are equal, i.e. in an utterance consisting of one clause realized by one word realized by one syllable, for example >no<. In such a case the absolute maximum of the reading score (121.22) is reached. (Note that the number of words cannot be smaller than the number of sentences and the number of syllables cannot be smaller than the number of words.) This is the easiest-to-read text one can think of. On the other hand, values smaller than 0 are also theoretically possible in short texts. If we take for example >computers are unbeatable< we get a reading score of -21.81. The value by itself would suggest that the text is practically unreadable. From this we can see that the length of a text poses theoretical and practical problems for reading scores.

There are many other reading indexes of which I only want to mention the index by Coleman/Liau (1975), which is based on the ratio of characters per words, in contrast to Flesch's ratio of syllables per words. Like the Flesch formula, the one by Coleman/Liau also uses three (different) constants for its index:

$$\text{readability score} = 5.89 \left(\frac{\text{characters}}{\text{words}}\right) - 0.3 \left(\frac{\text{sentences}}{\text{words}}\right) - 15.8$$

Figure 5.4: The Coleman-Liau Index

As the title of their article ("A computer readability formula designed for machine scoring") already suggests, this formula is designed for computer-readable input and therefore easily carried out on personal computers. Particularly in America, but also in other countries, the readability of texts is a concern for many companies and organizations. Therefore, before texts are published, they have to undergo one of the available readability tests in order to be optimized for the intended readership if necessary.

5.4 Questions and exercises

1. Analyse examples (3) and (4) in terms of constituent phrases and clauses, as was shown in examples (17) and (18).

2. Identify left- and right-branching structures in text samples from a novel and a book on linguistics or on some other technical subject.

3. Calculate the Flesch Reading Ease Score and the Coleman-Liau Index for three text excerpts of about 500 words and compare the scores with your impression.

5.5 Further reading

Kreyer (2008) offers a psychologically plausible network model to show how semantic, structural and frequential aspects of text production and recognition can interact. Kreyer (2008: ch. 3) gives an excellent survey of processing principles. See Schäpers (2006: ch. 4) for a detailed discussion of complexity metrics.

6 Textual Intentions

Having dealt with formal texture, semantic texture and decoder-orientation in the preceding chapters we will now turn to the concern of the text-producer, namely what he intends by producing a text. In other words: why is the text-producer producing the text? We have seen in section 1.2 above that the study of textual intentions is one of the main trends in text-linguistics. Van Dijk, one of the proponents of this trend, views linguistic actions as a special kind of action performed by human beings. He (1980: 76) points out that actions are guided by intentions: "Handlungen [sind] von *intentionaler* Art." Linguistic acts can be described as having local and global meanings. Therefore, van Dijk (ibid.: 75) assumes that texts can have both local intentions and global intentions:

> Neben den lokalen Intentionen für die einzelnen Handlungen nehmen wir daher auch das Vorhandensein einer vorausgehenden globalen Intention und Absicht an.

He views texts as being systematically connected with global units of linguistic actions of one or several speakers:

> Texte [hängen] systematisch mit globalen Einheiten von sprachlichen Handlungen desselben Sprechers oder verschiedener Sprecher zusammen. (ibid.: 212)

There are various attempts to classify the intentions of text-producers in terms of 'global text functions'. These are sometimes called *genre* or *text-type*. Unfortunately, these two expressions are highly polysemous. In the present account of text-linguistics we have understood *genre* to designate external and sometimes semantic classifications of texts as, for example, the components of corpora (cf. section 2.3.1.3 above). On the other hand, the expression *text-type* designates "groupings of texts that are similar with respect to their linguistic form" (Biber 1988: 70). Referring to the speech-act-like function of whole texts, I prefer to speak of 'global text functions' (and not 'text-type' as some authors do) in order to to avoid confusion.

Among the earliest and most influential accounts of global text functions are those by Longacre (1976) and E. L. Smith (1985) on the one hand, and by Werlich (1976) on the other. The categories that are proposed in the two approaches are listed in Figure 6.1.

Longacre (1976)/Smith (1985)	Werlich (1976)
expository	description
narrative	narration
hortatory/behavioral	exposition
procedural	argumentation
	instruction

Figure 6.1: Some global text functions

Even the two short lists of global text functions in Figure 6.1 demonstrate two things: Firstly, there seems to be a basic set of global text functions with recurring items, in our lists: exposition, narration and instruction (cf. hortative/ behavioral). Secondly, the number of global text functions varies.

In the Longacre and Smith approach the global text functions are called "deep structure genre" and "discourse framework" respectively. They try to capture the essential, global text functions with the help of features, e.g. 'temporal succession'. These will be discussed in section 6.1. On the other hand, Werlich's global text functions (which he calls "text-types") are related to general cognitive processes. They are summarized in Figure 6.2.

Global text functions	Cognitive processes
description	perception in space
narration	perception in time
exposition	comprehension
argumentation	judging (in answer to a problem)
instruction	planning

Figure 6.2: Global text functions and related cognitive processes in Werlich (1976: 39-41)

Both the Longacre-Smith approach and Werlich's approach have in common that their global text functions are high-level abstractions from actual texts and their surface properties. This dichotomy has led to the important distinction between the so-called 'discourse type' (i.e. 'global text function') and the 'text-type', as proposed by Virtanen (1992). The interplay between abstract 'discourse type' and more concrete 'text-type' will be described in section 6.2.

6.1 Deep structure genres

Longacre (1976: ch. 5) distinguishes four kinds of deep structure genre which have had a long tradition. They may be understood to represent different global speech acts: in a 'narrative' discourse we recount events, in a 'procedural' discourse we tell someone how to do something, in a 'behavioral' discourse we try to influence someone's conduct, and if the discourse is 'expository' we explain a subject matter (cf. Longacre 1976: 201). Longacre points out that these genres are universal. They are not language-specific and not necessarily tied to specific surface forms (ibid.: 202):

> We aim at universal characteristics of language rather than at the characteristics of any one particular language. [...] It is admittedly the deep structure characteristics, not the surface structure characteristics, which best distinguish the discourse genre.

Longacre distinguishes four classificatory dimensions along which the four deep structure genres are characterized: (1.) 'person', (2.) 'orientation', (3.) 'time', and (4.) type of 'linkage' (cf. Figure 6.3 below). It is therefore possible to characterize the four genres with respect to values along these dimensions.

	+ AGENT ORIENTATION	- AGENT ORIENTATION
+ CONTINGENT TEMPORAL SUCCESSION	NARRATIVE	PROCEDURAL
	1. 1/3 person	1. Non-specific person
	2. Agent oriented	2. Patient oriented
	3. Accomplished time	3. Projected time
	4. Chronological linkage	4. Chronological linkage
- CONTINGENT TEMPORAL SUCCESSION	BEHAVIORAL	EXPOSITORY
	1. 2 person	1. No necessary person reference
	2. Addressee oriented	2. Subject matter oriented
	3. (Mode, not time)	3. Time not focal
	4. Logical linkage	4. Logical linkage

Figure 6.3: Four deep structure genres of monologic discourse (Smith 1985)

The four deep structure specifications of each genre try to capture some general properties of the linguistic patterning. For example, the dimension 'person' relates to surface pronouns, 'agent' and 'patient' relate to corresponding deep structure cases, 'time' relates to the linguistic choice of tense, and 'linkage' to the internal and external organisation of clauses. In a modified version taken from Smith (1985: 231) the deep structure genres are characterized as in Figure 6.3.

The information that is given by the values of the four dimensions and is used to characterize the four deep structure genres can be reduced to two binary distinctions, namely [+/- contingent temporal succession] and [+/- agent orientation]. The four results of this cross-classification define the four deep structure genres, as shown in Figure 6.4.

NARRATIVE	PROCEDURAL
+ contingent temporal succession	+ contingent temporal succession
+ agent orientation	- agent orientation
BEHAVIORAL	EXPOSITORY
- contingent temporal succession	- contingent temporal succession
+ agent orientation	- agent orientation

Figure 6.4: The four deep structure genres defined by two binary distinctions

Longacre not only recognizes deep structure genres but also 'surface structure genres' to allow for culture-specific variation and for variation in the actual linguistic codings. Longacre (1976: 205) gives some culture-specific examples of surface structure genres:

> We must remind ourselves that the classification into surface structure genre subsumes many specific types within various languages. In Western European literature, the variety of types is so great that it would require considerable time and effort to catalog them successfully.

He then goes on to list some of the more or less prototypical instantiations of the four deep structure genres (which he also calls 'discourses'):

> In the narrative genre we do not only have the fairy tale and myth, the short story, the short short story, the novel and various varieties of novels such as historical novels, gothic novels, detective mystery stories, etc. We have, in addition, first person accounts, newspaper reporting, and historiography which, as we have said, make pretensions to factuality. [...] Types of procedural discourse vary from the food recipe, to the how to do it book, to the instructions to a particular worker for his activities on a given day. [...] Expository discourse can range from the familiar essay to the scientific article. [...] Hortatory discourses can range from sermons, to peptalks, to addresses of generals to the troops on the eve of an important battle. At any rate it would appear that hortatory discourse is a cultural universal. We can scarcely conceive of a culture where somebody does not give advice to somebody else orally or urge on him a change

of conduct. The very idea of social control seems to imply this. (ibid.: 205-206)

The second area where the usefulness of the less abstract surface structure genres can be demonstrated concerns the variation in the actual linguistic coding. Longacre (ibid.: 203) gives the following example:

> The second person deep structure component of hortatory discourse can emerge in various ways in the surface structure of hortatory discourse. It may emerge simply as second person or it may emerge in somewhat softened down form as first person inclusive of second person, so that a speaker may avoid saying *You goofed up on this point*, and elect instead to say *We have goofed up on this point*. Or third person may be used to hold up the ideal participant, *A real American does so and so*, or *A good Huichol acts as follows*.

Even though there is no one-to-one relationship between deep structure and surface structure categories it is tempting to investigate just that.

Smith (1985) analysed instances of Longacre's genres, which were impressionistically classified by the speech act functions of texts from genetic research, in terms of 'text-type clauses'. These are clauses which show the typical properties of the genres. Here are Smith's (1985: 233-234) examples:

(1) They asked the Vice President for Research to help them implement this idea.

(2) The basic problem in reconciling such sharply divergent viewpoints is that in most cases both the benefits and the biohazards that have been ascribed to the development of recombinant DNA technology are highly speculative.

(3) When the two DNA molecules with the complementary single-stranded tails are mixed together under appropriate conditions, the complementary tails will form a double-stranded DNA molecule that will hold DNA X and DNA Y together.

(4) Science for other ends must yield to science for people.

Example (1) was counted as a narrative clause. The past tense verb and the third person agent subject of the tensed verb allow for the classification [+ contingent succession] and [+ agent orientation]. Example (2) shows three expository clauses with the binary features [- contingent succession] and [- agent orientation]. The clause complex in example (3) contains three procedural clauses with the features [+ contingent succession] and [- agent orientation].

Example (4) is a behavioural clause with the features [- contingent succession] and [+ agent orientation], which is primarily reflected in the lexical verb.

With regard to the match between deep structure genres and text-type clauses Smith (1985: 234) found out the following in his study:

> While the expository (E1) and narrative (N1) samples are composed primarily of clauses of their respective text types - E1 has 97% expository clauses and N1 75% narrative - the procedural (P1) and behavioral (B1) text samples are dominated by clauses of a text-type other than their own: expository. Sample P1 contains 76% expository clauses and sample B1 75%. However, the *relative* proportion of procedural clauses in P1 is greater (18%) than in any other sample. Similarly, the *relative* proportion of behavioral clauses in B1 is greater (19%) than in any other sample.

This shows that the attribution of genre labels in terms of speech act types (i.e. the functional classification) is not necessarily linked to the surface realizations of the deep structure dimensions or to the deep structure dimensions at all.

In order to accommodate these facts Smith (ibid.: 242) introduces the notion of 'discourse framework'. Discourse frames determine how a writer intends his whole text or part thereof to function in a given situation. This intention may be expressed verbally in an advance organizer, as in the following example (5), or not (cf. Smith 1985: 242):

(5) In this chapter we shall examine the views presented, consider the methods used in moving toward a resolution of conflicting ideas, and identify a few procedural problems that become important during this many-sided argument.

Smith points out that the text from which this passage is taken belongs to an expository deep structure genre. Nevertheless, example (5) does not show expository text-type clauses but rather narrative ones.

These observations indicate that the deep structure genres (i.e. narrative, procedural, behavioral and expository discourses) may be characterized at the highest level by abstract performative verbs (e.g. *examine*) and that given deep structure genres may have embedded in them passages of different, lower-level text functions. Therefore Smith (ibid.: 244) summarizes the situation as follows:

> Hence, the performative impact of a text may be changed by its incorporation into a larger text with a different overall purpose. [...] Thus, though the overall purpose of a text may be indicated by linguistic features, it may well be that that purpose is not established by numeric dominance, or by relative dominance, or even by any

explicit linguistic features at all. Rather the purpose is established by
the abstract performative at the highest level framework in which the
text is embedded.

This leads us to the more general question of the relationship between the global textual functions, i.e. intentions, categorized in terms of deep structure genres and the actual linguistic encodings in clauses and clause complexes. A valuable contribution in this area was made by Virtanen (1992), who uses the notions 'discourse type' and 'text-type' to refer to this dichotomy.

6.2 Discourse types

Virtanen describes conclusively the interplay between what has been termed so far 'global text function' or 'deep stucture genre' on the one hand, and 'text-types' that are based on their linguistic form on the other. The reader should not be confused that Virtanen introduces a partially different terminology with her notion of 'discourse type' which she contrasts with 'text-type'. Her 'discourse type' corresponds to the very abstract 'global text function' or 'deep stucture genre' while 'text-type' can be understood much in the same sense as has been done so far in this book, i.e. it refers to concrete linguistic forms which instantiate the more abstract 'discourse type'.

In Virtanen's (1992: 293) model "text types [are] characterizable with the help of text-internal criteria." She does not describe text-types, as Biber did, in terms of corpus-based calculations of co-occurring linguistic items (cf. section 2.3.1.3 above), but rather concentrates on good or stereotyped examples, which for her are clear and salient instances of abstractions, i.e. prototypes. Virtanen relates prototypical exemplars of text-types to intertextuality and the processing ease for the text decoder:

> Various text types – prototypical abstractions – may be used as heuristics in the process of text production and text comprehension. This obviously relates to 'intertextuality', i.e., the dependence of one text on other, previously encountered texts. [...] Making use of the possibility of producing a prototypical text structure is a way for the text producer to maximize receiver-orientation. The way in which the text producer gives the text receiver information may thus facilitate her/his task of interpreting the text, of building around it a text world and a universe of discourse (Enkvist, 1989). A text that conforms to a prototypical structure obviously contains less information than a text full of surprises, which, in terms of information theory, carries a lot of information (Enkvist, 1991). The interpretive effort that the text receivers need to make in the processing of 'unusual' texts may be

hypothesized to involve the matching of such texts against a prototype. [...] The choice of text type and the degree of prototypicality must be part of the process of text-strategic planning, and it is in this sense that the product of that process – the text – may be viewed as an actualized instance of a particular text type. (Virtanen 1992: 297-298)

Virtanen uses Werlich's five designations of global text functions, which were listed in Figures 6.1 and 6.2 above, to distinguish five text-types: narrative, descriptive, instructive, expository and argumentative. For illustration she uses five text fragments "showing near-prototype characteristics" (ibid.: 299). They are rendered as examples (6) to (10) below. In example (6) there is a match between the narrative text-type and narrative discourse type (global text function); in (7) to (10) there are corresponding matches of discourse type and realization by text-type which result in 'direct' or 'primary' uses of the respective text-types.

(6) My eleventh day opened on a cloudy sky and four more little boys pursued me on bicycles, screaming *'Gaijin! Gaijin!* (Foreigner! Foreigner!)' When they had overtaken me, they locked my path with their bicycles and stood scowling up at me open-mouthed: '*Ufu! Mile! Eigo no hito da!* (Ugh! Look! It's an English-speaker!)' I suggested to them in Japanese that they might like to move their bicycles. They turned away crestfallen: '*Ara! Eigo ja nakatta!* (Oh! It wasn't an English-speaker)' (Booth 1985: 23)
[narrative discourse realized by narrative]

(7) In the silent gardens of the old houses in Kakunodate the tops of the stone lanterns are lumpy and green, the stone wells drip with dark water drops that congeal in the summer heat. The moss is black-green and thick as a poultice. Not a single flower blooms, though the cherry trees are in full leaf, and beyond the mounds of twig and rock stands a small, empty veranda from which to view their blossoms. (Booth 1985: 89)
[descriptive discourse realized by description]

(8) Melt the butter or margarine in a large saucepan. Add the onion, celery and potato. Cover and cook gently for 5 minutes. Add the stock and the stock cube. Simmer for 15-20 minutes or until the vegetables are tender. Allow to cool. Purée the soup in a liquidizer or food processor with the cheese until smooth. Season to taste. Return to the pan, and reheat gently without boiling. Serve garnished with chopped parsley or celery leaves. (Swann 1987: 42)
[instructive discourse realized by instruction]

(9) Dialects. Japanese can be divided into two major dialect groups: those of the mainland and those of the Ryukyu Islands. The mainland dialects are divided by some scholars into three groups – Eastern, Western, and Kyushu. In other systems, however, they are classified into the Eastern division and the Western division, which is then split into the Kansai (including the Chūgoku and Shikoku dialects) and Kyushu dialects. (Encyclopædia Britannica, Macropædia 10: 93)
[expository discourse type realized by expository text-type]

(10) But in plucking verbal foliage away from its cultural soil, his trenchantly expressed commentaries carry curiously little suasive weight. It is easy to concur with a swipe at an author when we are predisposed to share –'s scepticism; when we are not, it is easy to reserve a feeling that the roots of the problem have been left untouched. (Bell 1990: 1316)
[argumentative discourse realized by argumentation]

The point of Virtanen's argument is that realizations of the five surface 'text-types' do not always have to be instantiations of the five 'discourse types' (global text functions):

The superordinate discourse type need not always be realized through the corresponding text type. An apparent mismatch of a discourse type and the corresponding text type may be accounted for in terms of notions such as the 'direct' and 'indirect', or 'primary' and 'secondary' uses of various text types. (Virtanen 1992: 298)

Examples of 'indirect' or 'secondary' uses can be shown in examples (11) to (14), taken from Virtanen (1992: 300-301):

(11) *Kitagawa Utamaro,* also known as UTAMARO (b. 1753, Japan – d. 1806, Japan), one of the greatest artists of the Ukiyo-e movement (paintings and wood-block prints of the 'floating world'), known especially for his masterfully composed portraits of sensuous female beauties.
    Probably born in a provincial town, he went to Edo (now Tokyo) with his mother. There, under the name of Toyoaki, he started painting and designing rather unoriginal wood-block prints of women. He also occupied himself with nature studies and published many illustrated books, of which *Gahon chūsen* (1788; *Insects)* is best known. Around 1791 he gave up designing prints for books and concentrated on making halflength single portraits of women rather than prints of women in groups as favoured by other Ukiyo-e artists. In 1804, at the height of his success, he made some prints depicting the military ruler Toyotomi Hideyoshi's wife and concubines. Consequently, he was accused of insulting Hideyoshi's dignity

and ordered to be handcuffed for 50 days. The experience crushed him and ended his career as an artist. (Encyclopædia Britannica, Micropædia 5: 840)
[expository discourse realized by narrative]

By its global intention, example (11) explains a certain subject matter which the reader seeks to be informed about and to comprehend. It can therefore be regarded as an instance of expository discourse or global text function. The striking thing is the fact that at the level of surface structure we find a predominant feature that is typical of narrative text-types, namely past tense forms indicating temporal succession. It is because these surface characteristics are not used in a narrative discourse but rather in expository discourse that Virtanen speaks of an 'indirect' or 'secondary' use of the text-type narrative.

(12) STEP 1
When the design was finally settled (4), with the tesserae lying face upwards, and properly spaced (2 mm or 1/16 in. should be allowed for grouting) the area was carefully measured, allowing 6 mm (1/4 in.) extra all round.
STEP 2
The blockboard was then cut to this final size - 470 mm x 930 mm (18 1/2 in. x 37 in.) - and the design squares marked on it (50).
STEP 3
The legs were then screwed on (51).
STEP 4
Tracing paper squares were now cut to a unit size of 305 mm x 228 mm (12 in. x 9 in.). (Hutton 1977: 51)
[instructive discourse realized by narrative]

Example (12) is taken from the book *Mosaik Making Techniques* and is a piece of instructive discourse which tells the reader how he should plan his actions (cf. *STEP 1* etc.). Again, it is the narrative surface features that are used indirectly.

(13) A farmer went out to sow his seed. As he was scattering the seed, some fell along the path, and the birds came and ate it up. Some fell on rocky places, where it did not have much soil. It sprang up quickly, because the soil was shallow. But when the sun came up, the plants were scorched, and they withered because they had no root. Other seed fell among thorns, which grew up and choked the plants. Still other seed fell on good soil, where it produced a crop - a hundred, sixty or thirty times what was sown. He who has ears, let him hear. (Matthew 13:3-9)
[argumentative discourse realized by narrative]

The text from the Bible in (13) is a piece of argumentative discourse in which the reader or hearer is asked to judge in answer to a problem. Again, the argumentation is presented with narrative features.

(14) *[HOW DO THEY LIVE?]*
It's still the middle of the night but suddenly and simultaneously Mr and Mrs Saito are awake: earthquake! The floor is moving underneath them and the wooden posts and beams are squeaking and groaning.
    After a few seconds it stops. Neither of them has moved - they quickly judged it was only a small quake - but their pulses are racing all the same. There are three terrifying things, the Japanese used to say in the old days - earthquakes, thunder and a father's anger. The latter two don't bother anybody much these days, but nobody gets used to earthquakes. (Popham 1984: 41)
[descriptive discourse realized by narrative]

Example (14) is from the travel guide *The Insider's Guide to Japan*. Its concern is to give a description of interesting localities in Japan. In this case the narrative features result from the narrative present tense, which indicates temporal succession.

(15) From Haymarket station Dairy Road strikes south-west, and leads to the main exit routes to the south-west, to Kilmarnock and Lanark. On the north side in Distillery Lane is the CALEDONIAN DISTILLERY (1855), one of two in the city, producing bulk grain whisky by the continuous patent-still process for blending. When built it contained the largest whisky still in Scotland. By the gate is a traditional farmhouse of 1740 recently restored as an architect's office. Off Dairy Road in Orwell Place is DALRY HOUSE, a mid 17th-century mansion restored and somewhat altered in 1969 as an old people's day centre. The house is an oblong 3-storey block with 2 semi-hexagonal towers capped with ogee roofs; the one at the south-west corner is a 19th-century addition. Inside is a notable 17th-century ceiling.
(Hamilton 1978: 158)
[instructive discourse realized by description]

Example (15) is from another travel guide, *Essential Edinburgh*. This time the concern is to 'guide', i.e. 'instruct', the reader how to plan his tour through Edinburgh. The surface features are mainly typical of a descriptive text-type: they give spatial orientation.

(16) *Sightseeing Highlights*
Tsukiji: If you're an early riser, go down to Tsukiji Fish Market at first light (or before) to see more fish than one can ever imagine in the ocean - a daily

haul to feed one of the world's largest population centers. Almost all of Tokyo's fish comes from this neighborhood. The action starts before daylight and is worth getting up early for. Join the fishmongers for an excellent and reasonably priced lunch (their dinner) in the neighborhood. Don't worry; it's immaculate and doesn't even smell of fish. You'll find the market just to the south of the Tsukiji stop on the Hibiya Line, in southeastern Tokyo. (Old 1987: 37)
[instructive discourse realized by argumentation]

The main intention of example (16), from the travel guide *Japan in 22 Days: A Step-by-Step-Guide and Travel Itineary*, is again to instruct the tourist what to do. However, this time the surface forms are typical of an argumentative text-type: there is a condition (*If you* ...) and a refutation (*Don't worry* ...). It is as if the author engages in a dialogue with the reader.

Virtanen's examples show clearly that a two-level model as advocated here is needed to describe independently the overall intention of a text and its more or less prototypical realization by surface forms such as choice of past tense (narrative), present tense (description and exposition), imperatives (instruction), conditional/concessive conjunctions (argumentation), spatial orientation (description). Virtanen (1992: 302) concludes:

Discourse types, connected with discourse functions, may be assumed to precede the level of text-strategic choices, thus affecting the whole strategy of the text. The choice of text type, on the other hand, has to do with the textualization process, which is determined by the text producer's text strategy. The text type of a particular text need not agree with its discourse type. Narrative texts may realize the argumentative discourse type, instructions may take the form of the description, and so forth.

Virtanen (1992) observes that the narrative text-type can be readily used indirectly to serve quite different discourse types than the narrative, whereas the argumentative text-type typically realizes argumentative discourse types. (Note, however, the exception in example (16), where we have an argumentative kind of instruction.) She explains:

The narrative type of text seems to be able to realize any type of discourse, i.e., argumentation, exposition, description, instruction in addition to the narrative discourse type. The argumentative type of text, again, seems to be more or less restricted to direct use, i.e., to the realization of the argumentative discourse type. (Virtanen 1992: 303)

These findings are graphically represented in Figure 6.5.

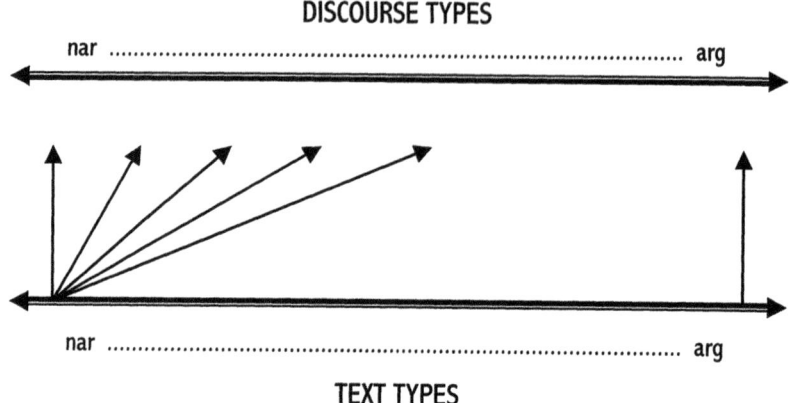

Figure 6.5: Text-types in the service of discourse types (Virtanen 1992: 303)

The multifunctional use that can be made of the narrative text-type leads Virtanen to speculate that the narrative text-type can be regarded as a 'primary' or 'basic' text-type (Virtanen 1992: 304). Furthermore she notes about the narrative discourse type (ibid.: 304-305):

> As a discourse type, narrative thus also shows a conspicuous characteristic in not allowing actualization through text types other than the corresponding narrative one: It cannot surface through a non-narrative type of text without a minimal narrative frame text.

Finally, the special status of the narrative text-type is also borne out by the fact that it can be regarded as a universal text-type, especially in its iconic representation of world experience.

6.3 Questions and exercises

1. Find a short story and the instruction manual of an electric device, and apply the binary distinctions given in Figure 6.4 in order to establish the deep structure genre to which these texts belong.

2. Take two travel guides and two recipes from cookery books. What are the discourse types, and to which text-types do the textual implementations belong?

6.4 Further reading

The relation of speech acts and texts is described in van Dijk (1980: ch. 3). Enkvist (1991) investigates discourse strategies and discourse types. Smith (2003) introduces the notion of 'discourse mode' which describes how speech-act-like text functions are textually implemented. She is interested in questions similar to Virtanen's, although the latter is not quoted. Relevant for our purposes are her chapters 2 and 11.

List of References

Abercrombie, D. (1967): *Elements of General Phonetics*. Edinburgh: University of Edinburgh Press.
Adamzik, K. (2004): *Textlinguistik*. Tübingen: Niemeyer.
Arnold, R. & K. Hansen (1996): *Englische Phonetik*, 10th ed. Leipzig: Langenscheidt, Verlag Enzyklopädie.
Beaugrande, R. de (1980): *Text, Discourse and Process: Toward a Multidisciplinary Science of Texts*. London: Longman.
Beaugrande, R. de (1994): "Text linguistics", *The Encyclopedia of Language and Linguistics*, ed. R. E. Asher. Oxford: Pergamon Press. 4573-4578.
Beaugrande, R. de (1997): *New Foundations for a Science of Text and Discourse: Cognition, Communication, and the Freedom of Access to Knowledge and Society*. Norwood, NJ: Ablex Publishing.
Beaugrande, R. & W. U. Dressler (1981): *Introduction to Text Linguistics*. London: Longman.
Bell, J. (1990): "'Stemming the sententious': Rev. Ronald F. Englefield, Critique of Pure Verbiage: Essays on Abuses of Language in Literary, Religious, and Philosophical Writings, ed. G. A. Wells & D. R. Oppenheimer (Peru, ILL: Open Court, 1990)", *Times Literary Supplement* Dec 7-13, 1316.
Bellert, I. (1970): "On a condition of the coherence of texts", *Semiotica* 2, 335-363.
Bernstein, B. (1971): *Class, Codes and Control*, 4 vols: *Volume One: Theoretical Studies Towards a Sociology of Language*. London: Routledge & Kegan Paul.
Biber, D. (1986): "Spoken and written textual dimensions in English: resolving the contradictory findings", *Language* 62, 384-414.
Biber, D. (1988): *Variation Across Speech and Writing*. Cambridge: Cambridge University Press.
Biber, D. (1989): "A typology of English texts", *Linguistics* 27, 3-43.
Biber, D. & E. Finegan (1986): "An initial typology of English text types", *Corpus Linguistics II*, ed. J. Aarts & W. Meijs. Amsterdam: Rodopi. 19-46.
Biber, D. & E. Finegan (1988): "Drift in three English genres from the 18th to the 20th centuries: A multidimensional approach", *Corpus Linguistics, Hard and Soft*, ed. M. Kytö, O. Ihalainen & M. Rissanen. Amsterdam: Rodopi. 83-101.
[Bible] (1987): *The Holy Bible*, new int. vers. London: Hodder & Stoughton.
Bolinger, D. L. (1958): "Intonation and grammar", *Language Learning* 8, 31-37.
Booth, A. (1985): *The Roads to Sata: A 2000-Mile Walk through Japan*. Harmondsworth: Viking.

Brown, G. & G. Yule (1983): *Discourse Analysis.* Cambridge: Cambridge University Press.

Burchfield, R. W. (ed.) (1989): *The Oxford English Dictionary,* 2nd ed. Oxford: Clarendon.

Burnard, L. (1995): *Users Reference Guide for the British National Corpus.* Oxford: Oxford University Computing Service.

Bussmann, H. (1996): *Routledge Dictionary of Language and Linguistics.* London: Routledge.

Butler, C. S. (2003): *Structure and Function: A Guide to Three Major Structural-Functional Theories,* 2 pts: *Part One: Approaches to the Simplex Clause.* Amsterdam: John Benjamins.

Carey, P. (1997): *Jack Maggs.* London: Faber & Faber.

Carter, R. A. & K. Malmkjaer (2002): "Text linguistics", *The Linguistics Encyclopedia,* ed. Kirsten Malmkjaer, 2nd ed. London: Routledge. 540-551.

Chafe, W. (1992): "Discourse", *International Encyclopedia of Linguistics,* ed. W. Bright. Oxford: Oxford University Press. 355-358.

Clark, H. H. & Eve V. Clark (1977): *Psychology and Language: An Introduction to Psycholinguistics.* New York: Harcourt.

Coleman, M. & T. L. Liau (1975): "A computer readability formula designed for machine scoring", *Journal of Applied Psychology* 60, 283-284.

Croft, W. & D. A. Cruse (2004): *Cognitive Linguistics.* Cambridge: Cambridge University Press.

Crystal, D. (1969): *Prosodic Systems and Intonation in English.* Cambridge: Cambridge University Press.

Crystal, D. (1990): *The English Language.* London: Penguin.

Crystal, D. & D. Davy (1969): *Investigating English Style.* London: Longman.

Daneš, F. (1964): "A three-level approach to syntax", *Travaux du Cercle Linguistique de Prague* 1, 225-240.

Daneš, F. (1970): "One instance of Prague School methodology: functional analysis of utterance and text", *Methods and Theory in Linguistics,* ed. P. L. Garvin. The Hague & Paris: Mouton. 132-146.

Daneš, F. (1974): "Functional sentence perspective and the organization of the text", *Papers on Functional Sentence Perspective,* ed. F. Daneš. The Hague: Mouton. 106-128.

Dijk, T. A. van (1977): *Text and Context: Explorations in the Semantics and Pragmatics of Discourse.* London: Longman.

Dijk, T. A. van (1980): *Textwissenschaft: Eine interdisziplinäre Einführung,* transl. Christoph Sauer. München: Deutscher Taschenbuch Verlag.

Dijk, T. A. van & W. Kintsch (1983): *Strategies of Discourse Comprehension.* New York: Academic Press.

Dijk, T. A. van (1997): "The study of discourse", *Discourse as Structure and Process*, ed. T. A. van Dijk. London: Sage Publications. 1-34.
[Encyclopaedia Britannica] (1983): *The New Encyclopaedia Britannica in 30 Volumes*, 15th ed. Chicago: Encyclopaedia Britannica.
Enkvist, N. E. (1973): *Linguistic Stylistics*. The Hague: Mouton.
Enkvist, N. E. (1989): "Connexity, interpretability, universes of discourse, and text worlds", *Possible Worlds in Humanities, Arts and Sciences: Proceedings of Nobel Symposium 65*, ed. S. Allén. Berlin & New York: Walter de Gruyter. 162-186.
Enkvist, N. E. (1991): "Discourse strategies and discourse types", *Functional and Systemic Linguistics: Approaches and Uses*, ed. E. Ventola. Berlin: Mouton de Gruyter. 3-22.
Esser, J. (1984): *Untersuchungen zum gesprochenen Englisch*. Tübingen: Gunter Narr.
Esser, J. (1988): *Comparing Reading and Speaking Intonation*. Amsterdam: Rodopi.
Esser, J. (1993): *English Linguistic Stylistics*. Tübingen: Niemeyer.
Esser, J. (2006): *Presentation in Language: Rethinking Speech and Writing*. Tübingen: Gunter Narr.
Euler, B. (1991): *Strukturen mündlichen Erzählens*. Tübingen: Gunter Narr.
Fellowes, J. (2005): *Snobs*. London: Phoenix.
Fillmore, C. F. (1977): "Scenes-and-frames semantics", *Linguistic Structures Processing*, ed. Antonio Zampolli. Amsterdam: North-Holland Publishing Company. 55-81.
Fillmore, C. F. (1985): "Frames and the semantics of understanding", *Quaderni di Semantica: Rivista Internazionale di Semantica Teorica e Applicata* VI (2), 222-254.
Firth, J. R. (1957): "Modes of meaning", *Papers in Linguistics 1934-1951*. London: Oxford University Press. 191-215.
Flesch, R. (1948): "A new readability yardstick", *Journal of Applied Psychology* 32, 221-233.
Fries, U. (1990): "Two hundred years of English death notices", *On Strangeness*, ed. Margaret Bridges. Tübingen: Gunter Narr. 57-71.
Gibson, W. (1966): *Tough, Sweet and Stuffy: An Essay on Modern American Prose Styles*. Bloomington, IN: Indiana University Press.
Gimson, A. C. (1980): *An Introduction to the Pronunciation of English*, 3rd ed. London: Arnold.
Greenbaum, S. (1991): *An Introduction to English Grammar*. Oxford: Oxford University Press.
Greenbaum, S. & J. Svartvik (1990): "The London-Lund Corpus of Spoken English", *The London-Lund Corpus of Spoken English: Description and Research*, ed. Jan Svartvik. Lund: Lund University Press. 11-59.

Grice, H. P. (1975): "Logic and Conversation", *Speech Acts*, ed. P. Cole & J. L. Morgan. New York: Academic Press. 41-58.
Grimes, J. E. (1975): *The Thread of Discourse*. The Hague: Mouton.
Halford, B. K. (1996): *Talk Units: the Structure of Spoken Canadian English*. Tübingen: Gunter Narr.
Halliday, M. A. K. (1961): "Categories of the theory of grammar", *Word* 17, 241-292.
Halliday, M. A. K. (1966): "Lexis as a linguistic level", *In Memory of J. R. Firth*, ed. C. E. Bazell, J.C. Catford, M.A.K. Halliday & R.H. Robins. London: Longman. 148-162.
Halliday, M. A. K. (1967): "Notes on transitivity and theme in English", pt. 2/3, *Journal of Linguistics* 3 (2), 199-244.
Halliday, M. A. K. (1985): *An Introduction to Functional Grammar*. London: Arnold.
Halliday, M. A. K., A. McIntosh & P. Strevens (1964): *The Linguistic Sciences and Language Teaching*. London: Longman.
Halliday, M. A. K. & R. Hasan (1976): *Cohesion in English*. London: Longman.
Halliday, M. A. K. & R. Hasan (1985): *Language, Context, and Text: Aspects of Language in a Semiotic Perspective*. Deakin University, VI: Deakin University Press.
Hamilton, A. (1978): *Essential Edinburgh*. London: André Deutsch.
Harris, Z. S. (1952): "Discourse analysis", *Language* 28, 1-30.
Hawkins, J. A. (1994): *A Performance Theory of Order and Constituency*. Cambridge: Cambridge University Press.
Hawkins, J. A. (2004): *Efficiency and Complexity in Grammars*. Oxford: Oxford University Press.
Hobbs, J. R. (1985): "On the coherence and structure of discourse", *Report No. CSLI-85-37, Center for the Study of Language and Information*. Stanford: Stanford University.
Hoey, M. (1991): *Patterns of Lexis in Text*. Oxford: Oxford University Press.
Hoey, M. (2005): *Lexical Priming: A New Theory of Words and Language*. London: Routledge.
Hoey, M. (2006): "Clumsy English", *The European English Messenger* 15, 48-57.
Hoffbauer, B. (2003): *Text-Constructional Units: Exploring Written Communication*. PhD thesis, University of Freiburg i. Br.
Hornby, A. S. (1995): *Oxford Advanced Learner's Dictionary of Current English*, 5th ed. by J. Crowther. Oxford: Oxford University Press.
House, J. (1994): "Text/Rhetoric", *The Encyclopedia of Language and Linguistics*, ed. R. E. Asher. Oxford: Pergamon Press. 4581-4585.
Hulse, M. (2002): *Empires and Holy Lands: Poems 1976-2000*. Applecross: Salt Publishing.

References

Hünig, W. (1980): "Der Paragraph als pragmatische Einheit zwischen Satz und Text", *Linguistik und Didaktik* 43/44, 295-318.
Hutton, H. (1977): *Mosaic Making Techniques*. London: Batsford.
Jansson, T. (2006): *A Winter Book*. London: Sort of Books.
Jones, L. K. (1977): *Theme in English Expository Discourse*. Lake Bluff, IL: Jupiter Press.
Kallmeyer, W. & R. Meyer-Hermann (1980): "Textlinguistik", *Lexikon der Germanistischen Linguistik*, ed. H. P. Althaus, H. Henne & H. E. Wiegand, 2nd ed. Tübingen: Niemeyer. 242-258.
Kay, P. (1977): "Language evolution and speech style", *Sociocultural Dimensions of Language Change*, ed. B. G. Blount & M. Sanders. New York: Academic Press. 21-33.
Kennedy, G. (1998): *An Introduction to Corpus Linguistics*. London: Longman.
Kimball, J. (1973): "Seven principles of surface structure parsing in natural language", *Cognition* 2 (1), 15-47.
Knowles, G. (1991): "Prosodic labelling: the problem of tone group boundaries", *English Computer Corpora: Selected Papers and Research Guide*, ed. S. Johansson & A.-B. Stenström. Berlin: Mouton de Gruyter. 149-161.
Krause, W.-D. (2000): "Text, Textsorte, Textvergleich", *Textsorten: Reflexionen und Analysen*, ed. K. Adamzik. Tübingen: Stauffenburg. 45-76.
Kreyer, R. (2006): *Inversion in Modern Written English: Syntactic Complexity, Information Status and the Creative Writer*. Tübingen: Gunter Narr.
Kreyer, R. (2008): *The Nature of Rules, Regularities and Units in Language: A Network Model of the Language System and of Language Use*. Habilitation thesis, University of Bonn.
Kreyer, R. & J. Mukherjee (2007): "The style of pop song lyrics: a corpus-linguistic pilot study", *Anglia* 125, 31-58.
Langacker, R. W. (1988): "An overview of cognitive grammar", *Topics in Cognitive Linguistics*, ed. B. Rudzka-Ostyn. Amsterdam: John Benjamins. 3-48.
Leech, G. N. (1983): *Principles of Pragmatics*. London: Longman.
Leech, G. & J. Svartvik (1994): *A Communicative Grammar of English*, 2nd ed. Harlow: Longman.
Leech, G. & M. Short (1981): *Style in Fiction: A Linguistic Introduction to English Fictional Prose*. London: Longman.
Lewis, W. J. (1977): *People Speaking: Phonetic Readings in Current English*. Oxford: Oxford University Press.
Lipka, L. (2002): *English Lexicology*. Tübingen: Gunter Narr.
Lodge, D. (1978): *Changing Places*. Harmondsworth: Penguin.
Longacre, R. E. (1976): *An Anatomy of Speech Notions*. Lisse: Peter de Ridder Press.

Longacre, R. E. (1979): "The paragraph as a grammatical unit", *Syntax and Semantics, Volume 12: Discourse and Syntax*, ed. T. Givón. New York: Academic Press. 115-134.

Louw, B. (1993): "Irony in the text or insincerity in the writer? The diagnostic potential of semantic prosodies", *Text and Technology: In Honour of John Sinclair*, ed. M. Baker, G. Francis & E. Tognini-Bonelli. Amsterdam: John Benjamins. 157-176.

Lyons, J. (1972): "Human Language", *Non-Verbal Communication*, ed. R. A. Hinde. Cambridge: Cambridge University Press. 49-85.

Lyons, J. (1977): *Semantics*, 2 vols. Cambridge: Cambridge University Press.

Mair, C. (2003): "Language, code, and symbol: the changing roles of Jamaican Creole in diaspora communities", *Anglistentag 2002 Bayreuth: Proceedings*, ed. E. Mengel, H.-J. Schmid & M. Steppat. Trier: WVT. 247-257.

Mani, I. (2001): *Automatic Summarization*. Amsterdam: John Benjamins.

Mann, W. C. & S. A. Thompson (1988): "Rhetorical Structure Theory: toward a functional theory of text organization", *Text* 8, 243-281.

Mann, W. C., C. M. I. M. Matthiessen & S. A. Thompson (1992): "Rhetorical Structure Theory and text analysis", *Discourse Description: Diverse Linguistic Analyses of a Fund-Raising Text*, ed. W. C. Mann & S. A. Thompson. Amsterdam: John Benjamins. 39-78.

Mathesius, V. (1975 [1961]): *A Functional Analysis of Present Day English on a General Linguistic Basis*, ed. J. Vachek, transl. L. Duškova. The Hague: Mouton.

Matthiessen, C. M. I. M. & S. A. Thompson (1988): "The structure of discourse and subordination'", *Clause Combining in Grammar and Discourse*, ed. J. Haiman & S. A. Thompson. Amsterdam: John Benjamins. 275-329.

McCarthy, M. J. (2002): "Lexis and lexicology", *The Linguistics Encyclopaedia*, ed. K. Malmkjaer. London: Routledge. 339-346.

Minsky, M. (1975): "A framework for representing knowledge", *The Psychology of Computer Vision*, ed. P. H. Winston. New York: McGraw-Hill Book Company. 211-277.

Monschau, J. (2004): *Input and Output in Oral Reading in English: The Interaction of Syntax, Semantico-pragmatics and Intonation*. PhD thesis, University of Bonn. Available at <http://hss.ulb.uni-bonn.de/diss_online/phil_fak/2004/monschau_jacqueline>, accessed 08 July 2008.

Mukherjee, J. (2000): "Krisis at Kamp Krusty: deviant spellings in popular culture as examples of medium-dependent graphic presentation structures" *Arbeiten aus Anglistik und Amerikanistik* 25, 161-172.

Mukherjee, J. (2001): *Form and Function of Parasyntactic Presentation Structures: A Corpus-based Study of Talk Units in Spoken English*. Amsterdam: Rodopi.

Nash, W. (1980): *Designs in Prose: A Study of Compositional Problems and Methods*. London: Longman.

Novak, V. (1996): *Form, Bedeutung und Funktionen von Nomen-Nomen-Kombinationen*. Frankfurt/Main: Peter Lang.

Obendorfer, R. (1998): *Weak Forms in Present-Day English*. Oslo: Novus Press.

Old, D. (1987): *Japan in 22 Days: A Step-by-Step-Guide and Travel Itinerary*. Santa Fe: John Muir.

Palmer, H. E. (1922): *English Intonation*. Cambridge: Heffer.

Peters, P. (2002): "Textual morphology from Gutenberg to the e-book", *Text Types and Corpora: Studies in Honour of Udo Fries*, ed. A. Fischer, G. Tottie & H. M. Lehmann. Tübingen: Gunter Narr. 77-90.

Plett, H. F. (1975): *Textwissenschaft und Textanalyse: Semiotik, Linguistik, Rhetorik*. Heidelberg: Quelle & Meyer.

Popham, P. (1984): *The Insider's Guide to Japan*. Hong Kong: CFW.

Propp, V. (1990 [1968]): *Morphology of the Folktale*, 2nd ed., ed. and rev. L. A. Wagner. Austin: University of Texas Press.

Quirk, R. & J. Svartvik (1979): "A corpus of modern English", *Empirische Textwissenschaft: Aufbau und Auswertung von Text-Corpora*, ed. H. Bergenholtz & B. Schaeder. Königstein: Scriptor. 204-218.

Quirk, R. & S. Greenbaum, G. Leech & J. Svartvik (1985): *A Comprehensive Grammar of the English Language*. London: Longman.

Reis, K. (1978): "Textsortenkonventionen: Vergleichende Untersuchung zur Todesanzeige", *Le Langage et l'Homme* 36, 60-68.

Robins, R. H. (1980): *General Linguistics: An Introductory Survey*, 3rd ed. London & New York: Longman.

Rohdenburg, G. (2003): "Cognitive complexity and *horror aequi* as factors determining the use of interrogative clause linkers in English", *Determinants of Grammatical Variation in English*, ed. G. Rohdenburg & B. Mondorf. Berlin: Mouton de Gruyter. 205-249.

Sandig, B. (1986): *Stilistik der deutschen Sprache*. Berlin: de Gruyter.

Sandig, B. (2000): "Text als prototypisches Konzept", *Prototypentheorie in der Linguistik: Anwendungsbeispiele, Methodenreflexion, Perspektiven*, ed. M. Mangasser-Wahl (in collaboration with U. Bohnes). Tübingen: Stauffenburg. 93-112.

Schank, R. C. & R. P. Abelson (1977): *Scripts, Plans, Goals and Understanding: An Inquiry into Human Knowledge Structure*. Hillsdale, NJ: Lawrence Erlbaum.

Schäpers, U. (2006): *Nominal versus Clausal Complexity in Spoken and Written English*. PhD thesis, University of Bonn.

Schneider, K. P. (forthcoming): *Introduction to English Pragmatics*. Frankfurt/Main: Peter Lang.

Sinclair, J. (1984): "Naturalness in language", *Corpus Linguistics: Recent Developments in the Use of Computer Corpora in English Language Research*, ed. J. Aarts & W. Meijs. Amsterdam: Rodopi. 203-210.
Sinclair, J. (1990): *Collins Cobuild English Grammar*. London: Collins.
Sinclair, J. (1991): *Corpus, Concordance, Collocation*. Oxford: Oxford University Press.
Sinclair, J. (ed.) (1995): *Collins Cobuild English Dictionary*. London: Harper Collins.
Slobin, D. I. (1975): "The more it changes ... on understanding language by watching it move through time", *Papers and Reports on Child Language Development*, September 1975. Berkeley: University of California. 1-30.
Smith, C. S. & A. van Kleeck (1985): "Linguistic complexity and performance", *Journal of Child Language* 13, 389-408.
Smith, C. S. (2003): *Modes of Discourse*. Cambridge: Cambridge University Press.
Smith, E. L. (1985): "Text type and discourse framework", *Text* 5, 229-247.
Stiff, P. (1996): "The end of the line: a survey of unjustified typography", *Information Design Journal* 8, 125-152.
Stubbs, M. (1996): *Text and Corpus Analysis: Computer-Assisted Studies of Language and Culture*. Oxford: Blackwell.
Summers, D. (ed.) (1995): *Longman Dictionary of Contemporary English*, 3rd ed. Harlow: Longman.
Svartvik, J. & R. Quirk (ed.) (1980): *A Corpus of English Conversation*. Lund: CWK Gleerup.
Swann, D. M. (1987): *Cranks: Soups and Starters*. Enfield: Guinness Publishing.
Tench, P. (1996): *The Intonation System of English*. London: Continuum.
Thomas, S. (2007): "Can we have a word?", *Woman's Weekly*, 22 May, 24-25.
Thompson, S. A. & W. C. Mann (1987): "Rhetorical Structure Theory: a framework for the analysis of texts", *IPRA Papers in Pragmatics* 1 (1), 79-105.
Townsend, S. (1983): *The Secret Diary of Adrian Mole Aged 13 3/4*. London: Methuen.
Vater, H. (2001): *Einführung in die Textlinguistik: Struktur und Verstehen von Texten*, 3rd, rev. ed. Stuttgart: W. Fink.
Virtanen, T. (1992): "Issues of text typology: narrative – a 'basic' type of text?", *Text* 12, 293-310.
Wasow, T. (1997): "Remarks on grammatical weight", *Language Variation and Change* 9, 81-105.
Wells, J. C. (1990): *Longman Pronunciation Dictionary*. London: Longman.
Werlich, E. (1976): *A Text Grammar of English*. Heidelberg: Quelle & Meyer.

Widdowson, H. G. (1978): *Teaching Language as Communication*. Oxford: Oxford University Press.
Wode, H. (1966): "Englische Satzintonation", *Phonetica* 15, 129-218.
Zipf, G. K. (1972 [1949]): *Human Behavior and the Principle of Least Effort: An Introduction to Human Ecology*, reprint. New York: Hafner.

Index

acceptability 16
allo-sentence 27-29, 178
ambiguity maxim 172
anaphoric reference 35
antithesis 153
appropriateness 19
argumentation 190, 193
autonomous style 36

background relation 144
balance 153
base 139, 142
basic text-type 194

cataphoric reference 49
chain 151
choice of characters 96
citation form 118-119
clarity principle 171
clause 25, 147
clause complex 25, 50, 178
clause element 27
clause pattern 26
cluster analysis 85
co-classification 45
co-extension 45
coherence 15, 20, 140
cohesion 13, 20, 30, 140
Coleman-Liau Index 180
collocation 68
comparison 39
complexity principle 177
compression 119-120
concession 153
conjunct 51-52, 56
connected speech 117
context form 118-119
contrast relation 145

coreference 34-35, 45
corpus 60
corpus norm 79, 92

death notice 115
deep structure genre 182-183, 185
description 189, 192
determiner 37
dialect 77
discourse 4-5
discourse framework 182, 187
discourse type 188
domain 139

Early Immediate Constituents 174
economy principle 172
elaborated code 36
elaboration relation 145, 147
ellipsis 41
enablement 147
end-nucleus 121
end-focus 121
end-focus maxim 168, 173
endophoric reference 35
end-weight 170
evaluation relation 143
everyday meanings of discourse 4
everyday meanings of text 3
exemplification relation 145
exophoric reference 35
expository text-type 190
expressivity principle 173
external macrostructure 111
eye-dialect 100

factor analysis 80
factor score 82
field of discourse 78

first order word list 65-66
Flesch Reading Ease Score 179
formal texture 10
frame 136, 139
Functional Sentence Perspective 31, 121, 158

genre 75-76, 181
global text function 181-182
graphic presentation 116

hypertheme 161

iconicity 171
informativity 17
instantiation 25-26, 166
instruction 189
intentionality 15
interpersonal rhetoric 165
intertextuality 18

layout 104
letter-type 97
lexeme 23
lexical cohesion 42
lexical patterns 61-62
lexical priming 132
lineation 108-110
list 147

macroproposition 154
macrostructure 155
major talk unit 127
maxim of end-focus 168
maxim of end-weight 170, 173
maxim of reduction 172
medium-dependent 20, 74, 95, 113
medium-dependent character 97
medium-independent 20, 25, 74, 95, 98, 102, 113
medium-independent word-form 23, 118

medium-transferability 24
Minimize Domains 176
minor talk unit 127
mode of discourse 78

narrative 7, 189, 191-192
naturalness 70-71
neutral tonality 125
non-autonomous style 36
normal intonation 125
notional paragraph 108
nucleus-satellite 147, 149

objective order 31, 122, 159, 168
orthographic paragraph 95, 107
orthographic sentence 95, 100, 102, 179
orthographic word-form 95, 179

page 95
paradigmatic choice 59
parallel relation 144
phonetic coherence 141
phonological word-form 96, 117, 119
phrase 25
place relator 45
pop song 99
priming 132
principle of end-focus 168
principle of end-nucleus 169
Principle of Immediate Textual Integration 178
Principle of Least Effort 177
principle of resolution 123, 169
probability rank 69
processibility 173
processibility principle 168
profile 142
profile-base 138
progression with a continuous theme 33

Index

progression with a derived theme 160
pronoun 37
propositional development 30-31
punctuation unit 95

rank 6, 25
readability 179
reference 35
register 75
restricted code 36
rheme 32, 121, 159
Rhetorical Structure Theory 146, 158
right-branching 175

scene 136
script 137
script unit 103
semantic and pragmatic coherence 141
semantic association 134
semantic texture 11
sense-lining 110
sentence theme 161
simple linear progression 32, 159
situationality 17
spacing 107
spelling reform 98
spoken presentation 117
spoken word-form 23, 96
stack 152
step 150-151
stretched sentence 113
style of discourse 78
style 91
stylistic coherence 141
subjective order 31, 122, 159
substance 23

substitution 41
superstructure 7, 155
surface structure genre 185
syntactic coordination 50-51
syntactic subordination 50, 53
syntagmatic relation 60

talk unit 125-126
text 4-6, 8, 34
text as a prototype category 9, 12
text classification 73
text language 99
text theme 161
text-type 75-76, 91, 181, 188
text-type clause 186
textual intention 11
textual linkage of clause complexes 57
textual rhetoric 165
textuality 12
thematic progression 32
theme 32, 121, 159
time relator 47
tone unit 117, 120
tone unit sequence 120
transparency maxim 171
type-area 105

universal text-type 194
use 77
user 77

violated expectation relation 146

word 25
word frequency 64
written presentation 97
written word-form 23, 95, 97

Textbooks in English Language and Linguistics (TELL)

Edited by Joybrato Mukherjee and Magnus Huber

Band 1   Ulrike Gut: Introduction to English Phonetics and Phonology. 2009.
Band 2   Jürgen Esser: Introduction to English Text-linguistics. 2009.

www.peterlang.de

Information Distribution in English Grammar and Discourse and Other Topics in Linguistics

Festschrift for Peter Erdmann on the Occasion of his 65th Birthday
Edited by See-Young Cho and Erich Steiner

Frankfurt am Main, Berlin, Bern, Bruxelles, New York, Oxford, Wien, 2006.
315 pp., num. fig.
ISBN 978-3-631-55130-1 · pb. € 53.–*

This book is a Festschrift for Peter Erdmann on the occasion of his 65th birthday. It contains contributions by former students, as well as by close colleagues from various phases of his academic life. The broad range of topics addressed is a reflection of Peter Erdmann's wide ranging interests in both synchronic and historical linguistics, extending mainly to English and German, but including numerous other languages as well.

Contents: J. Beatty: Tehenrahsahkwa – Story Variations and Personalities · S.-Y. Cho: Frequency, Productivity and Lexicalization of Complex Premodifiers in English · S. Diemer: The Polysemy of over in Late Middle English Verb-Particle Combinations · W. Kühlwein: Bede's Narrative on Cædmon: A Semiotic Analysis · M. Mangold: Final Devoicing according to SIEBS and Deutsche Rechtschreibung 1996 · K. Maroldt: Word Order in West Saxon Prose · E.-A. Müller/R. Charlton: Some Standard of Vowel systems of English: A Typology-Oriented Approach · E. Nowak: From Morpheme to Utterance – Information Structure and Polysynthesis · H. Pishwa: Tense and Aspect: Source of Information · J. Pocklington: Bewerben auf Englisch: Stages of Development in a Dictionary, Guidebook and CD-Rom Publication · E. Steiner: Construing Contextualization through Meaning: Some Thoughts on a Semantics for Theme · E. Teich: Information Load in Theme and New: An Exploratory Study of Science Texts

Frankfurt am Main · Berlin · Bern · Bruxelles · New York · Oxford · Wien
Distribution: Verlag Peter Lang AG
Moosstr. 1, CH-2542 Pieterlen
Telefax 00 41 (0) 32 / 376 17 27

*The €-price includes German tax rate
Prices are subject to change without notice
Homepage http://www.peterlang.de